THE EARLY MODERN EUROPEAN ECONOMY

Peter Musgrave

Lecturer in Economic and Social History
University of Leicester

St. Martin's Press
New York

THE EARLY MODERN EUROPEAN ECONOMY

St. Martin's Press, Scholarly and Reference Division, 175 Fifth Avenue, New York, N.Y. 10010

First published in the United States of America in 1999

This book is printed on paper suitable for recycling and made from fully managed and sustained forest sources.

Printed in Hong Kong

ISBN 0–312–22331–5 clothbound
ISBN 0–312–22332–3 paperback

Library of Congress Cataloging-in-Publication Data
Musgrave, Peter, 1947–
The early modern European economy / Peter Musgrave.
p.   cm.
Includes bibliographical references and index.
ISBN 0–312–22331–5 (cloth). — ISBN 0–312–22332–3 (pbk.)
1. Europe—Economic conditions.   I. Title.
HC240.M793   1999
330.94—dc21
                                                99–12189
                                                CIP

CONTENTS

PREFACE AND ACKNOWLEDGEMENTS

It is as well to begin by stating clearly what this book is not; it does not, on the one hand, make any claim to be an extensive or comprehensive 'Economic History of Early Modern Europe', covering in detail the development of all major sectors of the economy, nor the development of every region of Europe. Such a book, which would be very useful, but also very difficult to write, would be much larger in scale than this and would also involve a much greater level of qualification to the main thrust of the argument than this book permits itself. On the other hand it is not a contribution to what might be called the 'Debates in...' type of history. Although I have relied extensively on the work of other historians, my concern has not been to debate the detail of their work, nor yet to discuss the ways in which their work complements or contradicts the work of others. Rather I have operated on the principle that behind many of the more modern studies of aspects of the early modern period there lies a developing pattern of broader interpretation which is sharply distinct from the earlier underlying assumptions. What I have attempted to do in this book is to express and formulate that underlying pattern. I am very conscious that in doing so I may have either falsified or distorted the assumptions of other authors; to them, in advance, I apologise.

A book such as this cannot be written without the help, assistance and support of others; in identifying a few people to list here, I am very conscious that they are only a small proportion of the very large number of colleagues and friends who have helped with the development of the ideas I express here. It is to my colleagues at Leicester that I am most indebted. Derek Aldcroft, Huw Bowen, Peter Clark, Philip Cottrell, Peter Fearon, Francesco Galassi, Paul Griffiths and Charles Phythian-Adams have all endured listening to me on the topics developed here, not only during the writing of the book but previously. In a sense, the true originator of this book was the late Ralph Davis, who taught me the importance of looking behind the surface of detailed studies to the theoretical assumptions which lie behind them all; Ralph would have hated this book and its theoretical approach, but without his encouragement of a particular approach, it would never have been written. Ralph's insistence on seeing the events of economic history within a broader conceptual framework chimed closely with the insistence of my earliest university teachers, in particular Jack Plumb and Simon Schama, that the historian must always relate the events he or she is studying to a wider intellectual and conceptual framework.

My Heads of Department at Leicester, Derek Aldcroft, Huw Bowen and Peter Fearon, have helped immeasurably in the production of this book, not merely by their encouragement but also by making it possible for me to find time in a busy teaching and administrative programme to do the reading which the preparation of the book required and also to write it. I am pleased to acknowledge the support of the Staffing Committee of the University of Leicester which has granted me study leave. Gillian Austen and Lynne Haynes have performed miracles with my ham-fisted word processing.

The final, but most important thanks must, however, go to my wife, Sheena, who has been ever-patient and supportive throughout all the difficulties of this long process. She has been my greatest supporter and my greatest and most constructive critic and I owe her a great deal.

In the end, the ideas and interpretations expressed in the following pages are my own and I take full responsibility for them.

Peter Musgrave

INTRODUCTION

As in so many areas of historiography, the years since 1980 have seen major changes in the treatment of the European economy between the end of the Middle Ages and the Industrial Revolution. This change has not simply been one of new insights replacing the old as a result of the extension and refinement of knowledge about the period. What has happened has been a complete restructuring of the basic ideas and analytical structures within which historians' understanding of the period is organised. This restructuring is much more than a simple revision of ways of looking at the period because it involves changing perspective on much of the history of the economic development of Europe since the Middle Ages. This new perspective changes the way in which the operation of societies in this period is perceived and interpreted.

At the beginning of Chapter 3 of his mammoth *Civilisation and Capitalism*, Fernand Braudel admits: 'Whether through caution or negligence, or because my subject matter did not seem to require it, I have only used the word "capitalism" five or six times so far, and even then I could have avoided it. "Why didn't you!" may be the reaction of all those who would like to ban this "fighting word" for good.'[1]

Like most other historians of the economy and society of early modern Europe, Braudel found the lure of an analysis based upon the development of capitalism irresistible. The period between the end of the Middle Ages and the onset of 'industrialisation' and 'modernisation' at the end of the eighteenth century (or possibly later) has traditionally been seen as the period in which the feudal economy of the Middle Ages gave way to a new type of economic and social organisation, out of which was to grow, as an inevitable consequence, the economy of the nineteenth and twentieth centuries. That new structure had a special form, neither the feudal structures of the Middle Ages, but quite clearly not the fully developed structure of industrial and financial capitalism. The new capitalism had grown out of the

1

commerce and agriculture of the Middle Ages by a process which was inevitable, a consequence of the internal tensions of the feudal economy. In the same way, the new capitalism of the early modern period contained within itself all the tensions and structures which would metamorphose it into the even newer capitalism of the modern period. That metamorphosis was as inevitable as the transformation of a chrysalis into a butterfly. Braudel was talking about an inevitable historical process, in which individuals were swept along by the tide of history, in which individual decisions and choices can only be seen in terms of single, simple imperatives.

Why should Braudel have wanted to keep capitalism out? Why indeed should any student of the early modern economy wish to reject this simple, elegant and above all logically structured pattern of development? This question lies at the very centre of the re-evaluation of the economic and social history of the period which has taken place since Braudel wrote. Economic and social historians no longer feel able to accept the simple Marxian pattern described above without at least considerable modification, and for many the whole structure is flawed from the very beginning.

This book is an attempt to bring together much of that new work. Two things must be emphasised. The first is that, while the older 'Marxian' interpretation has frequently been brought together into a clear structure (most famously of course by Marx himself), the newer interpretations have yet to be put together as a coherent whole. This book is an attempt to do so, and in doing so, to draw out and examine some of the further implications of those new approaches. Most of the work on which the newer interpretations are based is essentially small-scale and monographic, and hence this book has to make connections which are not explicit in the originals. It is designed to be essentially a work of synthesis, offering an analysis of the underlying structures and arguments of recent material.

Unlike other books in this series this one does not set out to discuss and comment upon individual studies or on the ideas of individual historians. There are a number of reasons for this. First, because the central aim of the book is to put material together and to elucidate the implicit new interpretation, to look at the detail of each study would be to emphasise the differences rather than the common features. It would also bury the force and intellectual structure of the new interpretations which would inevitably lead to a loss of direction. The second reason is one of length. It is difficult to confine a study of the history of the economy of the whole of Europe for a period of three or four centuries – almost twice the span of time which has passed since the Industrial Revolution – within a single book of manageable proportions. Dealing in detail with a large number of monographs would produce a book of unmanageable length.

The starting point of any discussion of the early modern European economy must be a definition of the two key terms; what was the early modern period and what was Europe in the early modern period? Both questions are by no means simple and are bound up in the whole issue of interpretation. In the older interpretations the answer to the question of what was the early modern period *was* simple and grew out of historians' understanding of the historical development they were both charting and explaining. The early modern period was that period of history which saw the replacement of feudalism as the leading form of economic organisation by bourgeois or commercial capitalism. It was the period in which the economic and social system was dominated not by the owners and controllers of land but by the owners and controllers of capital which was employed in small-scale industrial production, in international and regional trade and in finance and banking. This change was seen as an inevitable and necessary part of the transition to modern industrial capitalism. Without breaking the chains of feudalism and without creating the mechanisms which were necessary to generate the financial and capital base of the new industries, further economic development was not possible.

The chronological span of the early modern period was then clear, at least in theory. It stretched from the end of feudalism as an effective system of economic and social organisation (the two were regarded as being essentially the same) until the onset of industrialisation and modernity. The endpoint, too, was clear. Conventionally, the early modern period was held to have ended either with the onset of industrialisation in England in the middle years of the eighteenth century, or with the political revolutions of the last decades of the eighteenth century and the first years of the nineteenth, which were in some way connected with the change to economic as well as political and social modernity. The beginning of the early modern period was always much cloudier, if only because there was no clear political event to use as a signpost. If the end of feudalism was the key point, what did that mean? Feudalism as a legal system did not end in most of Europe until the eighteenth or nineteenth centuries. Even in England its last vestiges did not disappear until the middle of the seventeenth century.

If the end of feudalism as an effective system of economic organisation is meant, just when did that occur? It is quite clear, within the older interpretations themselves, that the development of different regions moved at different rates and therefore the date of their transition from feudalism to commercial capitalism occurred at different chronological points. Should, then, the beginning of the early modern period be placed at the point at which the leading economies of Europe moved out of feudalism? The problem here is that the leading European economy of the late Middle Ages, that of northern Italy, had in many ways not had a true feudal period, and had emerged from that 'feudal' age in the eleventh or twelfth centuries, a time when feudalism was at its height elsewhere in Europe. Should the starting point be when other major regions – Spain, or France or Germany – emerged from feudalism? Here again the problem is a complex one. Did the crucial point come when a part of those economies became post-feudal, or was it necessary for the whole or the majority of the economy to have done so?

The solution which was adopted by most of the older historians was to link the start of the early modern period with one or both of two events, neither of which was specifically or directly economic. The first was the Renaissance, the change in European consciousness and culture which occurred in the fourteenth and fifteenth centuries. Traditionally regarded as a shift from a theocentric to a humanist perspective, the Renaissance was seen as being very much a triumph for rational and urban culture, and so the beginning of the new capitalist economic rationality which was both the keynote and the essential ingredient of economic advance towards modernisation. The second event, possibly related to the Renaissance, was the great expansion of European contact with the non-European world which came with the Iberian discoveries of new routes to Asia and of the Americas in the middle and late fifteenth century. The new imperialism and the new openness were interpreted as both signs of and causes of a new pattern of economic consciousness in Europe.

A third possible starting point, and the one which is perhaps most commonly adopted by those historians who do not completely accept the Marxian structure of the old interpretations, is the great demographic catastrophe which struck Europe between the 1340s and the 1430s. The crisis and its effects changed the whole structure of society and the economy. The loss of population and the shortage of labour it engendered meant that, despite attempts by ruling elites to reinforce or reintroduce feudal structures in the late fourteenth century, the old service-based and fixed structure of feudal society and the feudal economy collapsed in many parts of Europe. In its place a new structure of society and economy developed, much more open and much less controlled by the owners of land. Furthermore, the breakdown of both feudal society and the feudal state meant that the economic power of the feudal elite, based on their ownership of land, or more strictly on their control of seigneurial rights, broke down. Economic power, including the ownership of land (and the control of seigneurial right, which continued to be of importance in much of Europe until the nineteenth century) increasingly passed into new hands, particularly into the hands of the urban wealthy and commercial and rentier capitalists.

The older historians were reasonably clear about what constituted the separate identity of the early modern period, even if any definition of what that identity meant in terms of real starting and finishing points was not easy. More recent historians in some ways find it more difficult to point clearly to the uniqueness of the early modern period, if only because they do not see it as a clearly defined stage within a more general pattern of development. They reject, either implicitly or explicitly, the idea of the early modern period being the necessary preliminary for the Industrial Revolution, in which all that was significant was what led towards industrialisation. They see industrialisation as being only one of a series of possible outcomes for the early modern period and one whose triumph only developed very late. They are concerned with the issues of how the economy worked and the contexts which made possible, although not inevitable, one outcome rather than any other. At the centre of this argument lies the conviction that what were of crucial importance were individual choice and strategy. The development of the economy was not the inevitable working-out of impersonal and universal economic laws, but rather the result of an almost infinite series of small-scale decisions taken by individuals and groups within the framework of their perceptions of their situation and in accordance with their ideas of what was possible and what was acceptable, as well as what was likely to be the outcome of any action. This framework was as much social and cultural as economic, but central is the idea that individuals and groups have choices, that they are not so constrained by either economic laws or by economic and cultural conditions that they have no real choice of action. What distinguish the early modern period are the nature and the range of the choices available.

The 'Middle Ages' were distinguished by a very limited range of choice for most individuals and groups. The essentially agricultural, subsistence-based economy meant that for most people there was little choice but to cultivate the land and to cultivate it in ways which were acceptable to the rest of their communities. The commercial and urban sector was, in part as a result of the subsistence nature of the economy, small. It depended upon very low levels of effective demand, mainly from the wealthy and powerful. The commercial and industrial economy, therefore, offered few choices to the mass of the population, which remained locally based and tied to the land. The economic realities of the system were recognised in the form of feudal organisation and serfdom, in which the restriction of choice was institutionalised, and the relative security of the community was substituted for choice and for other forms of strategy. Choice in the Middle Ages was limited and hence economic strategies were relatively unimportant.

This medieval economic structure was shattered by the demographic crisis of the fourteenth and the early fifteenth centuries. Recent historians consider the demographic crisis important not because it marked the triumph of capitalism, as earlier historians thought, but because it massively widened the choices available to large numbers of people. The population collapse blew apart the old communal structures of land holding and management. It led to the construction of larger landholdings and to the possibility of great commercial involvement, as well as to the possibility of paid employment for a greater part of the population and to the possibility of greater variations in crops and farming methods. It led to a redress of the Malthusian balance and hence to greater prosperity, a prosperity which was increasingly expressed in a new way as labour demanded payment in cash rather than in kind or rather than being provided as part of a service economy. This newly monetarised prosperity led to new forms of demand and new patterns of distribution, and so to new forms of production and new industrial development. The breakdown of feudal restrictions made it much easier for people to move in search of work, both to the towns and also to other rural areas.

In short, the early modern period was one of expanding choice for much of the population and, despite some periods of difficulty, one of improving standards. What is striking and what, in the newer interpretations, distinguishes the early modern period from what went before and what went after, is the way in which this range of choice was used. Early modern Europeans were conscious, perhaps more than anything else, of the impermanence and insecurity of their world. This was not a literary conceit or a moralist's warning but a strongly felt part of the reality of the world about them. Much of their economic action and economic strategy was dictated by this fear and its corollary, a deep-felt need for stability and security. Because of the particular circumstances of the early modern period, the solutions which most Europeans found to this lay in a greater variety of activity, a conscious rejection of the specialisation which had been enforced by the conditions of the Middle Ages and which, in very different circumstances and with very different aims, was to be the keynote of the modern period.

The starting point of the early modern period, in the later fourteenth century and, more particularly, in that most revolutionary of all centuries, the fifteenth, is relatively clear. Its endpoint is much less definite, except in the sense that the chronological boundaries which have been imposed by tradition clearly dictate that the early modern period must have ended around 1800 and that what followed was in some way 'modern'. The problem is that there is no clearer definition of 'modern' in historical terms than there is of 'medieval' or 'early modern'. Was the modernity of the modern period political, cultural, economic or social? Can a nation, a region, a continent be said to be modern when only parts are modern, or does it require a total modernisation? The endpoint of the early modern period considered as something other than a historian's convenient way of organising the past is unclear. It can be argued that the early modern period in most of Europe, and in many parts of the most 'modernised' regions, did not end until the second half of the nineteenth century. For some regions, for instance Spain or much of France, economic, social and political structures which were typical of the early modern period lasted well into the twentieth century.

If the question of the nature and timing of the early modern period is a complex one, so too is the whole question of what constituted Europe during this period. If the early modern period is taken to cover roughly the period from 1450 to 1800, a period which is common to virtually all attempts to define a separate early modern period in economic terms, Europe's boundaries were not fixed. At the beginning of the period, Europe's boundaries were shrinking. The continuing advance of the Iberian kingdoms against the Muslim states of southern Spain was massively outweighed by the threat from the east. In 1453 Constantinople fell to Mohammed II. The Turks had been established on the European side of the Bosporus since the late fourteenth century, but the destruction of the last remains of the Byzantine Empire marked a new period of Ottoman expansion in the Balkans and central Europe which was to end with the Turks reaching the gates of Vienna and laying siege to Malta. On Europe's steppe frontier it was only during the reign of Ivan III (1462–1505) that the tide of Mongol expansion was finally turned. Even Iberian expansion was threatened in the fifteenth century by the growing power of the Islamic states of North Africa, in particular Morocco, and by Turkish expansion along the Mediterranean littoral in the sixteenth century. It was not really to be until the definitive turning-back of Ottoman power in the last decades of the seventeenth century and during the first decades of the eighteenth that Europe's eastern frontier became secure. Until the end of the real Turkish threat it is difficult to see large areas of Hungary and the northern Balkans as being truly European, in that the society of this region was still predominantly a military one, still basically defensive rather than expansive, with a very different set of choices to the more settled areas to the west.

The process of 'refeudalisation' in central and eastern Europe in the seventeenth and eighteenth centuries also points to, if not the 'non-Europeanness' of these areas in the early modern period, at least to the existence of two Europes: one Europe in the West and parts of the South, belonging to this new world of choice and variation; the other Europe, involving the East and South-east, and possibly even including some areas of southern Italy and Sicily, belonging to a much more closed and restricted world in which a combination of economic, social and political factors had reduced rather than increased the range of choice available, tying individuals to particular types of relationships with landlords and with the state, which made it difficult or impossible for them to follow anything other than predetermined patterns and strategies.

Two things need to be said about this distinction between an eastern and a western European pattern. The first is that this distinction is a very different thing from the distinction between South and North in Europe which has been an important part of some interpretations of the early modern European economy. The western European pattern includes most of the areas which make up the North and South of the old interpretations. It should be emphasised that the difference between them is not a difference determined by levels of modernisation or progress but a much more profound difference of economic system and economic structure. The second point is that, ironically, it is in some ways the eastern model which is nearest to the model of the early modern economy suggested by many traditional historians. Here, rather than in the West, was the sharp polarisation and deep customary social distinction which was supposedly so typical of the whole of Europe during this period. Here too was the very slow growth or stasis, in which virtually any economic improvement was immediately skimmed off by the landlords or by the state, in which poverty was rife and expanding and in which consumption for other than subsistence was small. Here too was the very simple economic structure in which broad basic economic laws could theoretically operate at their crudest and most brutal. Finally, it was in the East that, in some senses at least, the specialisation which was typical of the European Middle Ages and was again to be typical of the modern period survived and indeed expanded.

Just because eastern and south-eastern Europe do not fit with the patterns of western Europe, it would be wrong to exclude them from consideration. Despite the fact that it had a different economic system, eastern Europe had close links with the rest of the continent. Eastern and south-eastern Europe were and continued to be important to Europe throughout the early modern period as major suppliers of grain and cattle, of raw materials, and to some extent, at least, of labour. Indeed one of the major reasons why it is so difficult to develop a clear definition of Europe in this period is because of the complexity of Europe's links with areas beyond its borders. North and West Africa were closely linked into the European economy at least until the end of the seventeenth century, when they became more closely linked to the developing economies of the Americas. The Americas themselves were linked intimately with Europe economically and socially throughout the early modern period, to the extent that it is often more accurate to refer to an Atlantic economy, or rather a series of Atlantic economies, than to a purely European economy or economies.[2] The European significance of those Atlantic economies, or at least their 'Atlanticness', declined in the eighteenth century as both Latin American and North American colonies developed much more independent economic and social systems. Until then it may be more appropriate to include them in a broader European economy rather than to see them as separate.

Perhaps inevitably, the coverage of the economic history of Europe in this period is by no means complete, and in some areas, for instance Germany, little is as yet available. Equally, some topics have been covered in much more detail than others. Population has been intensively studied, in particular in France,[3] while topics such as distribution have been largely ignored. Any discussion and any interpretation of the history of the early modern economy based on more recent work have to be provisional, based upon a very partial coverage and with a very large element of speculation and theory to fill in the gaps. This cannot be avoided, but it must be made clear that what is happening is not an attempt to replace an interpretation based upon wide detailed and general knowledge of the period, essentially empirical and analytical in its operation, with one which is based upon a small amount of 'real' knowledge and a great deal of theory. In fact, both new and old interpretations are as much theoretical as they are empirical. They both rest upon fundamental assumptions and on fundamental patterns which are much more a matter of historical interpretation than they are a matter of that which is historically directly demonstrable. Historians, when they interpret the past, which in the end they can only know very indirectly, are inevitably as much creatures of their own age as they are dispassionate observers of the past or interpreters of it to the present. It is almost as important to study the historians and their assumptions as it is to study the past.

A very large proportion of the newer interpretations of the early modern economy are not what might be called strict economic history at all. They do not rely solely upon the economic context of the events and movements they are describing, but insist that they have to be understood in a much wider social, political and cultural context, that those 'non-economic' factors are central to the ways in which decisions were made, courses of action or inaction evaluated. In a very real sense the divisions between economic history on the one hand and other forms of history, especially social and cultural history, are being broken down and the economic sphere is being reintegrated into the broader pattern of society and culture. At the same time, this reabsorption of the economy into a broader spectrum of behaviour raises a question which many social scientists believed had been solved many years ago. If economic activity can only be understood in its social and cultural contexts, what then is the relationship between those differing types of activity? Since the time of Marx there has been a general, if tacit, agreement among economic historians that it was the operation of the economy, and above all particular types of economic relationships, which ultimately determined both social and cultural structures. If the newer interpretations of the economic history of the early modern period are valid, that simple, convenient solution is no longer available. The changing interpretations of early modern economic history have implications which stretch well beyond its limited scope and begin to involve the totality of early modern history.

Finally, the rise of the new interpretations has left historians without a clear vocabulary in which to discuss the period. 'Post-medieval', 'pre-modern' or 'early modern' are the labels conventionally used of this era. They all have the disadvantage of being inherited from the older interpretations. They imply that this period is merely a historical corridor where 'medieval' mutated into 'modern' and that its historical usefulness lies in the viewpoint it provides retrospectively on the Middle Ages and gestationally on the Age of Industrialisation, that it is an age which lacks a character of its own. More recent historians have increasingly insisted on the separateness and individuality of these 350 or 400 years, that they have an economic (and social) history which is *sui generis*. They have as yet failed to develop a vocabulary of their own, even a name for the period itself. In this book I have retained familiar terms such as 'early modern'. I would, however, suggest two new labels to encourage recognition of the independent status of this period. 'The Fourth Age' is neutral, simply indicating that this period is of equal status to and follows the Classical Age, the Dark Ages and the Middle Ages and precedes the Modern Age. 'The Polymorphic Age' is descriptive, stating the salient characteristic of economic (and social) phenomena during this period. As I hope to show in this book, the Fourth Age is the quintessential multivariate age in Europe, distinguished from other ages by its extraordinary diversity of economic and social forms, aims and activities. This is true whether its economic history is studied at a local, regional, national or continental level.

Cogent analysis of the history of the Fourth Age has been seriously impaired by the lack of a terminology appropriate to describe its polymorphic character. The application of terminology derived from the medieval and modern periods results in confused thinking and confusing arguments because the key concepts have to be repeatedly qualified or redefined when trying to apply them to different kinds of economic aims and practice. The Fourth Age is very different from what went before and from what came after; it needs a vocabulary of its own. The acceptance of the old vocabulary in this book should not be seen as excusing political and cultural as well as economic and social historians from the task of finding a proper and expressive vocabulary, which allows the study of the period between the end of the European Middle Ages and the onset of some version of modernity in the nineteenth century to be conducted in terms of the individuality of the period, and not solely in terms of its relationships with what went before and what came after. The new interpretations of the period have changed our perceptions of what it was about and how it worked, but those changed perceptions will never have their full force until a new vocabulary has been developed to match them.

1
DEVELOPMENT AND CHANGE

All historians, even the most vehemently anti-theoretical, operate within a framework of ideas, assumptions or theories about the way history and historical process work and about what is and what is not of significance. Economic historians have a much greater tendency to operate within theories than most other types of historian. There are two key reasons for this.

The first is the close historical linkage of the subject to economics itself and to the other social sciences. Even at its most descriptive and historical, economics is not strictly concerned with understanding history or historical process, but with identifying the underlying structures of economic activity, to construct general hypotheses about the way economies and the people in them are organised and work. Economic historians have been used to working within the vocabulary of economic theory and the vocabulary inevitably brings with it an intellectual burden. A great problem which has faced economic historians in the past decade has been the development of a new type of economics which is no longer concerned with historical or quasi-historical analysis, but with mathematical modelling and the insights which can come from it. Economic history and economic historians have to some considerable extent been left with a theoretical background and structure which are now for economists something of a historical curiosity. Although the insights of modern economics provide some useful tools for the economic historian, they do not, except indirectly, offer any new theoretical structure with which to understand the past. Economic history still holds on to old intellectual structures which belong to the economics of Marshall rather than to those of the later twentieth century.[1] Its historically close links with economics gave economic history a tendency to see historical process in theoretical terms, and a great deal of that theory has now sunk into the deeper consciousness of economic historians, so that it should perhaps be described as unconscious assumption rather than theory.

The second reason why economic historians tend to adopt a theoretical approach lies in the subject's own historical bias, especially in the Anglo-Saxon world. At the heart of the development of economic history – as of social history – there lies a social and political crusade. Economic history was to be the history of the common man, of the everyday rather than of the elite and the privileged. Its origins in the 1920s and 1930s and the relationship of many of its early practitioners with the political Left was to give much of later economic and social history a distinctly polemic nature. Economic history was about the ways in which the worker or the peasant were oppressed and about the ways that oppression could be relieved.

History has always had a political dimension. All social groups create histories to validate matters important to them. It was through history and historical interpretation that political systems sought part of their legitimacy; history justified the existence of nations and national states. Even today, underlying some of the assumptions which historians make about the past are a whole series of political stances. Europe's economic leadership in the nineteenth century is used, openly or unconsciously, to justify Europe's political domination of much of the world and its consequences.

Disentangling these assumptions and the theoretical structures which both underlie them and also play a major role in the interpretation of the past is difficult enough. It is necessary to remember that anyone who attempts to do so is themselves basing their analysis on a further series of assumptions of their own. It is all too easy to dismiss older interpretations on the grounds that they are based on dubious and undeclared assumptions while forgetting that newer interpretations are themselves equally assumption-based. History cannot be an objectively neutral study of the past, however scrupulous the historian.

Interpretations of the economy of Europe during the early modern period have tended to be only a part of more general theories of economic and historical development. Historians saw the early modern period as distinctive because of the contribution it made to what were conceived as being the crucial elements in historical development. As such, the basic assumptions and theories fit broadly into what Sir Herbert Butterfield categorised as 'Whig' interpretations of history.[2]

In such interpretations, although the historical process is a continuing one, it is seen as one which is moving towards a goal, be it English parliamentary democracy, industrialisation and industrial society, or socialism. What are significant about the past are the process and events which lead to that goal; everything else, no matter how important it appeared to be to contemporaries, was insignificant in comparison. In their purest forms, these interpretations of history, and in particular of economic history, show history as the working-out of inevitable and inescapable historical or economic forces which lead events to an inevitable endpoint. That endpoint is usually good and the process is one of advance and 'progress'. What the historian is doing is elucidating and expanding on the laws of historical evolution, following a selective process which was predetermined.

Another characteristic of older interpretations is that they made claims to be scientific either overtly or by implication. They claimed to be scientific in the sense that they operated on the basis of universal laws of economic, social or historical development, a tendency which was strengthened by the close link with economics and with its desire to be scientific. Not merely was past historical event seen as part of the working-out of these universal laws, but in addition the laws which were developed by historical study could also be used, like any other scientific law, to predict future development. Though it now seems bizarre, historical patterns whose interpretation was based upon twentieth-century theory, were used as the basis for economic and social policies for developing nations.[3] In truth the past, the present and the future had become blurred into one ahistorical mess. The past was no longer a foreign country, to be understood with difficulty, but merely an annexe of the present, in which people wore funny clothes but were otherwise modern.

The most widely influential of these ideas, even amongst those who declared themselves non-Marxist or anti-Marxist, were those of Karl Marx and his followers. Two important points need to be made here. The first is that Marx's interpretation of both economics and history was something separate from the political system called Marxism which developed, particularly in the Soviet Union, in the twentieth century. The second is that, for all his profound influence, Marx was in his historical approach very much a man of his age, a Whig in method if not in political conviction.

A number of central themes and assumptions from Marx's approach have become embedded in the older interpretations of economic history in general and of the history of the early modern European economy in particular, and it is important to recognise them. The first, crucially central to Marx's whole approach, is the idea that at the very centre of all economies and all economic development lies the process of production. What is important is what is produced and how, and the related questions of how production is owned and financed and how it is organised, in particular how labour is organised and employed. So important is the question of production that it determines very largely the form of political and social systems; they are no more than an expression in differing areas of activity of the basic economic relationships centring around production. It is impossible to understand society or political systems without understanding the productive relationships which go to make them and which determine their form and structure. Economics, and especially the economics of production, replaced theology as the queen of the sciences, or at least of the social sciences.

According to this Marxist-derived approach, the ways that production had inevitably come to be organised meant that the economy and society of Europe, in the past as in the present, were profoundly and inescapably polarised into the few who had wealth, and with it, economic and social power, and the many who did not, and hence were essentially powerless and doomed to greater and greater subservience and impoverishment. For Marx, who took the idea from Hegel, this polarisation of the economy and society was not merely inevitable but also functional, since it was out of the economic, political and social tensions which this polarisation produced that change and growth came. Change was in itself good. Its form was inevitable, because of the laws within which all activities operated, and consisted of progress towards the inevitable goal of historical development.

By far the most important and the most revolutionary of all the changes which came over the European economy were those which began in England in the middle of eighteenth century and which gradually spread to much of the rest of Europe in the course of the nineteenth century. These changes had the profoundest effects on European society and economy and, by a process which itself was inevitable, on the rest of the world. Since the late nineteenth century economic historians have called these changes the Industrial Revolution. The Industrial Revolution produced social and political change, it produced 'industrial society' and therefore it produced the modern world, and 'modernisation' became a term of praise.

Traditional Marxist-derived economic theory stated that this process of modernisation and industrialisation was inevitable and was latent in earlier patterns of change. The 'pre-industrial ages', whether the 'feudal' Middle Ages or the 'commercial' early modern period, were no more than preparations for the great event of industrialisation, and their study could be no more than the isolation and the study of the preconditions of industrialisation. Historians had no independent role for an early modern period. The crucial events and crucial changes were those which marked the shift from 'feudalism' to 'capitalism' and above all to industrial capitalism. The early modern period was no more than the uncomfortable blur between the two forms of the organisation of production, rather than a segment of history with its own defining characteristics. At the same time it also had to be of special importance. It was out of the early modern period that industrialisation came, albeit inevitably, and therefore the early modern period must be of interest.

This perception of the importance of the early modern period and, in particular, of its end, is heightened and complicated by the nature of some of the political changes which came about in Europe in the late eighteenth and early nineteenth centuries. During these years Europe saw, in parallel with the economic changes which are so important in the Marxian analysis of the period, a series of profound political changes which may or may not have been related to or dependent upon the economic changes. The great mass of these changes were reactions to early modern patterns of political organisation. The new political organisations and entities increasingly sought their legitimisation not merely in the political wrongness and injustice of the systems of the past but also in their economic wrongness and injustice. This could take the form, as in post-revolutionary France or Spain, of pointing to the economic exploitation of the impoverished many by the privileged few, and to the 'anti-enterprise' and hence anti-modernising culture of the old systems or, as in new nations like Belgium, Italy or Germany, of pointing to the economic decline and catastrophe which were associated with political disunity and with foreign rule. In both cases, the early modern period was demonised to act as a sharp contrast to the brave new world. As the dreams of progress faded, so the early modern period became more and more reviled so that it could still be seen as worse than what came after.

The traditional view of the European economy during the early modern period owes as much to these underlying assumptions about the nature and process of economic change as it does to the material surviving from the period itself. They have played a decisive role in determining not merely how historians saw the period but also what features of the period have been considered worth studying.

Histories of the early modern economy tended to be heavily centred around the development of industry and industrial processes and, related to this, the development of particular types of financial organisation, culminating in 'commercial capitalism'. Other areas of economic activity, such as the service industries, distribution and the whole demand side of the economy, were largely ignored or relegated to a totally subordinate position.

In addition, these interpretations of the early modern economy were dominated by the experience of two economies, that of the northern Netherlands and, above all, that of Britain. These two economies provide the paradigm of successful economic development during this period. All other early modern economies were seen as being more or less 'backward' or 'unsuccessful'. The economic patterns they displayed were judged to be intrinsically inferior to those followed by the 'lead' economies. In particular their economies were seen as being especially dominated by production for subsistence, by economic and social constraints on change and by essential localism, a failure to expand economic activities beyond a restricted local framework.

If countries failed to modernise, to follow the paradigm of good economic development set by the northern Netherlands and England, this condemned them, and the people who lived in them, to what was basically economic misery. Because the unsuccessful countries failed to, or possibly were unable to, modernise and to change profoundly, the only forms of economic growth and economic improvement available to them lay in expansion within the old framework. That old framework was, however, one in which long-term success was not possible, at least for the great mass of the people. In the old system, improving economic conditions certainly could lead to improved living standards, albeit on a relatively limited scale, but those improvements were inevitably doomed to be reversed. In particular, increasing population as a result of improved nutrition and living standards inevitably meant growing pressure on resources which could only marginally be increased, and so, by the process expounded by Malthus in the 1790s, the improvements in living standards would be reversed.[4] Early modern economies other than the modernising ones were doomed to structural stagnation and, over the medium or longer term, to increasing levels of impoverishment and misery, even without the growing competition of the modernising economies.

The profoundly static nature of the unmodernised early modern European economies meant also that the amount of wealth in these economies was both limited and fixed. Any changes in the economy could come about only as a result of the accumulation of wealth by groups in the economy or society which were in a position to invest that wealth in new means of production (or in extending the old). This could only occur as a result of the redistribution of the existing stock of wealth. If the wealthy were to become wealthier, indeed if the economy were to be improved or modernised, that could only happen as the result of a decline in living standards for the great mass of the population, as more of the little they had was concentrated in the hands of 'capitalists' (or in the hands of greedy and parasitic states and nobilities).

In such a situation, in which the position of most of the population was inevitably going to grow worse, it followed that, for the great mass of the population, the question of bare survival became greater and greater. Be it in industry or agriculture, there was greater and greater pressure on the labour force to produce just to survive. In these circumstances the peasants and workers had less and less control over their day-to-day actions and were more and more closely tied to their landlords or to their employers. Equally, they could have little concern with consumption beyond the very basic, and no real aims except to survive the next day or the next week.

The early modern European economy was, then, one of growing impoverishment for the great mass of the population. Even when there was some improvement, as in the sixteenth or the eighteenth centuries, that improvement could only be short-term since its reversal was an inevitable part of the economic system. The only areas of Europe to escape this trap were the modernised economies of England and, to a lesser extent, that of the northern Netherlands, which provided the criterion against which all other economies in the early modern period should be judged. In both the modernised and the unmodernised economies, what was of crucial importance was production, be it of food or of manufactures, and the ways in which that production was organised. All other forms of economic activity were essentially subordinate to production. Demand and consumption were relatively unimportant since the structure of most economies limited consumption and choice to a very small sector. For most of the population, consumption was determined by necessity rather than by choice.

Many of these issues will be examined in much greater detail in subsequent chapters but a number of more general issues need to be raised and discussed at this stage. First is the question of the 'inevitable' nature of both economic change and economic stagnation in the early modern economy. The issue of whether any historical event or process is inevitable is a complex and difficult one, and one which cannot be discussed in detail here. Even if the possibility is accepted that some processes were inevitable, because of the working-out of either historical or economic laws, there remains the question of the means by which those inevitable results came about. Increasingly, economic and social as well as political historians have moved away from the idea of the great motive forces of history. They are concerned much more with the everyday detail of how history has worked and in particular of how decisions are taken. In economic history, of course, this issue of decision-taking and the context within which it occurs are of crucial importance, since so much of economics relies on the consequences of choice. Did the inevitability of historical development mean that at any point at which a decision had to be made only one possible solution offered itself? Or did it mean, on the other hand, that while several theoretically possible solutions offered themselves, in practice only one was possible within the economic context (or within a wider socio-political context)? This question is important not merely because it puts a practical side to otherwise theoretical considerations, but also because it points to a difficulty, perhaps even a contradiction, within the traditional interpretations. They placed great importance on the role of the entrepreneur in the development of economic modernisation, of the great investor, financier or visionary who sees the future and backs it. If, however, the path which was being followed by the economy overall was inevitable or preordained, the entrepreneur is hardly the heroic figure he was painted, but no more than the unconscious agent of historical inevitability.

The second major problem relates to the generation of the profound changes which were seen as being necessary for the process of modernisation. How could economies which were basically backward generate sufficient capital and sufficient demand to provide both the basis and the incentive for the process of modernisation? Since it is clear that, from very early on in the process of industrial expansion which was related to modernisation, the internal demand of the modernising economies was not great enough itself to provide the expanding demand which the modernisation process required, how was it that the essentially static non-modernising economies of the rest of Europe were able to generate sufficiently large expansions of demand? Given the static nature of demand within them and the fixing of patterns of consumption by growing impoverishment, how were they able to divert sufficient existing demand into demand for the new production of mechanised industry?

Related to this is the question of why only some countries, and only some regions within some countries, began to modernise at the end of the early modern period. It can be convincingly argued that, in the early and middle years of the eighteenth century, a number of countries were, within the framework of the older interpretations, on the edge of modernisation and industrialisation. It can be argued that in some parts of France, western Belgium and parts of northern Italy, the preconditions for modernisation were more evident and more strongly based than they were in contemporary England.[5] Why then was it that England modernised first? Was there some special ingredient in England, and if so, what was it? One possible answer is that it was chance or luck which determined that in England, rather than elsewhere, the 'take-off' occurred. This is not possible within the structure of the older interpretations, since to accept that argument is also to accept that industrialisation was not inevitable.

A fourth and final consideration remains to be noted. The older explanations relied very heavily on the universal applicability of economic laws and that, in its turn, relied very heavily on the idea that economic perceptions and aims remain fundamentally the same through history. What was universally true had to be true in the past. Therefore, economic decisions, conscious or unconscious, had to be taken on the same basis in the seventeenth century as in the twentieth. Historians are rightly deeply suspicious of such statements: at best they are questionable, at worst clearly wrong. It seems unlikely that perceptions and assumptions would remain constant over such a long period. It seems even more unlikely, given the depth and significance of the very changes which are being discussed and explained. Industrialisation or modernisation was not an economic process only. It had profound effects on perceptions and expectations in a wide range of economic and social status groups. To argue that the one area in which it did not have this effect was the economic sphere seems perverse. A further criticism related to this has considerable force. Many of the older explanations were based on the assumption that seventeenth- and eighteenth-century decision makers chose courses of action on the basis of what the outcome would be. They required people to know that a course of action would be successful because it was consistent with the development of a new economic system which would come to dominate Europe and indeed the world in the future. This clearly cannot have been the case, since no one knew (or knows) the future with certainty. It falsifies the precariousness of the early industrialisation process and devalues the courage of the investors and producers who took the risks which were necessary. Industrialisation was a gamble and, in seventeenth- and eighteenth-century eyes, a very risky gamble, certainly not a certainty.

In the 1980s and 1990s the former dominance of the older interpretations has been increasingly challenged. In part this change has been a result of the accumulation of more and more evidence. Much more importantly, it has been a consequence of wider changes in perceptions and approaches in history, in economics and also, and perhaps most importantly, in the wider world. It is important that the older interpretations should not be rejected because they were based on theories and assumptions which reflect an earlier stage of the development of ideas and perceptions only to be replaced by newer interpretations which are claimed to be more scientific. The newer interpretations are as much creatures of their age as the older ones were of theirs, and it is important to attempt to identify what features of the perceptions and consciousnesses of the 1980s and 1990s have played a role in the development of the new interpretations.

Perhaps the first and the most immediately obvious of these has been the decline of political Marxism, typified by the fall of the Soviet Union. The links between Marx and his historical analysis on the one hand and the political and economic system of the Soviet Union and the other communist states on the other is a complex and difficult one. Soviet communism, despite its rhetoric, was hardly Marxist and hence the collapse of its political and economic systems should not, of itself, have necessarily had any effect on the acceptance or otherwise of Marx or his intellectual followers' analysis of the causes and nature of economies and economic change. What the collapse of the Soviet Union has done, more than anything else, has been to bring into question the idea of generally applicable and universal laws of historical inevitability, to make it much more difficult to accept the idea that only one historical outcome is possible from any set of factors.

Second, the period since the oil crises of the 1970s has seen a very major change in perceptions of industrialisation and the industrialisation process. The great and expanding prosperity in the post-Second-World-War years encouraged a very rosy view of the industrial economy. Forgetting the difficulties and crises of the inter-war years, which could be explained as the consequence of poor economic management, it was possible in the 1950s and 1960s to see industrialisation as a process which had guaranteed massive improvements both in national and regional wealth on the one hand and personal living standards on the other. Furthermore, the apparent existence of 'self-sustaining exponential economic growth' offered the prospect of unstoppable and endless economic and social improvement simply through the working-out of the industrial system. In truth this had to be the system of the future, because once it had got under way it could not be stopped. In the evolutionary struggle there could be no doubt that the industrial system had won and would lead on to even greater heights of prosperity and achievement in the future. From the mid-1970s onwards, however, doubts began to appear about the inevitable success and the inevitable progress caused by industrialisation. For the first time in a generation, and despite all the most advanced means of economic management available, economic growth ceased and at least for a while was reversed; permanent unstoppable growth was no longer certain. Furthermore, the association of this decline with the oil supply crisis of the 1970s changed another element in the picture. Until that point it had been the virtually universal belief that industrialisation and its aftermath had made the industrial nations masters of the economic world. Their economic power was so great that they could effectively control the whole of the world economic system from the supply of raw materials to the markets for the finished products. Industrialisation could and would win everywhere because it controlled all the important variables. The realisation that at least some suppliers of raw materials still had the power to 'hold the system to ransom' meant that industrialisation was not all-conquering and did not in reality control the system absolutely. Once this is accepted the idea that industrialisation must inevitably succeed falls by the wayside. If this is so, it opens up the possibility that, in other conditions, other systems and other structures may have dominated, and also that future systems may develop out of systems which are now, or in the past were, subordinate to, rather than a product of, industrialisation.

If industrialisation was only one of a range of possibilities, rather than an inevitable outcome, it becomes possible to ask whether industrialisation was necessarily the right turning to take. The development of concern over the state of the environment, and in particular the contribution which industry and the industrialised nations make to damaging it, have increased this feeling that perhaps enthusiasm for the uncontrolled expansion of industrialisation was a mistake. Industrialisation might be sustainable in the world of theory, but in the real world a combination of ecological damage and the exhaustion of raw materials might make it not merely unsustainable but actively detrimental to the long-term prosperity, indeed survival, of a large proportion of the world's population. If alternative economic strategies may need to be found in the twenty-first century perhaps alternatives existed at earlier stages, in particular in the period during which the triumph of industrialisation began, that is, in the early modern period.

Third, the rise of environmentalism is associated with a major revision in the way in which evolution is looked at by historians. The earlier belief amongst social scientists in a kind of evolutionary triumphalism, an evolutionary structure in which there are clear winners and losers and in which the current leaders provide the basis of future development, is increasingly being replaced at the end of the twentieth century by a more truly Darwinian belief in a much more complex evolutionary process. This states that organisms (plants, animals, societies or economies) evolve to fit particular niches in which they are dominant so long as their niche exists, but which are so specialised that they are often unable to survive the disappearance or modification of their niche because they are so specialised. Future development may come from modifications in the leading organism (although that is unlikely, since it has evolved to fit a particular system and is best suited to maintaining that system in some form of stability), but is much more likely to come from some other less specialised organism which had been less success-ful than the leader exactly because it was less precisely adapted to that particular niche.

Fourth is the growing unwillingness of modern Europeans and Americans to be dismissive of cultures and societies which are not their own. Political correctness can be taken to extremes but it does imply a wish to respect the insights and understandings of others. With this goes a growing readiness to attempt to comprehend other ideas and approaches in their own terms rather than to dismiss them as primitive or misguided. This open-mindedness is increasingly being applied to the past as well as to the present. The inhabitants of the past have the right to be recognised as having been as rational and as intelligent as their twentieth-century successors. Their approaches to their econ-omy and to their society have to be seen not as quaint or strange but as valid and appropriate responses to the conditions of their world as they saw them.

At the end of the twentieth century Europeans are much less willing to be judgemental than they were and in particular they are much less ready to treat anything strange or foreign as wrong. Equally there is a growing reluctance to see the past in terms of right or wrong decisions or to see particular lines of development as being correct and others being incorrect or mistaken. There is no longer the desire to categorise economies and societies as good or bad, successful or unsuccessful. Increasingly it is possible to see differing patterns in the past in much more neutral, much less judgemental terms.

Fifth, in all the social sciences the concept of the great simple cause or the great simple structure is very much under attack. The failure of monocausal explanations of economic or social functions, a realisation that things are complexly interlinked and that therefore causation is likely to be complex rather than simple has come to the fore in many areas. Most strikingly, the growth of chaos theory in economics in particular has made the broad-sweep approach very much more difficult. The acceptance that great effects do not necessarily need great causes and that major changes in economic structure can be the result of the working-out of very small occurrences and decisions, possibly even of chance happenings unrelated except indirectly to the outcome, should change the way in which historians look at change in past economies. The great, inevitable cause needs to be replaced by a much more complex pattern of causation. At the same time, this realisation of the potential importance of small-scale events raises a second range of issues. If small, unconnected events can have great effects, what are the contexts in which those events take place? Obviously this cannot be known in every circumstance, but what does seem clear from experience is that the context of such events is itself complex, made up of a range of social and cultural ideas, assumptions, expectations and aims. Certainly the context was not a solely economic one, and hence it follows that the structure and the development of the economy, if it is still possible to talk about it as a separate entity, is not purely dominated by the laws of economics, any more than the rest of society was.

The sixth and final consideration is that, particularly in the 1980s and the 1990s, historians have become more concerned with what might be called the integrative forces in economies and societies, rather than in the tensions within them. This reflects a concern to understand how societies and economies held together and operated, rather than to understand simply the forces of change within them. This has led to, and has also been encouraged by, a much greater interest in local communities, in families and kinships and a declining preoccupation with class or economic or legal groupings. In social history this has led to far less emphasis on the polarisation of society and of power. In economic history it is increasingly having its effects in terms of the study of whole-family or whole-community economies, rather than of the individual or the productive unit. This integrative approach tends to see production, especially industrial production, as only a part, and possibly a rather small part, of the overall economic activity of a family, a community or a locality. Economies are no longer seen quite as crudely as confidence tricks played by the rich on the poor but rather as complex structures in which many sectors of the population achieve at least in part their aims and expectations.

These changing cultural and theoretical patterns mean that the newer interpretations of early modern European economic history are not in a strict sense directly comparable with the older ones. The older economic historians attempted to create a pattern which was both inevitable and universal, in which historical development moved through a series of states which were effectively predetermined by the operation of universal laws about the way economies developed. In that sense they were making contributions to a science of economics rather than attempting to interpret the operation and history of past economies. They effectively denied the existence of practical choices, points at which developments could have taken another line, and above all they denied any effective role for considerations and beliefs which were not economic. Economic historians presented a closed system and they aimed to be predictive as well as to interpret the past. They believed that they could provide a paradigm for future development as well as describing the past.

More recent interpretations of early modern European economic history are not concerned with prediction or the elucidation of permanent and fixed economic laws. They are much more open-ended and provisional than the old ones. They do not insist on an inevitable outcome but rather postulate a series of possible outcomes and attempt to explain why one happened rather than any of the others. In this sense they are much more descriptive and analytical, much more historical and therefore fixed in their period than the old ones.

The development of the newer interpretations does not mean that the old ones are necessarily wrong either in whole or in part. It may well be the case that in some parts of Europe, or in some sectors of economic activity, they are correct. In England, for instance, the logic of the economic, political and cultural situation may have made the development of particular patterns of production and particular patterns of economic development inevitable. It is important to recognise that what may have been inevitable for parts of England was not inevitable for the whole of Europe, or indeed for the whole of the world.

Recent economic historians start with the sound but all-too-easily forgotten historical principle that the past must in part be evaluated in its own terms, not just as a small part of a larger whole. In particular, if the actions of individuals and groups in the past are to be comprehended it is necessary to understand how those groups saw their own world and their place within it, since it was on that basis that decisions were taken and events explained. It is obviously important to see how early modern Europeans thought their economy worked and what preconceptions they had about likely outcomes of courses of action. It is also essential to bear in mind that in the early modern period as much as at all other times in history, people did not take economic decisions for purely economic reasons. Their social, religious and political beliefs and expectations also played a large part in defining their aims and the means they felt were appropriate or acceptable to achieve them. It is equally necessary to recognise that these economic and cultural notions are themselves rational, given the state of knowledge and experience of the age, and were seen by the people involved as full, convincing explanations of their situation. These concepts offered practical ways of dealing with the situation people believed themselves to be facing. Early modern Europeans were no less intelligent, no less practical, no less capable of dealing with their world than are twentieth-century Europeans. Finally, it should be noted that more than one perfectly defensible and logical rationality could exist simultaneously within Europe, indeed within the same country or possibly even within the same locality or community.

This complexity of contemporary rationalities mirrored the complexity of the economy. The economy was not just a subsistence-based agrarian system, nor yet one dominated solely by privileged landlords and emergent capitalists. In particular, the basic functional units of the economy – the family, the kinship and the community – were structurally complex, allowing a wide range of economic activity rather than restriction to a single one. For each economic unit there was, potentially, a range of possible courses of action, and this series of possibilities was exploited by the unit to form an economic strategy based upon choice and upon the weighing-up of potential outcomes.

The structural complexity of the basic economic units has another important consequence which is built very firmly into the newer interpretations. The units were complex not just in their personnel but also in their economic and social position and in their position vis-à-vis, for example, the ownership of land or of productive capacity. A single unit could fill a wide range of roles in the traditional social and economic categories simultaneously – for instance, members of a family could be landowners, tenants and wage labourers at the same time. As a consequence neither the economy nor the society can now be seen as being polarised in the way that earlier historians presented them. Both the social structure and the economic framework were much more intricate and much less rigid than traditional accounts allow. This complexity requires correspondingly complex interpretations of both social and economic actions. It is no longer possible to talk in terms of a 'natural' conflict between rich and poor or between labour and capital. Economic historians now deal with the notion of co-operation as well as conflict and with concepts such as community and family as well as those of class. Economic actions have to be understood in a much more transactional framework, in which what is important, indeed often decisive, in the operation of the economy is a complex mix of social, political and cultural factors rather than economic factors alone. The recent economic historians of the early modern period are attempting to reintegrate economic history with social, political and cultural history without, at the same time, claiming its priority over all of them. They are also moving economic history much more in the direction of Fernand Braudel's idea of 'total history' in that they argue that economic decisions and economic change can be understood in this period only within the whole pattern of beliefs, assumptions and expectations of the people involved in it.

Another characteristic of the new approach is that early modern society is no longer seen as operating within a basically static and stagnant economy. Although long-term growth in the early modern period was less than it was to be in the industrial world after 1800, and although change was less dramatic after the end of the fifteenth century, there was undoubtedly growth and change in the economy. This growth can be seen in a general improvement of living conditions over much of western Europe, not merely for the urban wealthy but also for the great mass of the population. It can be seen in the increasing number and complexity of belongings owned by the mass of the population, ranging from feather beds to textiles imported from Asia. It can be seen again in the population history of Europe: one of the most striking factors of the history of eighteenth-century Europe is its rapid population growth and also the continuation of that population growth beyond its previous Malthusian maximum. If Europe had not escaped the Malthusian trap it was operating with a new raised ceiling, which certainly had not been reached by the end of the eighteenth century. This improvement in living standards and levels of wealth and the increase in population affected the whole of Europe, and not just England and the Netherlands. In other words, it was not closely connected with industrialisation or the preconditions for it.

The concept of a Europe whose economy was growing, albeit slowly, has important consequences for a wide range of issues. General growth meant that economic activity was more than a squabble over static or declining resources. In particular it meant that the economic or social improvement of one group in society could take place without inevitably causing the decline of another. Rather than being tightly restricted, many individuals and families had a wide range of economic opportunities available to them, a number of different ways to achieve their economic aims. Furthermore, growth meant that for the majority of the population those aims were not and did not have to be solely dominated by short-term survival. In a situation where economic improvement on an individual or family basis was possible without inevitably depressing the economic position of another family or group, and where all groups and families, at least in theory, could improve their positions, the conditions for social conflict were much less than they were in the older interpretations. Co-operation and a sense of community which overlaid economic status could be found all over early modern Europe. Not merely was society less polarised than earlier historians argued, but its consciousness of itself as polarised was likely to be much less, especially where the broad cultural pressure was towards community rather than away from it.

This economic growth also meant that people had choices about what and when to consume. It is no longer feasible to argue that early modern Europeans, or at least the great mass of them, had no consumer choices since all they could do was consume at a basic level to survive. Therefore, questions of consumption were as important in the economy as were questions of production. In an economic sense the consumption of the early modern period was far from limited to goods. A very large proportion indeed of the early modern economy was taken up with service industries, whether the luxury industries of the cities, the 'religious service industries' of the churches and monasteries, the political services of the court and administration or, most important of all, domestic service at all levels of society. Non-productive consumption, and increasingly consumption which was affected by fashion and show as much as by function and use, was a major part of the economy. It is no longer sufficient to concentrate on the history of production in the early modern period without at the same time looking at patterns of consumption and the determinants of those patterns. Equally the ways in which the demand which was generated was serviced, for instance by marketing, wholesale and retail, by the spread of information, both to merchants and producers and to consumers, have to be seen as being of central importance in the economy and in economic development.

Early modern Europeans had a series of economic choices – they were not universally deprived of choice by the desperation of their economic situation, which made survival the sole possible aim, or by the operation of inevitable economic laws which meant that in any situation there was no real choice available. Choice meant that individuals, families or larger groups could formulate strategies to deal with their situations and to bring about their desired aims. These aims were set by their economic, social, political and cultural circumstances rather than by the inevitable working-out of the future development of economic systems. It was the agglomeration of these individual choices and strategies which determined the future development of the European economy rather than the other way around. Industrialisation was not the only economic strategy available. Other strategies probably seemed to early modern Europeans more appropriate and more likely to succeed. For instance, strategies which aimed for stability, security and equilibrium would certainly have fitted much more sensibly with early modern ideas about the dangers of change and about the observed insecurity of life and of economic activity. It can be argued that, in early modern terms, industrialisation with, in the early stages, its high risks and high costs and also its high commitment to specialised activities and to a single economic strategy, was a very bad bet, which could be followed only in very limited circumstances and probably then only by those who were willing to take a risk or who had no choice but to do so.

Economic historians increasingly tend to see industrialisation and the Industrial Revolution not as the central and defining events of the early modern period but as a very specific set of circumstances particular to time and place. They argue that the role of production and the social and economic ties which grew up around production were much less decisive than broader social and cultural issues in determining not merely economic but also social and political development. Perhaps the time has come to ask whether, in fact, industrialisation was such a key factor in Europe's development. It was important, and certainly in the nineteenth century it was to play a major role in the history of many parts of Europe, but it can be argued that changes in productive techniques and in the organisation of production should be seen even in the nineteenth century as only a part of the causation of the political, social and cultural changes which occurred in the 'century of industrialisation'.

In conclusion, it is important to stress again that the new and the old interpretations are seeking to do two very different things. The older historians believed that the European economy in the eighteenth century, or rather some economies or sectors of economies within that economy, constituted a paradigm which all other world economies can and should follow. That view rests upon a series of assumptions, some historical, some definitely ahistorical, about the way in which economies in general and the European economy in particular worked and work. What was being studied was not the specific features of a particular situation but rather a set of more general rules of economic development. More recently, economic historians have abandoned, at least overtly, the idea of elucidating general rules and general patterns of development. They seek rather to explain the particular structures and particular circumstances of the early modern economy, how they worked and how they gave rise to the situations which developed out of them. They stress the particular nature of the early modern situation, perhaps even its uniqueness, rather than its applicability as a universal paradigm to all possible economic situations and circumstances. Their work is descriptive rather than predictive. They do not argue that any one outcome was inevitable, but merely that one result, or indeed a series of results, occurred because of a particular concatenation of ideas, events and even accidents.

It is inappropriate to say that one or the other interpretation is right or wrong: what is true as a theoretical economic paradigm may not necessarily be historically true. It is important to recognise the time-based nature of these explanations in the sense that each belongs to its own age and each performs, or performed, a valid function in that age. Whether or not the old interpretations are now considered 'correct', it cannot and should not be denied that they were widely accepted in their own age, the age of high industrial optimism, as it can be called. During that period they played an important role in establishing a particular set of cultural values and assumptions which, in their turn, had considerable effects on the ways in which Europeans dealt with the non-European world, not merely in terms of their economic development but also in their assumption of the social and cultural superiority of European modes over all others. In this way the history of the old interpretations provides an illustration of the validity of the new interpretations' insistence on looking at a wider cultural context when attempting to explain economic phenomena.

2

STRATAGEMS AND SPOILS

The economic theories reviewed in the previous chapter saw economies and economic change as being driven by great general changes in the conditions in which the economy operated. Individuals were broadly at the mercy of those grand economic forces, having very little if any choice in the economic courses they followed. As a consequence it was difficult to explain the differences between economic systems. The interplay of inevitable economic laws and similar circumstances should produce similar results, whether at the same period or over time, but clearly the reality was, and is, very different. Economic systems and economic responses are clearly not the same but widely diverse, and that diversity clearly cannot be explained within the framework of general laws. This failure of traditional economic interpretation has led to a refocusing on the individual units such as families or communities which make up the economy and on the ways in which, and the frameworks within which, they take the crucial economic decisions which go to make up the wider patterns of the economy and its operations. This has major implications for the ways in which historians see economic change, and in particular how economic change, or lack of change, are generated. The key concept is that individuals and groups, and hence the whole economy of which they form part, are not constrained by some ineluctable historical or economic force to move in one direction and in one direction only. Rather they have choices between two or more possible courses of action, which are determined by the existing state of the economy, their perception of that situation and its possible outcomes, and the individual's (or group's)[1] own aims and intentions. Which of the possible lines of action (including inaction) is followed also depends on the individual's evaluation of likely outcomes and on

33

their own aims and hopes. It is important to remember that, in a historical context, the one factor the individual making the decision cannot bear in mind is what the historical outcome will be. The decision maker may make assumptions about the future but cannot know what lies ahead. An investor choosing whether or not to put money up for new factories or new machines in the mid-eighteenth century could take many things into consideration, but one thing he or she could not know was the 'fact' that an industrial revolution was about to take place.

Economists and economic historians have to insist on the rationality of economic choice and decision making. If all economic decisions were made on the basis of whim, or irrationally, neither discipline could be any more than a chronicle of unrelated and inexplicable events. This essential rationality of economic choice, however, involves the introduction of a further complexity into the situation. Rational behaviour requires that each decision should not be taken in isolation from all other decisions but has to be seen as part of a whole, even if the rationale behind that whole is not openly expressed, or even consciously acknowledged. Individuals and groups took decisions within a wider context of aims, hopes and perceptions, a complex which can be taken together and called strategies. The past, like the present, operates within economic, social and cultural structures through which individuals order their lives and activities and in the formation of which they are at least a part. To understand the way economies operated and changed in the past, it is not enough to try to isolate and understand the great movements of economic history such as industrialisation or the rise of capitalism. It is necessary to attempt to isolate and understand the strategies with which people in the economy worked, and which added together to make up the great movements and also helped people come to terms with and relate to those movements.

This concentration on individual decision and individual strategy has been a key element in the development of games theory in economics. Games theory is concerned with the development and operation of individual and group economic strategies and aims and the ways in which they are pursued; rather than seeing economics in terms of broad historical or theoretical movements, it seeks to model the ways these structures of individual choice and strategy work and how, collectively, they produce the broad observed patterns of particular economies and economic situations. This new set of insights provides a new way in which economic historians can approach the early modern period. It is not, however, a way which is easy or without problems.

First, although it is relatively easy to construct theoretical strategies for individuals in the past, it is much more difficult for historians to get direct supporting evidence for them in the form of surviving documentation or artefacts. Most of the strategies which were followed in the pre-modern world, as in the modern world, were not openly expressed by the people who were following them. In many cases these strategies were not perhaps even consciously formulated and followed and their coherence was the product of unconscious assumptions about what the world was like, about the ways in which economies and societies operated and about what is and is not acceptable behaviour. Therefore the evidence for strategies and their particular application is, and is likely to remain, indirect and inferential rather than openly documented. This does not make the new approach invalid, but it does mean that the historian has to be even more careful than usual that the strategies described and analysed are not in fact based on modern rather than early modern assumptions.

The second difficulty with the new approach is that the context in which an individual makes a decision is not a purely economic one. In deciding on a particular 'economic' course of action, an individual is almost certainly not going to consider only the economic dimension of his or her situation; political, cultural and above all social considerations will pay a part, and possibly a major part, in the decision. For example, is a particular economic action, no matter how profitable it is likely to be, one which is acceptable from someone in his or her social position or in the social position which he or she is hoping to establish? Will a particular economic decision lead to political difficulties, either with the state, the local authorities or in the local community? This non-economic dimension of economic activity was rather grudgingly recognised by the traditional interpretations in the portmanteau term 'the residual', meaning all those things which did not fit neatly into a broad economic explanation of the situation.[2] The residual tended to be ignored, even though in some traditional interpretations its importance was acknowledged. Recent historians bring this whole area back firmly into the centre of the discussion and, by doing so, reunite economic and social history. The economic historian can no more ignore social history than the social historian can ignore economic history.

The greatest departure from traditional interpretations of the early modern period lies in the discovery of the wide range of choice available to individuals at all levels of pre-modern society. The traditional view tended to emphasise the essential poverty and lack of economic opportunity of most of the population. This opinion seriously distorted our understanding of the nature and the operation of the early modern economy.

In the traditional view the great majority of the population of early modern Europe were seen as being locked into a struggle for survival. Above all this was a rural population, largely isolated in settlements which were not closely linked to towns and cities and which were dependent upon a system of agricultural production which was, at its best, precarious, and at its worst, below subsistence level.[3] For the great mass of the rural population the only occupation available was agricultural labour, either for subsistence or on the lands of the landlord, who was usually noble and usually monopolised the supply of both land and employment in the area. The only alternative to this was effectively destitution, either starvation in the home village or vagrancy in search of charity, in effect a form of refugee status.[4] In the towns the position for the majority of the population was much the same: precarious and probably underpaid employment, with a very high risk of unemployment and destitution. The very high levels of poverty and destitution at times of economic crisis were said to point very clearly to the essentially insecure world of the early modern European. This was a world in which choice and strategy were limited to the choice between either accepting what was offered by the wealthy few when it was offered, or starving. In this traditional view, choice and strategic thinking were not realistic options for most of the population, who were compelled by the most basic economic needs into following what were essentially pathways set for them by the inevitable operation of the economic system.

This picture of the early modern economy is based upon the following set of assumptions about what was happening. The first is that the early modern economy was static: because it was not 'modern', it was unable to grow effectively over a long period. Inevitably this meant that, as the population increased, there was, in the long run, a proportionate decline in their prosperity. Since the economy was basically a subsistence economy, this impoverishment expressed itself in smaller and smaller landholdings and a more and more precarious level of nutrition for the population. The second is that, since the economy was not growing consistently or securely, any gains which were made by one section of the population could only be at the expense of other sections: that it was, in effect, a zero-sum game. So that the crucial changes in the economy leading to the rise of capitalism and of industrialisation could take place it was necessary for some sectors of the population to improve their position. It was an inevitable consequence that the rest of the population became more impoverished. The third assumption is that this was fundamentally a subsistence economy, based upon the production of food for auto-consumption. Any commercial production was essentially marginal to the producers' concerns and therefore the commercial and monetary economy was of little significance to most producers. Finally, it is assumed that the great mass of the population lived and continued to live in villages which were essentially closed economies and societies. People lived and worked in a single village, moving from it only rarely and very unwillingly. In that village the land was controlled either by a few dominant local families or, more usually, by a single absentee noble or urban landlord. The villagers' economic life was therefore closely defined by the village economy and its boundaries, beyond which they went only as a result of compulsion and, usually, as a sign of defeat.

This view of the early modern economy as essentially impoverished, unchanging and enclosed has been very powerful. It has on occasions been strengthened by arguments that the crisis of the seventeenth century in some parts of Europe saw an introversion of the European economy. It is claimed that the economic problems of the middle years of the seventeenth century saw many sectors and regions of many European economies turning back in on themselves, becoming more rather than less subsistence-based, less rather than more involved in the market economy.[5] Nonetheless, the evidence presented by recent economic historians increasingly points to a much more complex and much less gloomy and restrictive picture of the early modern economy.

As will be discussed later, the evidence for economic stagnation and for general impoverishment is unconvincing. Although the early modern economy may not have grown so dynamically or so decisively as the modern economy, there is evidence of firm long-term growth and improvement throughout the period, certainly until the last years of the eighteenth century. Documentation also points to a much more diverse pattern of prosperity in both rural and urban communities. Rather than communities being sunk into uniform levels of poverty and insecurity, there is clear evidence of differentiation of prosperity. This has two important implications. First, steady long-term growth of the whole economy means that this was not a zero-sum game. The growing prosperity of some sectors in rural and urban society did not mean the inevitable impoverishment of others. Second, historians have discovered that the complex dynamics and structures of village communities meant that in most cases there were close social and economic links between the more and less prosperous members and that the ranks of the more prosperous were not permanently fixed or closed. The importance of kinship and local ties meant that in many cases it was not simply individual action and the position of the individual which determined strategies and choices but the interrelated planning of a much wider group. These were not restricted to the home village. For instance, the connections formed by intermarriage stretched beyond the home village, often through a wide region, and also extended out of the rural context into the towns and the cities.

If it is no longer possible to accept uncritically the idea that the early modern period saw an impoverishment of the great mass of the population, nor that the improvement of the economic position of one sector of society necessarily involved the impoverishment of others, it is equally difficult any longer to see the early modern economy as being essentially a subsistence one, in which most economic activity took place in a non-commercial sphere within limited village contexts. Nor is it possible to see the early modern population as being essentially physically static, tied to the soil of their own home village for generation after generation and moving away from it with great reluctance only as a last resort, as a response to economic or political disaster. It is even possible to doubt the fundamental importance of the ownership of land as distinct from its occupation. It may not have been economically disastrous to lose the rights of ownership of land, to become a tenant rather than a landlord. Certainly there is much evidence from many areas of Europe of peasants selling their rights in land, not as a last resort after all else had failed, but as part of a clear economic strategy in which there were advantages for them in being tenants, or having the available capital that the sale of their rights could provide. The market in peasant[6] land was active throughout Europe. This was made possible by the complexities of feudal tenure, with its complicated separation of many of the aspects of 'ownership' and their distribution amongst multiple holders of rights in the same piece of land.

Equally certainly, early modern Europeans were not stay-at-homes. Many or most were part of family or kinship groups in which some members had voluntarily migrated elsewhere. Migration can no longer be seen as a desperate last-resort response to crisis. The evidence shows that early modern Europeans moved from place to place and did so frequently, wherever they were free to do so. Migration was limited only in those areas of Central and Eastern Europe where the early modern period saw a revival of feudal restrictions. Elsewhere this was a Europe of movement, not of stasis and stagnation. In some parts of Europe, such as Languedoc, rural workers 'commuted' into urban centres on a daily basis to work in service or industry.[7] Some migrations were either short-term and over short distances, for instance, agricultural workers moving in search of seasonal work to nearby villages, or were longer-term but seasonal, such as the migrations of pastoral farmers following their animals into the hills in the summer and back down on to the plains in the winter.[8] Other migrations were for longer periods, for example, rural workers moved into the towns and cities to spend some years in search of industrial or commercial work, or they were over longer distances, such as the migration of rural and small-town workers to the new capital cities or to the ports. Migrants were not only the poor and those at risk. Members of better-off rural families migrated into the towns and cities in search of social betterment, education or new commercial or professional opportunities. Migration was emphatically not a purely male activity; indeed in many areas of Europe migration may well have been predominantly female.[9] In particular the huge demands of the towns and cities for domestic servants (one family in seven in eighteenth-century Lyon employed some form of domestic servant)[10] and the trend towards the employment of female servants, especially amongst the middle and upper working 'classes', meant that many women and girls were attracted from the countryside to the towns and cities. Most of this migration was not caused by crisis but was part of the normal operation of the economic and social system. That in itself had important consequences. It meant that, in general, migrants did not come from kinships which had been destroyed by economic hardship in their home areas, but had families there which continued to thrive. As a result, many migrants remained in contact with their home kinships and home bases and their earnings could contribute to the local economy. This is most obviously seen in relatively local migrations, of workers, male and female, from the rural area around an urban centre where migrants could, and did, go home for holidays, for family events and, in many cases, to find their marriage partners. Even in longer-distance migrations, to the cities and ports, there is considerable evidence of continuing contact with the home kin and the home area.[11] Rather than emphasising migration as a symptom, and also a cause of the breakdown of the broader economy and broader society, it is now necessary to see it as part of the continuing strength of the economy. For many families or kinships, migration and employment of one or more of their members outside the village was normally a choice within a strategy rather than an obligatory last resort.

Migration was not the only form of choice available to individuals, households or kinships in the rural sector. The picture of the single-employment, single-employer rural community, with only a limited number of economic activities going on, is one which can no longer be defended, any more than can the idea of a roughly equal, and equally impoverished, peasantry. This picture arises from the same sources as does the overall picture of the economy. The economic structure was seen as being dominated and defined by the system of production and by the ownership of the means of production. In a basically agricultural system, the key determinant was the ownership of land, and society could be divided very sharply into haves and have-nots, the landed and the landless. Those with land – and that increasingly meant the wealthy outsider, the noble or the urban capitalist – had all the power. Those without land – those, that is to say, who did not possess legal rights of ownership in the land – were powerless. The landless were subject to the growing impoverishment which the concentration of ownership in fewer and fewer hands made inevitable, and were also without the means and the resources to develop their own economic and social base. The only way out of the trap for them was genuinely out – crisis migration. This picture of rural society and economy is very powerful and has played a very large role in the interpretation of the economic, social and indeed political history of the early modern period. It is, however, misleading in a number of complex ways.

The evidence shows that rural society was not uniformly impoverished. All over Europe, including the refeudalised areas of the east, what is clearly recorded during the early modern period is not equal impoverishment, but, very strikingly, growing differentiation within rural economies, not merely between the landed and the landless, but within the landowners as well as amongst the tenants and the landless labourers. In particular, the whole of Europe saw the development of the rich peasant,[12] peasants who came to occupy larger holdings than others, who had larger houses, wider economic activities and who in time often moved out of the rural context altogether to establish themselves in the towns and cities. These rich peasants were not only drawn from the group of small-scale landowners but frequently came from the tenants – from the have-nots of traditional interpretations.

Evidence for developing differentiation and developing wealth within local communities demonstrates clearly the fallacy of the concept of the universal poverty and universal impoverishment of the have-nots. It also suggests other, deeper objections to that analysis. It is striking that this landownership-based approach was one which was developed chiefly by British writers, such as Mill and Ricardo, and by those such as Marx who were heavily influenced by them. By the eighteenth century, England, and possibly the northern Netherlands, were strikingly different from the rest of Europe in that historical and legal development since the later Middle Ages had made 'ownership' a very clear and defined concept in law and reality. The early end of feudalism in any real sense in England meant that property could be clearly defined in law, and defined in absolute terms. On the Continent feudalism, or at least the legal and conceptual framework of feudalism, survived until the late eighteenth century, to be attacked by the antifeudal reforms of enlightened despots such as the Emperor Joseph II and by the ideals of the French Revolution. Ownership was a much more diffuse concept in a feudal system than it was in the more 'modern' English one. In English law rights to sell land, to draw rents from it and to decide who should occupy it as a tenant and at what rents were concentrated in the same hands, those of the landlord. Under the continental feudal system those same rights could be spread between a number of individuals. This meant that more than one individual could, and did, have rights in the same piece of land. These rights were saleable and were bought and sold like other commodities. Under the continental feudal system an apparently landless tenant could be legally entitled to sell the right to cultivate the land, and so the right to the greater proportion of its production independent of the rights of the land's owner.

In a feudal system landlessness was not necessarily powerlessness. Historians of the Third World have long recognised the difficulties and dangers which the colonial powers drew upon themselves in the nineteenth century by their insistence on seeing 'ownership' in the absolute English sense as being both crucially important and also inherent in all economic and agricultural systems.[13] It is not only in the modern Third World that this definition of ownership was foreign; it was as foreign over much of early modern Europe. If it had not been, the work of Joseph II or the agrarian reforms of the French Revolution would have been much easier.[14]

This diffuseness of ownership in most of continental Europe because of the legal framework of feudalism is important for the present discussion in two ways. The rural population was not simply at the mercy of landlords; tenants, even 'landless labourers', did have some potential for choice in their economic activities. In the early modern period the family and the kinship were important as economic units as well as social ones. If the individual had some range of choice, some scope for strategic planning and playing, that significantly increased the number of options available to the family and the kinship.

For a rural family these options could include a choice of whether to be tenants or labourers. In many cases they included choices such as which crops to cultivate, whether to engage in pastoral as well as arable agriculture, whether or not to engage, and to what extent, in commercial production as well as in production for subsistence. They also could include a choice about migration of the whole family or of single members. For the better-off, available options could include choosing to establish one or more members in the professions or in commerce. During the seventeenth and eighteenth centuries the range of economic choice open to a rural family was increased when industry, or at least some forms of industry and some industrial processes, moved to the countryside. This movement of industry, which has been called 'proto-industrialisation', should not be seen as a part of the impoverishment of the countryside, as the process by which urban capital and developing industrial capitalism brought more and more of the economy under its control in the early modern period. In the historical long run it may have been part of that process, but in the seventeenth and eighteenth centuries it contributed to the range of economic choice available in the countryside and widened the strategic choices available to rural families. It cannot be repeated enough that it is inappropriate and misleading to project back on to the economic activities of the early modern period judgements which are derived from the different economic circumstances of the Industrial Age.

It was not only in the countryside that strategic choices were possible. In the towns, too, people had the scope, and the need, to play the strategic game. One of the implications of the earlier discussion of migration and the continuing links between town dwellers and their rural homes is that in both social and economic terms the distinction between town and countryside has to be seen as a very imperfect and blurred one.[15] A sharp distinction, even a sharp conflict, between town and country, between 'bourgeois' and 'feudal', is implicit and important in the traditional interpretation, but like so many of these apparently sharp distinctions it is one which an examination of the evidence clearly makes impossible. Town dwellers had links with the countryside, and hence had choices and strategies which could be and often were linked to their rural backgrounds. They also had choices to make from a range of specifically urban economic opportunities. Many of these offered different choices from those in the countryside, for example, new kinds of employment, different lifestyles and a variety of consumer goods. And yet, perhaps surprisingly, the range of choices available in the town were less than those in the countryside, although the rewards for success in the towns were greater.

Another extremely important point to be made in this discussion is that for most individuals, and certainly for most families and kinships, choice was never restricted to a single choice between one activity or another. The idea that an individual has a single employment, or a single source of income, and that a household has a single breadwinner, is essentially a mid-twentieth-century one, based upon patterns of employment as they evolved in the later stages of industrialisation. Before industrialisation (and in some parts of Europe for quite long periods after industrialisation), individuals and families had many employments and many sources of income rather than a single one. The exclusive economic categories of the traditional interpretation, such as landlord, tenant, and wage labourer, cannot be applied to early modern Europe. A family could cultivate its own land, and hence be 'landed', and simultaneously hold land as a tenants and hence be landless. In addition some of its members could well work as wage labourers on the land of others, either for other members of the local community or for outside landlords, and hence be landless labourers, workers, even part of a developing rural proletariat. At the same time the family could employ workers to help on their land, either owned or rented, and hence be capitalists and employers. Additionally the family could include in its portfolio of economic activity the production of cloth or of industrial raw materials such as silk, and hence be proto-industrial workers. Other family members could engage in the professions and hence be part of a developing middle class. This diversity of economic activity cannot be discussed using the old categories based on notions of single, specialised economic roles.

Economic organisation is very closely bound together with social structure and with the political and administrative system. They are so interconnected that it is virtually impossible to separate them. According to the traditional view, in early modern Europe the economic condition of the majority excluded them from any active political role within the system. Their only political act could be rebellion against it. But the great mass of the population was not economically powerless, nor was it excluded from the exercise of political power within the formal political structure. The networks of patronage and clientage which linked village families and kinships socially and economically, also linked them politically into the wider structures of the state. Through them rural families could exercise political power not only in their own communities but also in the wider rural region and in the town. Here too the concepts of choice and strategy were significant.

In early modern Europe the political and administrative system was one in which everything operated on a personal basis and where information was limited. Personal recommendation and personal influence were crucially important, whether it be to set the government machine into action, to deliver the appropriate decision in a lawsuit (or even to bring the suit to trial or to prevent its being heard), or to reassess taxation. In most European countries during the early modern period, the state, in the person of the monarch, was the chief granter of benefits and rewards, economic and social as well as political. The only way that the wishes and requests of the lower levels of the structure could reach the higher levels, and the only way in which they stood any realistic chance of a favourable response, was through the support of powerful patrons higher and higher in the system. The patronage system, and the clientage system which was its essential corollary, were the essential bond holding the system together and the essential lubricant which made it functional. Without them it is difficult to see the early modern state, economy or society working.

The patronage system was by its very nature unstable. It relied on patrons being sufficiently effective to give their clients what they wanted and on the clients being able to give their patrons sufficient support and status. The patronage/clientage system was a two-way system. The clients gained advantages from their connection with powerful patrons who themselves were normally the clients of even more powerful patrons. The patrons gained political and (in the last resort, especially early in the period) military or physical support from their clients. It was also a system in which patrons were competing with other patrons for clients. Clients were constantly on the look-out to see if their present patron was successful or failing, and whether some other patron was likely to be more effective. This was a system in which power and choice were not monopolised by one level in the social, political or economic hierarchy but much more diffuse in distribution and much more complex in operation. The patronage system meant that for most families, even at the lowest levels of society, choice and strategy were important.

The choice of patrons, the ability to keep the patron happy, were important economic as well as political factors. Even where a family's own activities extended to government and administration, in isolation its resources were few. Alone, it could not easily get officials to operate on its behalf; it could not effectively protect and expand its own position without patronage. The family and kinship provided not merely ties of affection but also economic structures and political networking. The worst fate which could befall any early modern European was to be left to face the world alone.

The study of strategies, political and social as well as economic, in the early modern period is only just beginning and is extremely difficult and full of pitfalls. Most people, most families and groups, even though they have strategies upon which they base important, and less important choices, very rarely express those strategies openly or in any coherent way. The nature of historical record, especially of the myriad of decisions which go to make up everyday life and hence strategies, means that the historian's picture of the actions of the past is very imperfect and very partial. It is possible to know who the children of a particular family married, but the record has very little to say about the reasons for those particular choices. It is for the historian to provide the context and the details of the family's strategy by inference from the recorded actions. For traditional historians the answer was essentially simple. People in the past obeyed the basic laws of economics which were universal and unchanging. If their actions did not fit with those rules it was because people in the past were ignorant, perverse or made wrong decisions. Recent historians reject this imposition of modern values and modern perceptions on the past. The danger is that, in rejecting one set of modern ideas, historians will simply substitute a different set of modern values, with the same essentially ahistorical result. In this process of defining and identifying strategies, the historian must be sensitive to the differences in approaches, perceptions and aims between the modern and the pre-modern world.

The types and patterns of strategy which were followed are only just beginning to be studied in any extensive sort of way, and this study is heavily slanted by the types of information which are most easily available. The most obvious and most easily accessible area has been that of marriage patterns and strategies. For early modern families the question of the marriage of the younger members of the group was not simply a matter of affection and attraction. Marriage involved a series of economic and social interrelationships which were of considerable importance.

It could, at the most basic level, involve the handing-over of dowries and other forms of wealth, and it could involve establishing some secure base for the husband or wife should the spouse die or prove unsatisfactory. It also involved linking families and kinships together, a process which could hardly avoid having important economic and political consequences. At all levels of society, so important were marriage alliances and the economic, social and political arrangements that they involved that, particularly in southern Europe, they were frequently formalised in the most official of all possible ways, through notarial instruments. It is these official records which form the basis of much of the study of marriage strategies.[16] Economic considerations and economic advantage were only a part of the complex of relationships and influences which contributed to the marriage strategies of early modern families. As so often happens, it is not possible to identify a purely economic form of strategy, nor one in which a simple economic rationality operated.

Even more complex, and even more difficult to study, are what can be called the wider economic strategies of early modern families and groups. Here the evidence is even more partial, even more random in its survival and even more difficult of interpretation. For those reasons it is even more at risk from the undeclared and unjustified importation of modern modes of thought. The early modern rural family had a wide range of choices, and hence a wide range of possible strategies open to it. At the most basic level was the choice of the form and pattern of agriculture to adopt: should it be as a tenant or as an owner? If as a tenant, what sort of tenant? Should it be paying a fixed money rent or, as a sharecropper, paying a fixed proportion of production? Should the holding be concentrated, with all the land in one place, making movement between fields easier and the planning of production more effective? Should the holding be dispersed, allowing for a range of crops on fields in different places with differing conditions of soil, water supply and exposure? Should production be essentially for subsistence or chiefly for sale into a commercial market? Should there be specialisation in a single crop for high returns or a wide spread of crops to reduce risk? Should the agriculture be essentially arable, pastoral, or a mixture? In addition, the family had to decide what other employment strategies to adopt. Should it employ people or work for others? When should labour be employed, and how much? Should members of the family seek employment locally or at a distance? Should the family become involved in urban activities, either by sending members to work in the town or by setting members up in the town in trades or professions? Should the family engage in industry and, if so, to what extent? Should members of the family, or indeed the whole family, migrate elsewhere in search of employment or new opportunities? All these questions were neither exclusive nor permanent and changing circumstances resulted in changing solutions. The balance of the family economy was never permanent but had to be constantly readjusted.

The question for the historian is: on what basis were these choices made? It is possible to identify a number of factors which played a role in those choices and which are therefore important elements in the development of strategies.

The first consideration must be local conditions, the particular circumstances in which the family or group found itself and with which it had to deal. The range of choice which was available to any family was determined by the geographical, physical and political conditions in which it found itself. These were not constant across Europe but varied from region to region, and often within regions. The ability of any family to choose the crops it grew and to vary and mix those crops depended upon the climate and soil of the area in which it lived. Where, as in parts of Italy and the south of France, climatic and soil conditions made it possible to grow a range of cereal crops, and also grapes and other fruit, and olives for oil, and to graze animals amongst the crops, the range of choice was high. Elsewhere, in parts of northern Europe for instance, climatic and soil conditions severely restricted the range of crops which could be grown, and hence choice was less. Market gardening or commercial agriculture were options more obviously available for a family with easy access to urban markets than for one more distant from markets. Upland areas offered different ranges of choices from lowland ones. The range of choice available in southern Europe was greater than in the North and, on this basis alone, it is fair to speculate that different strategies would be followed in the two regions.

The fluctuations of the local economy also affected the range of choice available. The early modern economy was no more stable, no less subject to boom and slump than the modern economy. The vagaries of climate were of much greater importance in both the agricultural and the commercial economy in the early modern period than in the modern. War in Europe was a much more common event. Larger-scale and longer-term elements of economic change, for instance, population movement, also played an important part in the range and the nature of choice available.

The second factor which played a role in making economic decisions is the particular condition of the family itself. Differing strategies were needed and were more or less attractive depending on the size of the family group, the age of its members, their physical condition, the social status of the family, its existing economic position and activities. If the family group included large numbers of young children, strategies dependent upon using large amounts of the family's own labour were much less attractive than they would be a few years later, when the children were older and more able to contribute, and when the women were released from the physical constraints of childbirth and childcare. If the family were of particular social status its strategy might have to be tailored to match and support or improve that social status. Strategies and choices were not merely specific to areas, they were also specific to family type and structure.

The third factor affecting economic choice concerns the mentality of the decision makers. Strategies are essentially about making choices in the present with the hope that in the future they will have particular outcomes which are considered advantageous. One of the great dangers which historians have to face in their study of the past is hindsight. As historians studying events in the past it is very easy to see a situation in terms of its outcome. The historian knows what the outcome of a decision was to be, what the future held for the person making the decision. It is all to easy to forget that he or she did not and by definition could not know whether the decision would produce the desired effect or prove to be a disastrous mistake. In discussing strategies and decisions, then, it is of vital importance to consider the framework of assumptions and expectations of the decision maker about the way the economic or political situation would work out. It is important too that the historian remains alert to the danger of unconsciously assuming that late twentieth-century notions of 'good' or 'bad' outcomes necessarily coincide with those of early modern people.

It is extremely difficult to look at the assumptions and expectations of early modern people with any confidence. It involves moving away from the safe haven of economic principles and the working-out of economic laws into a much more shadowy area of ideas, of cultural history and of popular culture and popular belief. Research is only just beginning into the question of popular perception of the economy. It is, however, reasonably clear that much, if not all, of the European population did not share the mid-twentieth-century expectation of continued and secure economic growth and prosperity. They had a strong expectation that, in the short term as well as in the medium and long term, the movement of the economy was probably more likely to be downwards than upwards. In other words, the normal expectation of the population was always that things were going to grow worse economically.[17] Before the late eighteenth century every European's perception of the way things naturally were centred on the view that today's prosperity was insecure and transient, that in the near future the wheel of fortune would inevitably revolve and things would deteriorate and deteriorate rapidly, probably disastrously. This perception was not limited to the most economically and socially precarious groups in society, those for who deep poverty and destitution were immediate threats. It extended throughout the social and economic structure, affecting the wealthy as well as the poor. Everyone felt, to some greater or lesser extent, insecure. It is important to point out that this consciousness of insecurity was not necessarily supported by the performance of the contemporary economy; it is all too easy to overestimate the precariousness and liability to catastrophe of the early modern economy. For most families slow and evolutionary change rather than sudden catastrophe was the normal pattern. Nevertheless, that general feeling of insecurity about the future was important in helping to determine the economic responses and strategies of early modern Europeans. As the history of the British economy in the 1980s and 1990s demonstrated, the threat posed by perceived insecurity can play a very major role in the economic and social strategies of those who are in fact economically secure.

For most early modern Europeans the economy and their economic future was insecure. Therefore they could not base their strategies on the expectation of inevitable future improvement, nor indeed on future economic stability. The only sector of the early modern economy in which there could be said to be any expectation of stability and continuity was amongst the landowners, especially amongst the great landowners. Land was both the greatest store of wealth and the most secure way of holding it available to early modern Europeans. The owner of land had a commodity which was likely to retain its value in some form, whatever the vagaries of the economy, and it was a commodity whose ownership conferred stable social status. Landowners sought to make their position and that of their families stronger by preventing the sale of the land which was the basis of their position, so that, at least in the broadest economic terms, landowners were able to face the future with some feeling of security. Hence it should have been the landowners who were most able to adopt more risky economic strategies, for instance to invest in industrialisation, rather than the merchants or bankers, the new capitalists who were caught in the insecurity trap as much as any other section of the population.

The fourth major factor in the development of strategies consists of the aims of the people involved in making economic choices. Strategies are the means for getting to those aims. If the problem of identifying and describing strategies is a difficult one, the same is even truer of aims. The aims of individuals and families are never simple and are not simply economic. In the early modern period families wanted prosperity or growth because of what it allowed them to do. The uses to which prosperity or security could be put were an important part of their economic thinking, and those uses were not exclusively economic nor determined by economic factors, but were prompted by much wider social and cultural concerns. Social and cultural aims helped to define what forms of economic activity and what economic decisions were acceptable or possible for a family.

It is at this point that newer interpretations of early modern economic and social history depart most radically and most significantly from the traditional. Older historians thought that the actions of individuals and families were constrained by the operation of the economy: they had no choice, since the theoretical and historical inevitability of each situation defined very tightly what should be done; to act differently was folly, based upon ignorance or perversity. More recently, historians accept that early modern decision makers had to make a choice between a number of courses of economic action. They recognise that for the people actually taking the decisions the choice was not obvious, predetermined or inevitable, but had to be made on the basis of the best information then available to them. This included their best guess as to what the future was going to be as well as information or rumour about the present situation. Their decision had to be made in the context of a pattern of aims and beliefs which was culturally and historically determined, and not solely in a context of immutable economic laws and principles. At this crucial point the distinction between academic types of history – economic, social, political, cultural – blurs and disappears.

It is important to appreciate this distinction between the new and the old interpretations since it lies at the centre of another crucial difference between them. For the traditional historians much of the behaviour of people in the early modern period is explicable only by treating it as folly. Such historians saw people in the past as essentially less intelligent, less able to act rationally than those in the modern world. This arises because much of the economic behaviour of early modern people is apparently in direct opposition to what 'economic inevitability' dictates. For the more modern historian this is not seen as evidence of irrationality but rather it is evidence of a different form of economic rationality, which it is the job of the historian to attempt to understand.

The search for profit maximisation was as valid an economic objective for early modern Europeans as it is for the modern world. It would certainly be wrong to argue that at no time and in no place in early modern Europe did people or families set out to improve the performance of their own private economies by seeking and following the sort of opportunities which were to lead on to the industrial developments of the nineteenth and twentieth centuries. This economic aim could be followed sensibly in an early modern context only in certain limited and specific circumstances. The sorts of specialisation and relatively fixed investment which it required introduced huge danger into an economic strategy, as did a massive dependence on market conditions and on the terms of trade in those markets. The experience of the modern developing world indicates clearly that the 'Industrial Revolution Model', far from being a guarantee of certain success, is deeply flawed, not least because it carries a high risk of economic disaster. The early modern world placed greater emphasis than the modern world on stability and security. 'Industrialisation' was too risky an economic strategy to be adopted by successful economies and successful individuals. The economic historian has to identify the conditions which made the sorts of gamble inherent in the search for expansion through specialisation possible and acceptable.

The first possible situation in which the higher levels of risk were acceptable is one in which the economic condition of economies, families or regions was so weak and so uncertain that the gamble appeared attractive. This implies that change only occurs when the existing system becomes so unstable or so risky that the risks of change and growth seem small by comparison, so that change only occurs in what, in early modern terms, were the least successful economies, those which were the most unstable and insecure. It was England which industrialised in the eighteenth century rather than other countries such as France, Italy or parts of Germany which appeared in some ways to be as close or closer to 'take-off' in the mid-century, because it was the English economy which was the most unstable. It had rapid population growth, an unhealthy over-reliance on fugitive external markets and growing problems with the supply of raw materials. All of these made the situation such that risk and change were the only alternatives to worsening crisis. It is interesting to compare England's successful response to crisis with examples elsewhere in Europe of unsuccessful specialisation and growth. For instance, the wheat agriculture of northern France was specialised much earlier than English agriculture, a specialisation largely forced on it by climatic and geographical conditions. During the eighteenth century this specialisation led to a series of crises culminating in the great subsistence crises of the 1770s and 1790s.[18] In early modern terms it was the least successful economies which 'modernised' rather than the most successful.

A second explanation sees the conditions for following a strategy based on specialisation as being dependent upon the reduction of risk. It is predicated upon changes in conditions for investors or producers, which meant that it was no longer as dangerous to invest or to alter production patterns or methods. To some extent it is true that the development of industrialisation provided its own form of risk reduction as changes in production techniques and structures allowed the development of new patterns of self-sustaining growth. But it was necessary for industrialisation to have begun for this factor to apply; it cannot be used as an explanation for the beginning of the process, but only for its continuation.

A third explanation is that financial and management structures were created which permitted a much lower level of individual risk. A single individual or family did not have to risk all their capital or all their income in a single risky venture, nor was all the capital for a venture provided by one individual. Partnerships and joint-stock financing were important not merely because they permitted wide pools of capital to be tapped but because they permitted a spreading of risk. According to this explanation, investment in industrial development and change was most likely to come from those people who possessed large amounts of wealth and who also had considerable security in their wealth. This would mean that much of the capital for industrialisation was likely to come not from the 'bourgeoisie' but rather from the landed and rentier classes. 'Gentlemanly capitalism' is perhaps a contradiction in terms, and certainly its use involves considerable re-evaluation of the earlier process of economic development, but it does seem to describe a great deal of the early finance of industrialisation in England (and elsewhere in Europe) and to fit well within this framework.[19]

The search for profit maximisation was just one possible economic objective for early modern Europeans. Other objectives were also available, and in many ways they were much more important in early modern Europe. Two aims in particular probably played a greater role in determining economic activity than did a desire to pursue specialisation.

A concern with security and stability lay at the very centre of much early modern thought, about the state, society and the family as well as about the economy and economic activity. Life itself was uncertain: disease was common and medical knowledge and skill were unable to deal very effectively with many problems. Death was a common feature of daily life. Prosperity was uncertain, not merely because of the sort of economic fluctuations which are common in the modern world but because of the uncertainty of food production and food supplies. Crop and animal varieties were much less resistant to bad weather and to disease than are modern varieties and their yields were much lower. The difficulties and high cost of the transportation of food over more than very short distances meant that local fluctuations in production were unlikely to be smoothed out by supplies from elsewhere. Trade, industry and commerce were precarious, not merely in the ways they are now precarious but because of the greater difficulties of transport, because of the more frequent interruption of trade and trade routes by war, disease or bad weather and because of the problems of dealing in markets which were distant and for which there was little or no up-to-date or clear information.[20] In economic as well as in other activities there could be no certainty, no security, unless activities were structured to achieve these goals, and even then the fear of failure and loss remained. A craving for security and stability which permeates much of early modern culture, both 'elite' and 'popular', is as rational an approach to the realities of the early modern world as a growth/development aim would have been. The early modern world and the early modern economy were not as unstable, not as precarious as the people who lived in it believed. To some extent they themselves operated on the basis that there was some stability in the system; it is hard to see how economic activity could have survived without that. Nonetheless their profound consciousness of the insecurity and instability of their situation played a role in creating a series of economic strategies in which the generation of stability and the reduction of risk were much more central than the creation of growth or the maximising of profit at all costs.

Strategies which reduced risk were of major importance in early modern economies, and the form such strategies took depended very much upon local circumstances. Geographical conditions dictated which crops could be grown successfully. Success was defined as much by security of performance in most possible climatic conditions as by prospects of high yields. Market conditions and the accessibility of markets helped to define whether or in what proportions crops were grown for subsistence or for market, and other factors, such as the need to pay rents or taxes in cash rather than in kind, also played a role here.

It is easy to forget that the early modern producer and consumer had other kinds of insecurity built into his or her life which are largely unknown, or of much less significance in the modern world. In particular, the flow and pattern of income were different in the early modern age and they were rather less stable than in the modern world. The changes in employment patterns and in methods of production which have followed industrialisation mean that for most people, in industry, service, commerce or agriculture, income is relatively stable and arrives at regular, relatively short intervals, every week or every month. Before industrialisation, patterns of income and employment were very different. In a basically agricultural economy, income can, and does, fluctuate, and often fluctuate sharply from year to year. In the early modern period that income came not in regular parcels but in large concentrated blocks at infrequent and, because of the uncertainty of the seasons, unpredictable intervals. That income was not necessarily or only an income in cash. A cultivator growing a single crop for a combination of auto-consumption and the market received an income, which fluctuated from year to year, on a single occasion, the harvest each year, a date which, because of the natural fluctuations of the climate and hence of the date of the harvest, was not fixed but could vary by as much as a month from year to year. During the time between harvests, the cultivating family had no income and had to rely on the careful management of the previous year's income, not merely for its prosperity but in many cases for its very survival. Housekeeping in the early modern period was not a marginal or unimportant activity but crucially central to the survival of families. This centrality of the management of household budgets is one reason why, whatever the legal role and status of women, they were so important culturally, socially and economically in early modern society.

Even for those families which did not directly cultivate the land to produce food for their own consumption and for the market, this seasonality of income and the problems of management it caused were of great importance. Agricultural wage labourers were not employed throughout the year but only as they were needed, and at daily or weekly rates of pay. In all agricultural economies demand for labour peaks at certain points, for instance for ploughing, sowing and harvest, and it is much lower for the rest of the time. Wage labourers therefore had peaks of employment and peaks of income followed by periods of little or no employment and hence little or no income. Trade and industry also responded to the demands of the seasons, perhaps not quite so directly as did agriculture, but nonetheless significantly. Demand was highest at times of high income, at or around harvest time. Trade was most easily carried out in the warmer, drier months of the year. For instance, the wind systems in the Atlantic dictated that most goods for the North American market would be dispatched in the spring and early summer. Industry had peaks of production to accommodate these peaks of demand and corresponding periods of slack working.

So early modern Europeans had to deal with a whole range of uncertainties which are much less common and much less significant in the modern Western European world. Inevitably they developed strategies to try to reduce the uncertainties and their effects, if not to completely remove them. One strategy was to find some way of becoming associated with some economic activity for which seasonal and longer-term fluctuations were less significant. Joining one of the great monastic organisations was one obvious solution, albeit one which in most of Catholic Europe was only open to the already relatively wealthy. Perhaps more important in terms of numbers was association with a wealthier and therefore, at least theoretically, more stable household through employment in domestic service. One of the peculiarities to modern eyes of the early modern world was the very large number of domestic servants. There was a continuing supply of willing workers in what we have come to regard as lowly and demeaning employment because of the relatively high social and economic status which many domestic servants then enjoyed. Service was popular because it was a way of avoiding or at least reducing uncertainty by associating with an economic unit which was more stable, which was more able to reduce the dangers of seasonal and annual economic fluctuations. So successful could such a strategy be that, in the eighteenth century in cities like Paris, higher-ranking servants were important consumers of luxury goods, as well as having their own servants, since they had relatively regular cash incomes.[21]

These strategies of association were available only to a minority. For most, other ways of reducing risk and uncertainty were needed.

The most obvious and the most important can best be described as strategies which reduced risk by spreading it. Rather than relying on a single activity, and therefore on a single potentially vulnerable income, families preferred to rely on a variety of sources, spreading the risk over a wide number of circumstances and, coincidentally but not unimportantly, over a range of times. Such a strategy does not tend towards the maximisation of income and profit which greater specialisation would allow. It substitutes for it something which was seen as being more valuable in the early modern period, that is to say stability and risk reduction. Strategies of this type may appear perverse when looked at from the traditional point of view, but in the context of their own age they were more rational, more intelligent and more sensible than more modernising strategies would have been.

Risk-reduction was not the only reason why early modern Europeans followed different economic strategies. Economic success was not the only goal that early modern Europeans thought it worthwhile to pursue. Social status, for instance, could be just as important as economic prosperity and the pursuit of improved social status might well involve economic strategies and economic choices which were at variance with the idea of profit maximisation. In the nineteenth and especially the twentieth centuries, social status and wealth have become intricately interwoven. Social status is not solely defined by wealth, but wealth is an important component in it. In the early modern period, social status was in many ways much more complex. Wealth certainly played a part in it, but of equal or greater importance were legal status, relationships with higher levels of society, employment and lifestyles. In particular, certain types of economic activity were considered to be of lower social status than others, and engaging in them constituted a bar on social advancement; equally, some types of employment or activity were a help to greater social status, even if they were a bar to greater wealth or, indeed, a cause of declining wealth. In such a situation individuals or families could follow strategies which were designed to improve their social status at the expense of their economic position. The best-known form of this type of social strategy was the widespread desire of many families to establish themselves in the nobility. Over much of Europe there was a prejudice, and in some cases an absolute prohibition against noblemen and women engaging in trade and commerce; if a commercial family wished to get into the nobility, or, having bought its way in, wished to be accepted within the nobility, it would do well to convert its economic base to one resting on landowning, or on the ownership of government debt, even though the profit and income from these sources was less (and in some cases less secure) than from the commercial activities they had been involved in. Hence, a social aim led to 'non-economic' or 'perverse' actions. The purchase of land, the abandonment of trade, the investment of commercial capital in government bonds had attractions which were non-economic, although the results of those actions were economic. It does not matter that many established members of the nobility were engaging in just those activities that aspirants were feeling compelled to abandon. Strategies depend upon perceptions and expectations as much as they do on demonstrable facts.

The idea that the development of the early modern economy should be seen in terms of the working-out not of grand economic factors but of individual strategies, some of them purely 'economic', but most of them with a very large non-economic content, has many important consequences. First, and perhaps most importantly, it suggests very clearly that the course which the European economy was to follow in the later eighteenth century and afterwards was not an inevitable and predestined one, but rather one which it followed as a result of the cumulative effect of a large number of strategic choices. Had those strategic choices been different, the course of development would have been different. The second is that in order to understand the way the economy operated and the ways in which it changed, it is not enough simply to look at the economy. It is necessary to look at the much wider social and cultural dimension to understand the framework underpinning the setting of economic aims and the methods for achieving them. Third, the idea of alternative economic goals and their working-out through alternative strategies allows the economic historian to restore to early modern Europeans the basic dignity of being recognised as rational beings who pursued rational, logical, and certainly comprehensible (and in some cases laudable) aims. They should no longer be stigmatised as automata subject to the inescapable operation of the economic system or, even worse, as too ignorant and too stupid to understand the advantages of a new economic pattern which was fated to rule the world.

Finally, the idea of a system based on strategic choice and on strategies based on the idea of gaining advantages from the system points crucially to two related points of the greatest importance. The first is that, certainly in the medium and longer term, that this was by no means a closed system, a zero-sum game in which one player could only gain at the expense of all others. The evidence shows that the early modern economy was capable of, and actually was, providing growing advantages – spoils – for large sectors of the economy without depressing the rest. Second, it relies upon all players in it having some flexibility and some scope for action. In other words, it relies on every player having some kind of 'power' and 'control'; perhaps not a great deal, but some. The game requires a situation, social and political as well as economic, in which power is not all concentrated in one place and in which all the other players are powerless. Power can be of different types, since not all power comes from the control of the means of production, and the exercise of power is diffused throughout the social structure. The simple economic and social model of the haves and the have-nots, of elite and mass, rich and poor, and the inevitable conflict between them cannot exist in parallel with the strategic game.

3

THE RISE OF A CONSUMER SOCIETY

The older interpretations of the early modern European economy centred around issues of production: how goods were produced, how raw materials were supplied, how the industries were organised and financed, how labour was employed. Questions about the demand for the goods produced, about the market for them, who consumed them and why and how they reached the consumer were subordinated to the topic of production to such an extent that issues of demand and consumption were largely ignored.

The reasons for this concentration on production are many. First, the means of production and who controlled it were absolutely central to the older explanations and, indeed, to the whole tradition of economic and social history which developed round it. Second, the picture which the old interpretations offered of the early modern economy as essentially stagnant, dominated by poverty and subsistence for the huge majority of the population, did not allow for questions of consumption to pay any part. The population had to be impoverished (much of the model would not work if this was not so) and an impoverished population could hardly make choices about what and when to consume. Third, according to the old interpretations, it was only after the liberating effects of industrialisation and the social and economic changes which it produced had occurred that patterns of consumer demand and modes and structures of consumption could develop. To say that widespread consumer demand developed before industrialisation is to deny that industrialisation and the Industrial Revolution are at the very centre of that economic and social change. Fourth, the production side of the economy is much easier for historians to study, because it left more complete and more accessible records than did consumption.

Production was tied up in what can perhaps be called the formal and institutionalised part of the economy, involving national legislation and control and preserved in government and legal record. In contrast, the consumption side of the economy, including the ways in which goods were supplied and sold, belongs to a much more informal and often undocumented side of the economy. Where records exist they are much less complete and much more fragmentary, chiefly because private papers of this sort are seldom kept for long. Old account books and ledgers were of little use or interest in business.

Even when taken on its own terms, the production-centred approach has many problems and contradictions. First, economic historians are discovering an increasingly large amount of evidence that consumer demand in early modern Europe was not minimal, static or unchanging. Recent studies show that there were patterns of consumption and distribution throughout Europe which changed in nature and also grew during the early modern period.

Second, the older historians fail to explain convincingly where the production of industry went. It is clear that the production of industry increased during the early modern period. Industrial units grew larger and more efficient and in addition they increased numerically, so more and more goods were produced. If the normal processes of the economic system were to operate, those goods must have been bought by somebody. It is possible that growing demand was generated by the development of extra-European markets, in Asia or the Americas. The evidence suggests that, at least until the middle of the eighteenth century, Asia was better able to supply itself with manufactured goods than Europe was to supply them, and that although the developing American colonies, north and south, did undoubtedly provide an important market for Europe's industries, they were also developing their own production and certainly were not either able or willing to provide a sufficiently large market to explain the expansion of production in Europe. Again, it is possible that growing demand was a result of a growing population, although of course that growing population would in time lead to a further impoverishment of the population and hence to falling demand. Finally, Say's Law, that every supply generates its own demand, has to be called into play; the problem here is that Say's Law implies that any good will be consumed if its price is right, usually meaning if it is low enough. However, in the situation of stagnation and impoverishment described in the traditional interpretations of the early modern economy, the only way in which Say's Law could apply is by industrial producers constantly cutting prices, and hence reducing profits in a constantly downward spiral. This hardly seems likely to have produced an increase in industrial activity except in the very short run.

Third, the older historians needed to explain how and why industrial processes and industrial organisation changed during the early modern period, since without that change it was impossible for them to explain the beginnings of the Industrial Revolution. If there were no pressure from changes in demand and consumption to change production methods or the goods produced, they had to explain change as being the consequence of pressures within industry itself, above all as the result of bottlenecks and other problems in production caused either by shortages of raw materials or by the inefficiency of old techniques. These problems did exist and did sometimes lead to change, for example the development of coke iron-smelting in England in the early eighteenth century was a consequence of the desperate shortage of suitable timber for charcoal production, as the survival of charcoal-based iron production in areas like the Corrèze valley in France, where supplies of timber remained, clearly demonstrates.[1] However, it is also clear that many of the bottlenecks in industrial production were the consequence of the growing demand for products, and in particular for new products.

So the production-based interpretations fail to provide a satisfactory economic model because they focus almost exclusively on a single aspect of the early modern economy. This results in a distorted picture which is at variance with the documentary evidence. Furthermore, the production-based interpretations cannot fit within the world of strategic choice described in the previous chapter. If most people in early modern Europe were in a position to make choices and to follow their own strategies and aims, they must also logically have had choice in consumption, both whether to consume and what to consume. In such a situation production is going to be affected by the strategic and other choices which individuals and families make. That is not to say that historians should replace a purely production-based model with a purely consumption-based one. Production could never respond immediately to demand and to changes in patterns of consumption. Historians need to construct a model of the early modern economy in which both production and consumption are represented more accurately.

There is convincing evidence that, throughout Europe, especially in the later seventeenth century and during the eighteenth century, consumption expanded, in the sense that more and more families bought goods which were not purely the necessities of survival. There is also growing evidence of changes in consumption: new goods were available, people bought different goods and increasingly followed fashion. In addition, most strikingly in the eighteenth century but by no means limited to it, there is a growing 'leisure' industry, for instance, there were increased numbers of bars, eating places and cafés, as it became fashionable among all classes, not just the wealthy, to take daily promenades and Sunday outings. Most of Western and Central Europe was involved in this expansion of consumption and consumer choice. This was not something which was confined to 'developing' areas such as England and the Netherlands, nor was it confined to the eighteenth century and the 'beginnings of industrialisation'. The beginnings of this consumer society in England in the sixteenth century occur at a time when England was still one of the more backward regions of Europe economically.[2]

A general increase in consumption across Europe during the early modern period can be seen in the greater volume of manufactured goods produced and traded and in the growing development of new industries and in the expansion of old ones. It can also be seen most spectacularly in the growing amount of goods imported from the non-European world. During the sixteenth century, Europe's importation of spices from the East increased perhaps fourfold. It was the reason why the great Mediterranean cities such as Venice and Genoa were able to ignore the competition of the Portuguese, who had reached India via the Cape of Good Hope in 1498 and attempted unsuccessfully in the early years of the sixteenth century to monopolise the spice trade. After the 1520s the volume of spices brought round the Cape of Good Hope by Portugal remained roughly static for the rest of the century, while the trade of the Italian cities not merely recovered but in fact expanded massively during what has been called their final Golden Age.[3] In the seventeenth and eighteenth centuries Europe expanded massively its demand for and consumption of colonial products such as sugar and tobacco. New trades and new industries were to develop in relation to this massive expansion in demand for goods which were not necessities and which had previously been either unknown or rare and expensive luxuries. This increased level of consumption was not merely limited to manufactured or imported goods. Raw materials, too, were in greater demand, whether industrial raw materials, like wool or iron ore, or the raw materials for building better housing, bricks, stone, timber and glass, or the raw materials for everyday life, such as firewood, coal or charcoal for domestic heating and cooking.

A major increase in levels of consumption is also apparent from the inventories of relatively simple households preserved in legal documents. This is the best indication there is of consumption, but the collection of information from these sources has only just begun and is at present very limited in its scope, being rather heavily biased in favour of urban rather than rural households and towards the eighteenth century rather than to earlier periods. What has emerged, however, is that, throughout Europe, the early modern period sees a marked increase in the number of items possessed by each household.[4] Furthermore, not merely did each household have more goods, but it had goods of a much wider variety, of a much higher value and also of a much less utilitarian kind. More colourful and more decorative clothes had replaced rather simple, dull clothing, kitchen equipment was more specialised, household crockery was more likely to be decorated, there were more likely to be ornaments on the mantelshelf (and there was more likely to be a mantelshelf), curtains at the windows – even, by the later eighteenth century, paper on the walls – than had been the case in the sixteenth century. Items, too, were more likely to be changed periodically, before they fell to pieces. In the towns and cities, especially, the second-hand dealer was an important figure in most neighbourhoods, not just the poorest.[5] Throughout Europe, houses themselves were improved; English historians are used to the concept of a rebuilding of rural England in the sixteenth century, of the replacement of wattle and daub houses by stone or, later, brick ones, but a similar process seems to have taken place, perhaps over a longer time-span from the sixteenth to the late seventeenth centuries, over much of continental Europe.[6] Not merely were houses made of improved, more weatherproof materials, but their internal layout was changed, producing more specialised use of space which offered greater privacy and also encouraged the purchase and use of furniture and other household items which were of better quality and designed for a single function rather than being multi-purpose. At the end of the early modern period the average European family had better, or at least more, clothes, utensils and household goods than it did at the beginning. Furthermore, all these items reflected more closely changes in fashion, in form, decoration and use than previously.

Some of these changes were the result of changing patterns of international and regional trade or of changing technologies. Wider international and intercontinental trade made a more extensive range of goods available to the consumer. It is worth pointing out that just because goods were available they did not necessarily become major items of consumption, as the history of the potato demonstrates.[7] New technologies also led to changing patterns of consumer demand. For example, the development of the narrow, curved chimney in place of the medieval wide, straight chimney allowed a reduction in size of the fireplace and the safe use of coal rather than coke or wood. Now, a smaller fire could warm a room much more effectively and cheaply. In addition, the disappearance of the terrible smoke problem which had been associated with the old chimneys greatly increased domestic comfort and made possible not merely a rearrangement of the ways in which rooms were used but also created demands for new types of furniture and equipment for houses.[8] Again it is worth pointing out that the development of that new chimney technology did not mean that it would be adopted automatically and rapidly, nor that the changes in living arrangements which it made possible would actually take place. Individual home owners and occupiers had to choose to have a new chimney. Their decision was based not merely on the benefits they thought they would derive from it. They had also to have sufficient disposable income to pay for the chimney and its installation. They also had to believe that their future prosperity would be such that they would not regret the 'waste' involved in a non-essential purchase. The fact that changes in the availability of goods or technology did lead to changes in consumption patterns and ways of living clearly shows that many people in both town and countryside were able and willing to spend some part of their income on choosing to improve their standard of life.

An increase in levels of consumption can also be seen in the growing importance of leisure and leisure activities in early modern Europe. Leisure activities can be defined as non-productive activities engaged in for personal or group enjoyment. Many early modern leisure pursuits such as attending sermons, watching public executions or bear-baiting do not figure in modern ideas of leisure activity, but this is a matter of cultural difference. For the economic historian, leisure is important because it indicates a level of prosperity which does not require people to engage in productive activity the whole time. It is an indicator that a considerable proportion of the population is sufficiently prosperous to be able to engage in economically non-productive activity. If early modern people could chose to spend time not working, even spending money to engage in leisure activities, it is clear that they were not trapped in an economic situation where they could gain enough for bare survival only by constant toil.

It is necessary to be very careful about this. The idea that it was even possible to work all the time is a modern rather than a pre-modern one. In early modern Europe, much economic and productive activity was intermittent, dictated by the growth cycle of crops, by seasonal demand, by the effects of the seasons on transport and on commerce, by day length and by weather conditions. For the poorer members of society, the problem almost certainly was not a lack of leisure time but rather a surplus of it. What was important about leisure is not its existence, but rather the uses which were made of it. Even at the beginning of the early modern period people enjoyed a whole range of communal and religious activities and events such as religious festivals, village high days, church ales and so forth. Characteristically they were communally organised rather than being commercial undertakings. By the end of the eighteenth century all over Europe, although the traditional forms of leisure activity survived, they often did so in a truncated form, having lost many of the elements which had made them strikingly communal. Either they had been deprived of the involvement of the better-off and more socially aspiring parts of the population and had become no more than 'popular events', or, especially in the towns and cities, they had been taken over by the elite and had become displays of civic wealth and pride, in which most of the population were only involved as spectators. The great communal events of a city like Hamburg had become, by the eighteenth century, not events involving the whole community emphasising communal solidarity but rather great pieces of fabulously expensive civic show, in which the ruling civic elite demonstrated the power and the wealth of the city both to its competitors and to its population.[9]

As the role and nature of more traditional forms of leisure changed, new kinds of leisure activity were growing up to replace them. The new leisure activities took place much more frequently than the old: the periodical village event, happening perhaps once or twice each year, was replaced by the weekly Sunday promenade, or by the daily drink in the bar or café.[10] They were also much more commercial and monetarised than the old activities. Money was necessary to buy the drinks in the bar, or to visit the pleasure garden, and as a consequence the new forms of leisure involved a much more active economic decision, not merely to abstain from work and earning but also to spend money on leisure. Such a change indicates a relatively high level of prosperity compared with the supposed poverty of early modern Europeans. It also illustrates again the importance of individual choice in the operation of the early modern economy and the variety of ways in which that power was exercised.

New service or productive industries were created to meet the new demand for commercial leisure activities. For example, the adoption of the Sunday promenade in many towns and cities led to the development of new shopping areas, first with Sunday markets and then with shops opening in the areas where promenades took place.[11] It also led to the creation of new commercialised 'places of resort and refreshment', pleasure gardens, eating places and bars. Fashionable promenades required fashionable clothes, new or second-hand, preferably at relatively low prices so people could afford to change to the latest mode. In time this led to the appearance of workshops targeting production at this level of the market. The development of commercialised leisure was not limited to towns and cities. In many villages, bars and cafés opened in response to consumer demand.

A growing propensity to enjoy commercialised leisure activities and to purchase a widening range of consumer goods and services is often used as an indicator of greater economic wellbeing because it is most likely to occur in a society where prosperity is increasing. However, it can only take place when income not merely increases but increases in forms which make greater expenditure possible. In some circumstances, such as those which may well have applied in the first years of industrialisation in Britain, growing consumption, measured by the number and value of goods traded, can go hand in hand with falling incomes if it is accompanied by a profound change in the nature and form of income.

The whole question of how early modern Europeans earned their income and in what form is one of crucial importance to any interpretation of their economy and economic relationships. Payment in kind, that is in produce either from one's own fields or from other people paying for labour or services with their own production, produces an income which may well be high in value, but it gives no purchasing power, except through complex systems of barter. In a barter economy, incomes may be high, but levels of consumption of goods and services not locally produced are likely to be small because of the difficulty of agreeing comparable values for payment and the problems of handling payments in kind. On the other hand, payment in money, for labour and services or from the market sale of production, provides an income which it is much easier to spend. A cash income inevitably involves spending since money has to be spent to buy food and other goods which, in a barter system, would either have been produced by the consumer or bartered for other goods.

One explanation of the growing consumption of early modern Europe could be simply that more people were producing for the market or that more workers were being paid in cash rather than in kind and so they had more money to spend, and had to spend more money. Why might this process of commercialisation and of a shift to wage employment have been going on? The most usual answers are that there was a growing demand for production for an expanding market sector of the economy. This implies either genuinely growing demand from a rapidly growing population or from increasing prosperity. Both of these factors would lead to a rapidly growing industrial or service sector, both paying wages in cash rather than kind. This leads to the circular argument that this, in its turn, was caused by increased demand coming from either increased prosperity or from a shift to more disposable incomes arising from a greater proportion of cash payments. That is to say that the argument requires an increase in demand as a starting point for its explanation of increasing demand. Of course there is some truth in this; one element in the economic growth of the eighteenth century was undoubtedly that changes in one area of the economy had effects on the rest of the economy which, in turn, led to further growth and changes in the first area. On the other hand, it would certainly be going to far to argue that prosperity in the eighteenth century, and indeed the origins of the Industrial Revolution, were based entirely on the effects of a shift in the form of payment, which is the logical extension of this argument.

The question of the commercialisation and monetarisation of the early modern European economy is an extremely complex one. It has, as yet, received only sparse attention from economic historians, except in the context of the extension of sharecropping in southern Europe and in the revival of feudal relationships in Central and Eastern Europe. In both these cases, the shift which is being studied is one in which a formerly monetarised economy became less monetarised, more dependent upon barter and payments in kind or labour services. In those areas where this process took place, it is obvious that the shift to kind-based systems had important economic and social consequences. The barter base of the economy seriously reduced choice and limited the potential range of strategies available to families. In return they had much greater economic security, albeit with a significantly lower standard of living. For much of Europe, and, even for many people in areas like Tuscany where the shift from cash to kind was going on, historical experience was different.[12] The evidence points to a gradual but general shift to cash payments and cash trade over much of Europe. Like all such processes in the early modern world, change was not always in a single direction. There is evidence that, especially during the difficult years for the mid-seventeenth century, and in particular in areas like Germany or central Spain, some areas saw a brief reversal of that process, a growing introversion and reversion to production for auto-consumption, to kind payments and to barter.[13] In general these periods of reversal were local and temporary and gradually the general European shift to a monetarised economy reappeared.

In part this shift was a response to changing economic conditions, to a gradual expansion of the market sector of the economy, but other factors played a major role. In particular, political and social change led to a greater emphasis on cash payment and to a cash economy. The growing centralisation of the state and the growing specialisation and professionalisation of some of its functions meant it was no longer as willing as it had been to have its taxes and other dues paid in kind. What it now required was cash which could be easily transported to other parts of the state and beyond its borders, instead of food or services which could only be used in limited ways and in limited localities. If the state required cash, so did its closest servants, the nobility, and in particular the court nobility. The ideal picture of the medieval noble family showed it ensconced in its castle on its estates, supplied with food and wine by its own lands and farms which lay around the castle and which were worked by the feudal services of its tenants, who also provided it with the physical backing upon which its power depended. During the early modern period this image was replaced by a picture of the noble family at court, part of the great theatrical performance which surrounded the king, expressing and operating its power through the lavish expenditure of money on clothes, furniture, food and bribes. At a lower level, too, the wealthy family increasingly came to define status in terms of expenditure and on a lifestyle which was distantly related to that of the noble family at court. This essentially political and social change had major economic consequences; to maintain their new state the nobility, at court or in the provinces, required cash, not goods. This change was so great that for some Marxist historians, it constituted a fundamental change from 'feudal' to 'pre-capitalist' relationships based on cash and the market.[14]

The idea of this transition from a kind to a cash economy must not be taken too far. The economy of late medieval Europe was by no means one which was entirely based on kind payments and barter. The development of urban markets, for instance in Italy, the Low Countries and the Rhine Valley, meant that there was already a major cash sector in the economy. States and noble families did not merely want payment in kind in the Middle Ages and cash had become important then in many sectors of the rural economy as well as in the urban. It should also be noted that the economy of eighteenth-century Europe was by no means entirely monetarised and commercialised. Over large areas of Europe cultivators consumed a proportion and often the largest pro-portion of the food they produced themselves or exchanged it directly for other goods and services within the local context. Noble families and institutions such as religious houses or tithe gatherers still wanted payment in kind for certain purposes. There was still a large subsistence sector in the European economy even after the eighteenth century, but there had undoubtedly been a shift to a more widely distributed cash-based economy. For an increasing number of the population a greater and greater proportion of total income was taken in a form which made consumption easier and in particular made the diversion of income from pure survival to other forms of expenditure possible. It is difficult to see the 'modernisation' of European agriculture in the later eighteenth and nineteenth centuries taking place without this process of monetari-sation and commercialisation.

The monetarisation and commercialisation of the economy were only preconditions and not the sole causes of the development of consump-tion, any more than was an increase in real wealth. For a family to change from spending only on the basic necessities of life, hoarding any surplus against an uncertain but probably worse future, to the purchase of 'luxuries', 'goods of fantasy' or entertainment required more than a simple increase in disposable wealth, and certainly more than the mere availability of goods or services. It required a significant change in assumptions and beliefs which underlay that family's eco-nomic decisions. The miserly peasant living a life of poverty despite having both an annual surplus and a hoard of gold under the mattress, or his good counterpart, the thrifty peasant or tradesman not living 'too high', prudently conserving his goods against future problems, are both common features of the moral literature of the early modern period in most European languages. They are directly or indirectly being compared, and from the point of view of the moralist, being compared favourably with the spendthrift who is imprudent, spends all that comes in, does not save but wastes his (or her) substance and inevitably comes to a bad end. La Fontaine's grasshopper and ant embody in some senses the tension between the traditional society and its morality and strategies and a developing new society in which the old constraints on consumption were much less. For such a shift in behaviour to take place, for such different strategies to develop, there must have been major changes in people's perceptions, expectations or aims. It must have become acceptable over a wider range of society and over a wider range of economic levels to spend on immediate consumption rather than to save for insurance reasons.

There are two possible explanations for such a change in attitudes. The first is that it was the product of fatalism, stemming from despair and desperation. If things are bad and are inevitably going to get worse, there may appear to be no point in saving and no point in not spending now. In this situation, the growth of consumption would be no more than escapism, the perverse reaction of a populace to growing misery and impoverishment. This seems to be an unlikely explanation of the growth of consumption in early modern Europe. Although impoverishment has been seen as an important element in, for instance, the history of Germany during the mid-seventeenth century, rather than leading to a desperate increase in spending, it led to greater introversion and a decline in consumption.[15] The other explanation is that the change is a result of greater optimism about likely future development of the economy. The family considers that the future is likely to be an improvement on the present and that, if crises arise, they will be manageable, not catastrophic. Modern economic historians increasingly favour this second explanation, which accords more closely with the tone of contemporary sentiment. It would be tempting to link this change with wider European events such as the Scientific Revolution of the seventeenth century, but such explanations are much too simple. Again, it would be wrong to overestimate the unwillingness of Europeans before the seventeenth or eighteenth centuries to spend. What is clear, however, is that consumption did increase steadily during the early modern period, and that attitudes to spending and consumption were gradually changing, rather more rapidly amongst the mass of the people than amongst the elite.

Such a rise of consumption could not be without consequences for the consumer-oriented industries and services. In particular, given the important role of fashion in the new consumption patterns, industry had to be in a position not merely to produce more, but to change what was produced with some rapidity to meet new demands and new fashions.

Manufacturing industry did not begin either with the Industrial Revolution or with the early modern period. From the Ancient World onwards Europe had possessed a large number of industrial activities and large numbers of Europeans had been involved in industrial production. Much of that industrial production had been for essentially local consumption; the costs of transporting both raw materials and finished products over moderately large distances meant that most basic manufactures could not be transported outside local and regional markets without becoming uncompetitive. This did not mean that higher-value production, and the higher-value raw materials which were needed in many cases to produce them, were not transported from region to region. The glass and mirrors of Murano, the steel of Toledo and Brescia, the high-quality textiles of the Netherlands and, later, England were all traded widely throughout Europe. Raw materials, like the high-quality wool of England or Castile, the iron ore of northern Spain or the timber and tar of the Baltic, were all exported and traded widely from the Middle Ages onwards. The industrial town was hardly an invention of the Industrial Revolution. By the later Middle Ages many towns throughout Europe had a major industrial sector, employing a considerable proportion of the population and providing an important element in the urban economy. The industrial sector was so important that most towns and cities, and the people who were involved in industrial production, sought to ensure that this valuable component of urban life was protected from uncontrolled competition. To this end, industrial activity within the urban context was controlled, in the same way that most retail and service activities were controlled, by urban regulation and by restrictive organisations, the guilds or arts. Late medieval industry was urbanised, highly organised and highly restricted. The restrictions which the guilds, backed by urban governments, and in many cases by the state, sought to impose and to maintain covered all aspects of industry: the employment of labour and the transfer of skills, entry into industrial activity and wages are perhaps the most obvious. In addition the guilds sought to regulate both the quality and the type of goods produced, and governments sought to protect urban industry from external competition by tariffs and taxes.

Such a highly regulated structure had many advantages for those involved in the production of goods and for those trading in them and for the purchaser who knew that goods purchased from particular producers or from particular towns would be of a given, guaranteed quality and, perhaps equally when there was no standardisation of weights and measures, of guaranteed size. It was, however, a system which was designed to prevent, or at least reduce, the possibility of innovation and change. Innovation and change, in particular the development of new types of product, above all in the textile industry, were what the new patterns of consumption required. Industry had to be able to increase production rapidly, which was not easy when increasing the labour force involved the long and complex process of apprenticeship. The new consumer markets demanded relatively cheap products without the traditional insistence on quality and durability. If clothes were going to go out of fashion relatively quickly, there was little to be gained from insisting that they should be of such quality that they would survive in use for a decade or more. This meant changes in production techniques and in the ethos of production, and it meant falling wages for those employed in production since the jealously guarded traditional skills were much less in demand.

The demand for innovation and change and the reluctance or inability of traditional industry to respond to it helped to produce a major alteration in the pattern of industrialisation. One of the characteristics of the early modern period throughout Europe is the growth of industrial activity in the countryside outside the areas controlled by the guilds and arts. According to the traditional interpretations this spread of industrial production to the countryside is a significant step on the way to the new, nineteenth-century patterns of industrialisation and is called 'proto-industrialisation'.[16] It is seen as significant for two reasons. First, it involves industry and the capital on which the new ventures were based, breaking out of the medieval, 'feudal' restraints of the towns and cities to establish new structures of production and employment ruled by market relationships rather than by the traditional, customary relationships of the towns. Second, proto-industrialisation is seen as being industrialisation (whereas the production of the medieval towns was not), because the organisation of the new industries moved them a step closer to the control of the means of production by capital. Urban industry was essentially dominated by the small-scale master, working on his own account and employing no more than a few journeymen and apprentices, all of who could themselves hope to set up as masters on their own. This was replaced by a system of industrial production in which the trade was dominated by a few large-scale 'capitalists', usually cloth merchants (who were not themselves cloth producers), who provided the raw materials for large numbers of producers and in many cases also owned the machinery on which the goods were produced. The labour force was to become what the labour force of the urban industrial centres had not become, a proletariat tied to its employers, having therefore few means of escape and few possible areas of strategy and choice.

The whole issue of proto-industrialisation is a complex one. Undoubtedly industry, which had been largely absent outside the towns and cities, became established in the countryside and developed some new characteristics. Although industry appeared in the countryside it did not entirely disappear from the towns. Some of the textile towns of northern France, northern Italy or central Castile did see a sharp decline in both employment and prosperity in their traditional forms of production, but in few cases did this process go so far that it can genuinely be called total de-industrialisation.[17] Equally, the move to the countryside in part represented not the movement of traditional forms of production out of the towns, but rather the establishment in the countryside of the production of new textiles, metal or ceramics, which guild restrictions made it difficult to introduce within the towns and cities.[18] Furthermore, it was often the case that only some of the processes of a complex production moved to the countryside. New forms of cloth might be woven in the countryside, new forms of yarn spun there, but many of the dyeing and finishing processes continued to be based in the restricted and controlled towns and cities. In addition, before the arrival of proto-industrialisation, some of the processes involved in production, such as spinning, had been carried out on a putting-out basis in the countryside.

For proto-industrialisation to have some kind of special status it must be more than just a variation in production patterns introduced to make the development of new forms of production possible. It should clearly represent a new departure in the ownership of the means of production and, more particularly, in the relationship of workers to employers, of labour to capital. It is by no means clear that it does so. Even within the traditional interpretations, it is not clear that proto-industrialisation really does constitute a step on the way to the new relationships which are so vital to that interpretation. It almost looks like an attempt to integrate into the interpretative framework what strictly should not have happened, a movement of industry and production away from the sort of urban centres which are supposed to be so characteristic of industrialisation and bourgeois capitalism towards the backward and feudal countryside. Increasingly, economic historians find that they do not in fact need proto-industrialisation to square this particular circle. The movement of industry to the countryside, and the spread of industrial employment there are other strategies for both 'capitalists' and 'workers'. Far from marking a key stage in the subjection of the workers to the owners, the appearance of industrial employment in the countryside adds another element of choice to the range available to individuals and families. It is a particularly useful one, since industrial employment had its own seasonal and longer cycles which were different from those of the agricultural year. Agricultural workers did not, as a result of some process called proto-industrialisation, suddenly become industrial workers. Instead, in the complex economic strategy which most family units operated, rural industrial employment offered a widening of their opportunities and choices. Industrial employment was usually paid for in cash and this extended the monetarisation of the economy, especially for rural families, and hence aided the expansion of the range and importance of consumption.

Despite the traditional view that it was unable to do so, early modern industry managed to keep pace both with expanding demand and with changing patterns of demand. It was not totally inflexible nor yet completely tied to particular, outdated patterns of production. Even after the beginning of industrialisation in England in the eighteenth century, growing demand was, at least until the early years of the nineteenth century, met as much by the expansion of traditional, early modern methods as by the new industrial means.[19] On the Continent this continued to be the case well on into the nineteenth century. The processes which were revolutionised were the basic ones; finishing processes remained largely traditional for much longer. Nowhere was this truer than in the clothing trades, that is to say in those trades most heavily involved in the sort of consumer-related production which was the major change in patterns in the early modern period. Paris, for instance, remained dominated by small-scale producers, both of cloth and even more of clothing, into the twentieth century. The Paris uprising of 22–24 June 1848, 'the June Days', so central to the idea of 'modern' popular dissent based on class and on the new patterns of industrial production, largely involved traditional small masters and journeymen rather than factory workers, of which Paris had very few.

It was not enough to produce the goods for the new consumer markets; the goods had to get to the markets and, when there, they had to be sold. The importance of communications in any economy which is at a level anywhere above absolute self-sufficiency is clear. For there to be any more than a very simple local exchange of goods there has to be some system of moving them from place to place. The scale and efficiency of that system will play a very major role in determining both the nature of the goods which can be moved about and also the economic organisation and efficiency of the market which develops. As the market and trade sector of the economy expands so another form of communications becomes increasingly important. The participants in any efficient economic system require reasonably concrete, reasonably accurate and reasonably rapid flows of information. They need information about prices, market conditions, demand, the availability of raw materials, the action of princes, and so forth, upon which to make rational decisions about their economic activities. Without such information production and marketing become a game of guesswork and hunches that is unlikely to succeed.

Early modern Europe had adequate systems for the transportation of goods and for the gathering and exchange of information. The vast development of European industry and European commerce during the period could not have happened without effective transportation systems and without reasonably accurate and rapid systems for the communication of information. That these systems were less efficient, in particular in terms of transporting bulk production, than the systems of mass transport which developed in the nineteenth century is beyond doubt. That does not mean that they were ineffective in transporting the goods which did move about, merely that a different sort of goods, or smaller volumes of the same goods, were traded.

The nature of the communications system is one of the reasons why the older historians tended to dismiss it as ineffective. In itself this is a symptom of their insistence that what was important in the early modern economy was that which led on to the economic system which developed from the nineteenth century onwards. Since the early modern system made no real attempt to transport goods overland in bulk and could only do so at the cost of prohibitive increases in price to the consumer, it must follow that it was both inefficient and unimportant. Ironically, of course, it was this highly 'inefficient' system of transport and communications which made the first products of the Industrial Revolution available to most of Europe until the 1840s or even later.

Related to this point is the fact that the early modern transportation system differed very markedly from what followed it, or rather from what followed it in the perception of many economic historians. The age of industrialisation in the nineteenth century was seen as being intimately connected with bulk land transport and above all with the railways; the Age of Industry and the Age of the Railways are almost synonymous. Although other forms of transport, in particular water transport, were of much greater importance than the railways even in England until the 1830s and 1840s, and continued to be so in many areas of continental Europe for much longer, they have become to be regarded as no more than a side-issue, as an evolutionary dead-end and consequently of little or no importance. Early modern Europe had no efficient system of land-based bulk transport and therefore it could have had no efficient system of transport of any kind.

The older interpretation does have a number of valid points which should not be ignored. First, it is true that, although the transport of bulk goods, in particular of bulk raw materials over land in early modern Europe, did occur, it was a costly business, only to be undertaken when there was no effective alternative. This was particularly the case with food, especially grains and cereals. Despite the importance of food supplies in the overall economy, grain could not be transported over land easily or cheaply and the movement of large quantities of grain overland was something which could only be contemplated at times of great crisis. In the sixteenth century, the costs of transporting grain from Orléans to Lyon increased its price by 75 per cent.[20] The early modern transportation system was much more efficient at moving goods of relatively high unit value rather than goods of bulk consumption. Second, early modern communication was slow, be it over land or by water; it was not possible to rush supplies of goods or raw materials to markets or to producers to meet sudden peaks of demand or to deal with sudden shortages. In the sixteenth century goods moved overland from Lyon to the southern Netherlands averaged 44 km per day; by river they could be moved as fast as 90 km in a day downstream, but upstream they averaged no more than 15 km a day.[21] Even in the eighteenth century, movement away from the most important roads and rivers was slow: the fastest passengers could hope to get from Vannes to Rennes was 24 hours, while goods being moved by river took ten to twelve days, and the river route was only open for six months each year.[22] Third, the flow of information about market conditions and so forth was slow. There was no instantaneous information available and merchants and traders often had to rely either on the lessons of past experience or on trusted agents and partners operating directly in distant markets. All these factors made the early modern system less 'efficient' than a modern system would be. However, what is important is not that the early modern system could not do what the modern system does but that early modern traders, merchants and manufacturers were well aware of these problems and had developed strategies to deal with them. The specific difficulties of the early modern system might have proved insurmountable for a nineteenth- or twentieth-century businessman trying to operate in a modern way, but for early modern Europeans they were no more than a normal part of the overall situation, to be dealt with by the adoption of the appropriate strategies. As ever, it is important to attempt to see the system through the eyes of the people who were working it rather than as an inefficient precursor of a system which developed from it, in very different economic conditions.

Early modern communications were heavily dominated by water-borne transport. The coasts of Europe were obviously crucial in the movement of goods. Goods and raw materials produced in the interior were brought as quickly as possible to the coast so that they could be more effectively and cheaply transported. Coal from the mines of Northumberland and County Durham were brought to the Tyne and the Wear to allow its easy export; iron ore from the hematite mines of northern Castile was transported from Burgos to the Basque ports of the northern coastline, Bilbao, Santander and San Sebastián.[23] It was not only the major ports which played a role in this coastal trade. Coastal shipping was small, and most coastal places, whether they had harbours or not, carried on sea-borne trade.

Water was also used as the major route into the interior of Europe and as the major arteries of inland trade. The great rivers, the Gironde, the Loire, the Seine, the Rhône, the Scheldt, the Rhine and its tributaries the Meuse and the Main, the Weser, the Elbe, the Oder, the Vistula, the Danube and its tributaries, the Adige and the Po were all major highways for goods (and people) into the far interior of Europe. They constituted important routes along which the trade and production of the interior reached the coast and international markets. Nor was it only the major river systems which saw trade and navigation; rivers like the Charente, the Somme or the Ems were also important regional routes. The limits of navigation on all these rivers were much higher than they were to be in the nineteenth and twentieth centuries; Le Puy in the Auvergne, for instance, was the head of navigation on the Loire, at least in a downstream direction. River boats were much smaller, and smaller boats were much more economical than they were to become in the nineteenth century, when the need to compete with the railways meant that boats had be much larger. It is often forgotten that streams which are now too shallow for any form of navigation, and ones which have vanished through silting, land drainage or reclamation, were important locally and that methods of improving the depth of water, such as flashing, were used all over Europe, allowing even mountainous areas to served by water-borne transport, at least downstream.

River navigation was slow, especially upstream, where the need to make progress against the current meant that animals or human towers were necessary, increasing both time and cost. Although this was a major problem in the nineteenth century, especially as boats became larger and more expensive to build and maintain, during the early modern period it was less of a problem. If the journey upstream was too difficult or expensive, it was better to take a boat or other conveyance downstream and then return upstream overland, leaving the boat, or the wood of which it was constructed, to be sold.[24] In such circumstances the boat used only for travelling downstream did not have to be complex or even particularly well built because it had to survive only a single journey. On many rivers a considerable amount of traffic was carried on rafts, platforms of logs with basic navigation equipment, living quarters for the crew and basic storage for other goods.[25] The raft was not a survival of a primitive form of transport, indicating the backward and undeveloped state of transportation, but in fact an entirely practical solution to a common problem.

A second problem with river navigation was its seasonality. On all European rivers, but in particular those like the Loire where shallows and sandbanks were common, trade was only possible when conditions were right. The Alpine rivers, fed by mountain snows, were unusable during the winter when the cold locked up much of their flow. Rivers like the Elbe or the Vistula were largely unusable during the winter months because of ice, although some goods continued to be carried by sledge on the frozen rivers. Virtually all rivers were unusable, especially upstream, during the spring spates. Summer or autumn drought, which meant low water levels in the rivers, also slowed or stopped movement.[26] This seasonality of trade would obviously become a major problem in the nineteenth century when the new factory-based industries depended on year-round production and sales to service their immense establishment and financial costs, but in the early modern period this seasonality fitted well into a structure which was itself heavily seasonal. Again, the early modern system was efficient within its own terms. It is only when it is expected to carry out functions which were foreign to it that it begins to appear inefficient.

The problems of the water-based transportation system were not totally insurmountable, nor were no attempts made to deal with them, attempts which were in many cases successful. Early modern Europeans did not simply accept their transportation and communications system in a fatalistic sort of way but attempted to improve the situation. The river navigations themselves were improved by dredging, by piling and other forms of water management including, in some places, canalisation and the installation of locks to bypass rapids or to raise water levels. Increasing attempts were made to modernise the system by improving the connections between river systems. One of the untold stories of the Middle Ages and the early modern period is the process by which the gaps between river systems were bridged, for instance, the way in which the economic systems of the Loire, Rhône and Seine valleys were brought into contact. To move from river system to river system involved some kind of transport across the intervening land which, by its very nature, was hilly and difficult. In the early modern period these links not only existed but were of considerable importance. Towns like Roanne and La Charité-sur-Loire owed their prosperity to a major extent to their importance as transhipment centres.[27] The longest and most complex of these overland links were the ones which linked rivers over the Alps. The route from the head of navigation on the Adige at Bolzano over the Brenner Pass to the head of navigation on the Inn at Innsbruck was one of the major routes of European commerce. As the importance of these links, and of the interlinkages between regions, grew, attempts were made to improve them. In some cases this took the form of road improvements and the provision of larger and better teams of draught animals or of larger pack trains, but in others the importance of the link was so great that by the seventeenth century plans were being laid to develop water communications. The construction of the Canale de Briare in 1604 marked the beginning of a water communication between the Loire and the Loing and hence with the Seine and Paris. The new canal was striking both for its scale and also for the complexity of the civil engineering work involved. An even greater piece of linkage was the construction of the Canale des Deux Mers in southern France. Canal construction, of course, was not limited to France. In the Low Countries the construction of canals and dykes, used for both drainage and for transport, had been a common feature since the Middle Ages. In the northern Netherlands, for instance, the canal system played a major role in the transport of goods, including agricultural produce, to and from the cities of the western Netherlands, and also provided an efficient system of passenger transport.[28]

The water-borne system was in many ways well suited to the structure and organisation of early modern industry and commerce. It would be entirely wrong to suggest that goods were only transported by water, with land transport playing the role of local distributor to towns and villages off the main lines of river communication. Land transport did play a major role. In part that role was the linking between river systems mentioned above, but in some cases it went much further than that. For instance, even in the sixteenth century, much of the important trade between Lyon and the cities of the southern Netherlands, rather than following the longer water route via the Doubs and the Rhine, was taken, either by boat or by packhorse or cart to St Jean de Losne on the Saône and then by road via the upper Seine valley to Troyes, Reims, Laon, St Quentin and Guise. This was a sufficiently large and sufficiently established land-trading route for specialist 'haulage contractors' to have developed in the villages of the upper Seine valley around Bar-sur-Seine who contracted with the merchants to convey their goods over the whole journey.[29] Land-based trading could have a place in the system where the alternatives were either too long or too risky. It was much better to convey goods between the Loire and the Seine over land than it was to risk the dangerous voyage down to the sea and around Brittany.

Land-based trade occurred in other circumstances. In particular, goods which could move themselves, cattle and sheep, for example, were taken over land. Whatever the impression the older interpretations claimed, meat was an important element of consumption in early modern Europe. In an age without refrigeration, the only way in which fresh meat could be supplied was by taking the live beast to the consumer, or nearly so. For some towns and regions local supplies were enough, but for many of the expanding urban centres of the early modern period, local supplies were by no means adequate. English historians have long been used to the idea of the great cattle droves from the pastoral areas of England, Wales and, by the eighteenth century, Scotland to London. This movement of animals, however, was only one, and a relatively unimportant one, of many similar movements of cattle. Cattle from the pastures of the Limousin were already in the sixteenth century being driven to Bordeaux, Lyon and Paris; Lyon also drew important supplies both of cattle and of dairy produce from the Bresse and the western slopes of the Alps.[30] The Hohenlohe in south-western Germany raised cattle which were exported on the hoof to the towns of southern Germany, and to Strasbourg or even further.[31] Cattle and sheep were driven from Normandy to Paris or were driven to Picardy to be fattened before being traded to the Paris market.[32] Greatest of all, involving in some cases herds of 15 000 or 20 000 beasts, was the movement of cattle from Europe's 'wild east', the plains of Poland and western Russia, through cattle-trading towns and centres in Saxony and Thuringia, further west into Germany, France and the Netherlands.[33]

Early modern Europe's transportation system was by no means primitive or minimal. Goods did move about to a lesser extent than they were to do after the arrival of the railways and, as a consequence, there were still economic advantages in the relatively local production of the cheapest goods for mass consumption. Nonetheless, there was extensive trade in manufactured goods and raw materials, sufficient to allow the development of relative local specialisation in particular types of production, and certainly enough to allow the development of a consumer market in goods which were not locally produced. It is worth pointing out that the acknowledged problems and cost penalties of the long-distance transport of manufactured or colonial goods were not so great, or alternatively the poverty of early modern consumers was not so severe, as to prevent the development of large-scale consumption of these goods which lay outside the basic minimal consumption for survival.

Goods were not the only thing to travel. Information, economic as well as political, was of crucial importance. In the modern world, where so much information is available widely and immediately, it is very easy to forget how important information, about economic conditions, about the political situation in distant places, even about the prevalence of epidemic disease, was for traders or producers. Information about markets and demand in general was important, but short-term information, and the short-term advantage which came from having information (in particular correct information) before one's competitors, could be of great importance. Information in the early modern period moved in general no faster than the fastest horse.[34] As conditions on the roads improved, as they did over most of continental Europe, so the speed of information increased, but even at the end of the period, it was not so great that decisions could be referred back to the home base of a company if the market was to be played effectively. The development of a large, more fashion-influenced consumer market which was more likely to be fluctuating increased the importance of information and began the creation of what can be called an information industry. In particular the need of traders and merchants for accurate information about distant markets, and incidentally about the political and military situation which was a crucial element in those market conditions, led to the development of newssheets designed to provide just that sort of information. Some of the great trading and financial companies of the later Middle Ages and the sixteenth century, and indeed some of the states, had developed internal information systems. The great Fugger banking house of Augsburg collected information from its agents and correspondents all over Europe and circulated them internally. The Venetian Council of Ten, as part of its European-wide information network, collected commercial as well as political reports. It was in the seventeenth century, in part as a result of official action, but increasingly as a private commercial undertaking, that newssheets began to be published and circulated, listing prices in major centres such as Amsterdam and Hamburg. Increasingly these newssheets collected information from elsewhere in Europe. For the first time merchants and manufacturers could have – albeit somewhat out-of-date – information about prices and market conditions in Europe's major centres of trade and consumption without the expense of setting up their own networks.

If information was in short supply and expensive, rumour was in general in good supply and cheap, at least to purchase, if not in its consequences. One of the major issues which the earlier interpreters of the early modern economy never really tackled, and which even more recent ones are only just beginning to consider, is the role of rumour in economic decision-making. In the early modern period it was only possible long after the event to be certain whether information was correct. Usually, economic decisions had to be taken on the basis of information which could be totally incorrect, based on rumour, and in some cases on rumour maliciously spread. The degree of accuracy of any report was unknowable. This problem is most strikingly visible where the time-lag between events and information was very long, such as in the intercontinental trades with Asia or America.

The trading networks which have just been discussed were, in modern terms, wholesale networks, moving goods from region to region in bulk rather than distributing them to consumers within the region. Although some of the long-distance traders did engage in more local trade, the complexities of long-distance trade made concentration on it much easier than trying to combine it with other activities. Furthermore, the structure of long-distance trades tended to mean that all long-distance traders had to some extent to be general dealers rather than specialists. Although a trader might partially specialise, for example, in the export of textiles from his local economy, or in the import of spices into that economy, his need to maximise the efficiency of the operation of his trade meant that on the return leg of the trade he was likely to trade in whatever commodity appeared likely to be the most profitable or the most secure or to return his profits as cash.[35] Hence commercial specialisation at the highest level was uncommon. Since a particular retail buyer was unlikely to know what goods a particular trader was carrying on a specific trip, and was unlikely to be interested in dealing in all the goods he might carry, since it might range from spices to silks to iron goods from Sweden, there was a considerable tendency to specialise in either wholesale or retail trade.

The production-based interpretations of the early modern economy have tended to ignore the whole retail sector. Historians discussed how goods were produced but had little interest how they were consumed and how they got to the consumer, certainly compared with questions such as the supply of raw materials or of capital to provide machinery. Consideration of the distribution network was limited to a discussion of the great fairs, such as those of Lyon or Champagne, which were essentially wholesale and financial organisations, and of the local markets and of pedlars. Up to a point this concentration on the periodic markets is both valid and significant. In the sixteenth century and before, most retailing outside the largest towns does seem to have occurred within the framework of these weekly or less frequent markets. The periodic nature of these markets and hence of spending is a clear reminder of the periodic and seasonal nature of much income and expenditure, especially in the dominant rural sector. In the older interpretations the figure of the pedlar symbolised the relatively low levels of consumption in an economy dominated by subsistence, but may be seen rather more as the first stage of the development of a distribution network which reached far beyond the market towns and began to service rural consumer demand.

By the eighteenth century, however, this picture was changing not merely in the most 'advanced' areas of Europe but over most of the continent. Although periodic markets and pedlars still survived, their importance was declining. In many towns the permanent shop had begun to replace the market stall, and in some towns and cities, the shop had become something more than an enclosed version of a market stall; for instance shop windows and window displays had begun to appear. Shops also began to be seen in villages in the eighteenth century, earlier in some parts of Europe. At first these village shops sold only food and drink, but later much more complex general stores, selling haberdashery, textiles, metal and other household goods, began to appear. Village people began going to the shop for their needs rather than waiting until market day and making the trip into the market town for their purchases or waiting for the irregular and unpredictable visits of the pedlar.

This rise of the permanent shop has considerable significance for both the economy and for society. Permanent shops, with their higher overheads, imply a higher and more constant level of consumer demand, a demand which expressed itself in cash terms. That higher level of demand indicates either greater prosperity or a higher level of disposable income, or both. The permanence of that demand suggests either a very much higher level of income and a much higher security of income, or a profound change in attitudes to consumption and to saving, or both. The shops could provide credit and hence offer another way of tiding a family or an individual over seasonal or other crises. This local supply of easily available credit with no security may well have played a role both in generating a more permanent level of consumption and in creating the greater sense of security which was necessary for the generation of higher consumption.

Most of the changes in the retailing sector happened during or before the eighteenth century, that is, before any real process of industrialisation got under way in Britain and long before it occurred on the Continent. Yet these changes were said in the older production-based interpretations to be the consequences of industrial change and of the industrialisation process rather than precursors of it. It is striking that these changes in retailing, as well as the more general changes in patterns of consumption on which they closely depended, were not confined to the most 'developed' areas of Europe, that is, to the Netherlands or England, but can be identified over much of the Continent. It may well have been in some of the most 'backward' areas such as France and Spain which were dominated by 'feudalism' and by 'feudal values', or in Italy, whose merchant capitalist tradition was in the process of being 'betrayed' by a formerly commercial nobility which was being refeudalised, that the developments in retailing and consumption appeared earliest and developed most strongly before the nineteenth century. It can no longer be safely argued that change in early modern Europe, nor even change in a 'modernising' direction, were confined to a few particular areas in Protestant north-western Europe.

4

THE ROLE OF THE STATE

Nowhere is the distinction between the early modern and the modern period so clearly seen as in the role and nature of the state. The traditional start and finish of the early modern period have conventionally been defined by political events. For traditional economic historians with their bias towards a nineteenth-century viewpoint the French Revolution marked the divide between the early modern and the modern. Over much of Europe, the most profound consequences of the Revolution and of the French expansion which followed it were political and administrative rather than social or economic. Despite their normal rejection of the importance of political change and political structures in economic change, the traditional historians considered their role as crucial in defining the difference between the periods.

The importance assigned to the state and to the political dimension was heightened by the development of models of historical development in which the role of the state was great. It became an article of belief that the state had to perform certain roles and functions if the economy were to develop, grow and modernise. The traditional historiography did not ascribe to the state the dominating and controlling role which it was to play in Marxian theory, where it became the only force which could be effective. Nonetheless, the role of the state was central to the economy: as a consumer, as a collector and spender of taxes, as a regulator and controller of economic activity and as the operator of a clear and progressive economic policy. This view of the development and importance of the state was, by the 1970s, accepted, implicitly or explicitly, by virtually every economic historian.

Interestingly, this idea coexisted in tension with an older one, which goes back to at least Adam Smith, that the history of the development of the European economy and its infrastructure was, in essence, the history of the decline of the state and the reduction of its role in the economy to that of a regulator and a legislator, setting the basic conditions for the free operation of the economy. Given that the economy was a freely operating structure, self-regulating and, as a force of nature, too powerful to be controlled by any state, it was folly for the state to attempt to do more than to set and maintain the conditions in which the economy and its natural forces could operate safely and freely. Hence, 'liberal' or 'small government' states like England and the United Provinces were praised for their demolition of regulation and intervention, for being non-interventionist and allowing the economy to develop. The interventionist 'absolutist' governments, like France or Prussia, were criticised for over-regulation and over-interference – for acting like modern states. Underlying much of this are deeper assumptions about the nature of the state, about 'absolutism' versus 'freer' political structures, or even of Catholic against Protestant.

Until recently, the distinctions between the early modern and the modern state and their economic roles and functions were seen by historians in very sharp terms which were usually to the disadvantage of the early modern state.

The modern state was characterised, as much by implication as directly, as being efficient. It was able to make decisions on the basis of sound and extensive information, to convert those decisions into effective and structured policies which it put into effect because it possessed the mechanisms and the personnel to ensure that policy decisions produce commensurate action at whatever level in the economy or society. The modern state was seen as centralised, able to take a nationwide viewpoint, based upon consistent and accurate intelligence from the whole of the area under its control. It could assess and collect taxes fairly and efficiently, and so it possessed concentrated economic power which enabled it to play a major, indeed *the* major role in the economy. It was able to this because administration became a professional and specialised activity. The modern state was seen as having professional cadres whose loyalties were to the state and to its organisation rather than to family, local or political groups. This professionalism means that the modern state was able to follow consistent and active economic management policies, using its power and expertise to create the framework within which economic activity can happen. In addition, the modern state was able to control social and economic activity and it could also determine and direct economic and social change.

Management of the economy and economic policy lay at the very centre of the activity of the modern state. It was above all the success with which economic policy was directed which often determined the standing and overall success or failure of governments.

In contrast, the early modern state was characterised as failing to meet the standards which were deemed necessary for the creation of a healthily functioning economy and as having a number of additional failings. The early modern state was inefficient. It had an unprofessional administration which was dominated by clientage and essentially corrupt. The majority of the administrators of the early modern state were amateurs, members of local and regional elite groups linked to the state at the basic local level of its operation. At best they had clearly divided loyalties, and in most cases were seen as furthering their own ends rather than those of the state. At higher levels there was a professional administration, but it was tiny. It was too small to carry out effectively even the small amounts of activity which the early modern state was able to undertake and its personnel were more often placemen and the clients of the greater nobility than a professional administrative service. The early modern state lacked effective means to execute its policy. In most areas of government activity policy decisions largely had to be implemented by the local elites, who themselves would be affected by them and whose loyalty in a crisis could not be guaranteed. The early modern state lacked effective and speedy means of coercion in a crisis. It also lacked effective means for gathering and transmitting information so problems could not be dealt with rapidly before they became critical. The early modern state was regarded as failing to follow effective economic policies. It was too weak and too diffuse in political and administrative structure to pursue any central policy, as was the Venetian Republic, or it was too centralised and authoritarian, as was Habsburg Spain, or it was both at once, as was seventeenth- and eighteenth-century France. The early modern state was dismissed as not being, in general, interested in economic policy as such, but as regarding it as no more than a minor adjunct to other policies. The failure of the early modern state was epitomised for supporters of the traditional interpretation by the dominant economic theory of the seventeenth and early eighteenth centuries, mercantilism, against which Smith was to argue so forcibly in *Wealth of Nations*. Mercantilism saw the political and military success of the state as being the chief goal of government, and the development of commerce and the economy as being subordinate to this end.[1]

The early modern state was not seen simply as carrying out badly (or not at all) the same economic activities and functions as the modern state. In the traditional interpretation it also had damaging economic effects of its own. First, because the early modern state treated economic prosperity and economic development as subordinate to its other aims and purposes, it took political decisions without any concern for their economic consequences. For example, some states concerned with enforcing religious conformity expelled dissenters, despite the effects those expulsions might have on the economy. The expulsion of the Maranos from Spain and Portugal in the sixteenth century was to have major effects on the economies of the Iberian monarchies throughout the early modern period, and contributed to the massive rise of north-western commercial centres such as Antwerp, Amsterdam and Hamburg, where they settled. Whatever its political or religious justification, the expulsion of the Moriscos from southern Spain in the early years of the seventeenth century was an act of economic folly, ruining the agriculture and industry of one of the most productive areas of Spain. Although the Revocation of the Edict of Nantes in 1685 was the culmination of a century or more of political development, it ruined France's hopes of economic and commercial development for many years, and also gave France's European competitors a major injection of skills and entrepreneurship.

Second, the way the early modern state had to operate made it dependent upon sectional interest, and hence its policies were seen as being concerned with protecting those sectional interests. The economic consequences of this could be substantial, as it was, for instance, in many parts of southern France or in Saxony, where the state depended upon the support of the urban elites, both for the political control of the cities and towns and their hinterlands and also for the loans upon which it relied. The state became a protector of the privileges of those urban elites. It backed the urban guild regulations which local elites imposed on trade and manufacture to maintain their own positions, prevented the liberalisation of production within the towns and cities, and attempted to prevent unregulated development outside the urban areas.

Third, the early modern state treated taxation as no more than a way of financing its own activities rather than as a tool of economic or social management. The early modern state sought to balance its books by increasing taxation income to match expenditure, rather than by cutting expenditure to match economically beneficial or even sustainable levels of taxation. At the very end of the early modern period, the history of the last decades of absolute monarchy in France demonstrates the inability of early modern governments, even at times of terminal crisis, to control their expenditure over any more than a short period. As a result, early modern taxation was high, particularly for lower economic and social groups. Changes in taxation were related not to the state of the economy but to the demands of other aspects of state policy. For instance, the economic crisis of the 1690s in France was made worse by massive increases in taxation to finance the state's wars at a time when climatic and commercial difficulties had already made things difficult for the great mass of French people.

The traditional view was that in the early modern period taxation was high and also unfairly distributed. The archaic political structures of the early modern state meant that the great burden of taxation fell on the less well-to-do. This was often a consequence of the taxation privileges and exemptions of the nobility, the clergy and, in some parts of Europe, the urban elites. In Spain the richest 15 per cent of the population was able to claim exemption, and inevitably an unfair share of the taxation burden fell on the rest of society. The unfairness of the distribution of taxation increased when states like France and Spain resorted more and more to the direct sale of privileges, and hence of exemptions, to help them meet their increasingly urgent financial needs. Most taxes were taxes on consumption rather than on income or wealth. Their weight fell disproportionately on the less well-to-do and on the poor, since food and other necessities were taxed as heavily, or more heavily, than luxuries. Taxes were normally not collected directly by the state but were farmed out to members of the commercial, financial or political elite, so the tax burden on the poor was increased by the demand of the tax-farmers for profits from their taxation franchises.

The structure of the early modern state and of its government effectively precluded any real change in the sources and nature of its income. Throughout the early modern period states were moving away from medieval forms of government, of monarchy and of defence, but few of them succeeded in moving away from their medieval tax bases. This meant that the early modern state was regarded as having no real stake, and no real interest, in the expansion of new sectors of the economy, since they lay beyond its ability to tax.

This inability to expand the tax base at a time when the costs of the state were expanding rapidly meant that the early modern state had to cope with frequent and severe financial crises. In trying to solve its financial difficulties, the government could produce damaging economic effects. Trying to meet increasing costs, the early modern state could make use of expedients such as the sale of offices and of patents of nobility, but the only options it had for increasing its income substantially were either the reduction of the metallic content of the coinage or increased borrowing.

In the sixteenth century and the earlier part of the seventeenth, a favourite expedient was debasement. A reminting of the coinage with a smaller proportion of precious metal allowed the state to take for its own use the metal so removed. However, this inevitably led to major currency and economic crises. The effects of the 'Great Debasement' in Tudor England or of the *Kipper- und Wipperzeit* in early seventeenth-century Germany had profound social as well as economic effects.[2]

The early modern state found that borrowing was a more reliable method of increasing its income and government debt throughout Europe expanded rapidly. It was the reliance of states upon borrowing and the consequent expansion of national indebtedness which played a major role in the development of more modern banking systems in, for instance, the Italian Republics in the sixteenth century or the Netherlands and England in the seventeenth. The growth of state debt was seen as doing considerable damage to early modern economies. Capital was drained away from its potential use in industrial and commercial expansion because the states needed so much money that they took so much of the available wealth. In addition, because states had to pay high rates of interest (because in part there was a high risk they would refuse to repay loans in full or at all), investment in government securities was more attractive to investors than was investment in commerce or industry. The subsequent inability of the states to service their huge debts, because they could only pay off one loan by further borrowing, caused bankruptcies. This destabilised the structure of finance and banking across Europe because states tended, at least until the eighteenth century, to turn to large private capitalists for their funds, rather than a larger number of small investors. The great bankers of Augsburg and Nuremberg, for instance, were bankrupted by the failure of the princes to whom they had lent money, and the consequences of their failure had major long-term effects for the urban economies of southern Germany.[3] Not all state borrowing was voluntary. The forced loan was a major element in state finances throughout the early modern period and this played a major role in destabilising the financial system. It also maintained and increased the great distrust felt by most investors for loans which were not secured and not operated within a clearly personal relationship.

Fourth, it was not merely the excessive scale of the state's expenditure which was a problem for traditional economic historians but also the nature of that expenditure. Some of expenditure priorities of the early modern state seem almost quixotic to modern eyes. Even at the end of the eighteenth century and despite the attempts of reforming ministers to change the balance of expenditure, two elements of expenditure out-weighed all others: defence, and the maintenance of the royal court and the structures of monarchy. In the last years of the old monarchy in France, the upkeep of king and court amounted to more than a third of the government's annual expenditure, and in other states was an even greater proportion of the total. The costs of royal maintenance covered not merely the upkeep of palaces and the pomp and circum-stance which went on in and around them, but also the large subven-tions and gifts which the Crown made regularly to its supporters and hangers-on.[4] In terms of modern economic policy, the early modern state spent a huge proportion of its income on what could only be called conspicuous waste. Even if the large proportion of total govern-mental expenditure which was collected and expended locally is included, a very significant proportion of the share of production which was being taken in taxation was being used for unproductive, in some cases counterproductive, purposes.

It was argued that the monarchical nature of most early modern states and the political instability of many of the non-monarchic states such as the United Provinces or the Venetian Republic meant that most political decision-making was very short-term. The early modern state seldom formed or implemented long-term political, social or economic policies. One reason for this was the precariousness of the finances of most early modern states. Financial and economic policy was domi-nated by the urgent need to ensure that sufficient money was available to pay wages or to feed the court and its dependants that week, month or year. Longer-term considerations were inevitably subordinate to immediate crisis. For example, it was acknowledged at the time that expedients such as the sale of nobility or of offices were dangerous in the medium and longer term, but immediate needs outweighed longer-term fears.

Fifth, it was argued that the structure of the early modern state was such that government policy was often dependent upon personality.

The will or the whim of the monarch ruled absolutely and the continuity of policy could be dependent upon nothing more firm or more certain than the favour of the king. The history of French economic policy under Louis XIV or Louis XVI, or that of Spanish policy under the eighteenth-century Bourbon monarchs, clearly demonstrates that drastic changes of direction could be induced by no more than royal displeasure with an old minister or royal infatuation with a new one. The political structure of the central administration was focused upon a monarch enclosed in a faction-ridden court, with little or no access to any external advice or information. This guaranteed that the factional and personal in-fighting of the court was more likely to determine the fate of ministers and their policies than any dispassionate assessment of their success or failure.

Sixth, for the traditional historians, early modern government was corrupt. In the early modern period the concept of a government or a bureaucracy which was not swayed by considerations of personal profit and power was unknown. The court and the courtiers who dominated the early modern state and its policies were at the apex of a system of patronage and clientage which extended through the whole of society, linking clients in distant urban and rural localities, through complex intermediate patterns of patronage and clientage, to the court elite at the centre. It was the development and refining of this system, and the installation of the monarchy as the ultimate patron, the chief dispenser of bounty, which had been the great unifier of the early modern state, the great advance politically from the late Middle Ages. This had had two consequences for the way the state was able to operate. First, ministers were dependent for their position upon the support of the great patrons, and so they had always to consider how policy would be received by those great courtiers and by their extensive patronage networks. Sectional and personal interest were built into the system of government. Second, the implementation of policy in the regions and localities depended on the support and involvement of the patronage networks. Any government activity would inevitably necessitate the diffusion of advantage through the patrons to the networks, whether it was a share of any funds expended, a share of the proceeds of policy success, or a share of the proceeds of the offices created to put any policy into effect. The traditional interpretations argued that, even when, unusually, governments did attempt to implement policies of economic improvement, most of the beneficial effects of those policies leached away through the patronage system.

Seventh, the royal court at the apex of the early modern system had a restricted membership which was largely exclusive. Entitlement and appointment to office was not determined by merit or ability but by membership of the ruling group. All across Europe the courts were dominated, and became increasingly dominated by, the nobility. The nobility, and in particularly the court nobility, were a social and political group with their own interests and their own ethos and culture. Whether that ethos was based on rank and 'race', as in France and Spain, or upon service to the state and to the monarch, as in eighteenth-century Prussia or the Russia of Peter the Great, it was regarded by the traditional historians as having an essentially anti-commercial, anti-industrial and anti-financier outlook. The commercial classes were necessary for the prosperity of the state and hence for the proper operation of state policy, but that did not make them socially acceptable or even proper advisers for the king. As the early modern state became more and more organised, and as the nobility and the professional bureaucracy became more entrenched in its structure, so, it was argued, the state became more and more dismissive of the commercial classes and their concerns.

This general condemnation of the economic role of the early modern state in comparison with that of the modern state, as either marginal to the point of insignificance or actively malign in its influence, is unfair and needs to be reconsidered.

First, the basis of the comparison between the modern and the early modern state is unfair. What is being compared is not the practical functioning of the two systems but, instead, the ideal of the modern state is compared with the reality of the early modern state. We all know from experience that the modern state is not always an impartial and efficient organisation. The modern state does not distribute the tax burden equitably in society, nor is it able to gather all its revenues. The modern state is not able to maintain law and order throughout its territory at all times. Few modern states are able to exclude either sectional interest or short-termism from their policy-making structures: they are inseparable from a government's political self-interest and from the sectional interests of the bureaucracies upon which the modern state depends. It would be difficult to characterise the economic policies of a modern state as always based on rational argument, as always put into effect with success and as always having the consequences intended by government. It would certainly be impossible to argue that modern states have only pursued economic policies based upon fairness and equity. The modern state in practice is in many ways as imperfect as the early modern one.

Second, a great deal of the traditional contrast between the early modern and the modern state is based upon an anachronism, on the assumption that early modern states pursued, or should have pursued, the same objectives with the same methods as the modern state and should therefore be criticised when they failed to achieve them. An early modern state had different aims and objectives, and its society was organised with a different power structure and involved different practical considerations.

Third, the traditional contrast is based upon the profoundly illogical view that the early modern state was somehow separate from the nation it was governing. The ruling elite was isolated from the ruled and the different interests of the two groups were frequently in conflict. If the economic performance of the early modern state was poor, because it was profoundly dependent upon a system of patronage and clientage which stretched from the royal court to local communities, it could hardly at the same time be alien and distant from the society and the economy which it governed and controlled.

The traditional view is an expression of a broad refusal to accept that the early modern state differed from the modern one in its nature and operation as well as in its aims and objectives. It is also clear that the early modern state was not so economically disastrous nor economically unimportant as has been argued. In many parts of continental Europe, far from slowing down or impeding economic development, the state was an important factor in much economic change during the early modern period. Simply because the early modern state did not follow open and declared economic policies, that did not mean that it was in some way divorced from the economy.

In most European states during the early modern period the state was the largest single actor on the economic stage. Even though the power structure of the state was diffuse, and its use of its economic power was divided and sometimes incoherent, nonetheless its central institutions – the monarchy itself, the military and the bureaucracy – constituted both the largest single receiver of income and the largest single spender. In most early modern states, the only institution which could compete economically with the state was the Church. In both Catholic and Protestant countries, however, the Church did not exist as a single corporation with a single policy, but was rather a series of separate entities, each following its own economic or commercial policy, often operating in competition with other sectors of the Church. These discrete corporations were held together by their common privileged status rather than by any shared economic interest. In the early modern period, a great deal of the wealth of the Church was held in totally illiquid forms, in particular in land or land entitlements which were unsaleable and often limited by traditional rights and dues. One of the major sources of liquid wealth for the Church, the tithe, had been wholly or in part alienated and transferred to private, non-clerical owners across much of Europe. The liquidity of its financial position was one of the great strengths of the state, compared with the Church or with private individuals and 'capitalists'. The early modern state had few capital assets which could be realised; its wealth depended upon the liquid income from taxation, dues and the sales of privilege and office. Unlike a private capitalist, or pre-capitalist, unlike a prudent clerical or lay corporation, the early modern state did not normally think to increase its capital stock, to put money or assets on one side for insurance against hard times, or to build up a credit balance to provide for an increase in trading capital.[5] The early modern state took little thought for the morrow and spent all, and often more than all, its income immediately.

Because it was by far the largest spender of money, the state inevitably must have had major effects on the economy and its operation. The state was the largest consumer in an early modern European economy. This is as true for 'small government' states such as England or the United Netherlands as it was for the 'heavy government' absolutisms such as France or Prussia, and it remains true throughout the period. The state consumed huge quantities of materials; it required wood and metals, pitch and tar, minerals, grain, meat and dairy produce for the armed forces, it needed building materials, textiles, food, luxury goods, paper and a myriad other things to maintain the court and the monarchy. The establishment of new court centres and new administrative towns led to the development of industries and new agricultural systems to supply them, at first locally, but increasingly on a wider basis. For instance, the growth of Madrid in the sixteenth century led first to the development of new industrial and agricultural production in the neighbouring areas of Old and New Castile and then to the development of long-distance supply routes bringing food and other goods to the capital from Valencia and other areas of provincial Spain.[6] In France the growth of Versailles in the seventeenth century stimulated the industrial economy of the Paris region and also the agriculture of the whole Ile de France.[7] As the court increased its demand for more goods and for greater novelties, the net was spread wider and wider. By the 1680s wine was being brought to Versailles from the Rhône Valley and the Midi, by a combination of road and river transport, while cheese and other dairy produce was being brought from the Auvergne and cattle on the hoof from the Limousin.[8] Similarly, in the Kingdom of Naples the expansion first of Naples itself and then of the new royal centre, Caserta, in the late seventeenth and eighteenth centuries, led to a growing trade in grain from Puglia to the capital.[9]

The state was not merely important as a consumer; it was also the largest single employer of labour in an early modern European economy. For instance, the courts employed, either directly or indirectly, large numbers of people, of local origin at first, but increasingly drawn from a wider area. The state was the largest single employer of women, even though their role does seem to have declined in the pattern of service in the eighteenth century. The unpopularity of employment in the army and the navy should not hide the fact that military employment was an important element in the economies of many parts of Europe in the early modern period. For instance, the basically pastoral and almost certainly overcrowded economy of the Auvergne seems to have been heavily dependent for its survival upon the employment of large numbers of Auvergnats in the army and the navy.[10] In Spain, the poor western provinces of Castile, Extremadura and La Mancha were the major recruiting grounds for the *tercios*, the infantry upon whom Spain's military reputation depended in the sixteenth and seventeenth centuries, and these desperately poor regions depended above all upon military employment for their survival and moderate prosperity. Many of the Swiss cantons and many of the communities of the Tyrol also depended upon military employment for their economic survival. In all these cases the availability of military employment permitted the survival of population densities much greater than the soil could directly support.

The early modern state, then, played a major role in the national and international economy. Without the state as a consumer and an employer the overall pattern of most early modern economies would have been very different. It is, however, incorrect to see the early modern state as a totally passive or involuntary player in the economy. Although the aims and interests of the state were not in general directly economic (although they became increasingly so in the eighteenth century), nonetheless early modern states did undertake activities which had important economic effects.

The most obvious of these was the creation of new towns, most spectacularly the creation of the new court and administrative capitals, either like Madrid, grafted on to older, small towns or created completely afresh, such as Mannheim or St Petersburg.[11] In the short term, the building of new towns, or of great palace complexes like Versailles or, in a smaller state, Herrenhausen, required large supplies of labour and raw materials, which stimulated demand over wide areas and which also required the development of infrastructure to transport supplies to the site. In the long term the new towns became important centres of consumption, and hence of service, of employment, of demand for agricultural produce and of manufacture.

New capital cities and new palaces were not the only major building projects which the state undertook. The great refortification of Europe which began with the development of new forms of military architecture under Vauban was very expensive and involved high levels of employment, high demands for raw materials and, in many cases, quite considerable improvements in technology and skills. Of greater long-term importance for the economy was the creation of new ports and commercial centres by state action. The establishment in the late sixteenth century of what was essentially a new port, Livorno, by the Medici Grand Dukes of Tuscany, and the continuing history of that port's encouragement by the Grand Dukes, illustrates the importance that early modern states could attach to economic and commercial activities.[12] In France the establishment of Le Havre by François I as a deep-water port which allowed ships to avoid the shoaled approach to Rouen had major long-term consequences for the economy not merely of Normandy, but for the whole of northern France[13.] In the seventeenth century the establishment of ports such as Rochefort on the west coast of France[14] or Sète at the Mediterranean end of the Canale des Deux Mers[15] was vitally important for both local and regional economies.

In addition to establishing new towns and other centres of consumption, the early modern state was also active in the establishment of more effective inland transport infrastructures. The motives behind state intervention in road and river improvements were not necessarily wholly commercial. Greater speed and certainty in the movement of troops, more rapid transit for royal messengers, and greater ease on journeys for courtiers and the court were probably as high in the priorities of states as improvements in commercial opportunities when they decided to improve roads or rivers or to build canals. Nonetheless those transport improvements made the movement of trade easier, cheaper and more reliable. However, it would be wrong to give the impression that the early modern period saw large-scale improvement in the transport and communications network. Most roads continued to be badly maintained, if they were maintained at all. Even in the eighteenth century the roads from Amiens – one of the chief industrial cities of seventeenth- and eighteenth-century France – to its port St Valery-sur-Somme were so poor that merchants frequently paid local landowners to be allowed to take their carts through the ploughed fields rather than along the main road.[16]

One of the reasons why the road to St Valery was so bad was that river communication along the Somme between Amiens and the sea was so poor and unimproved that it could take goods eight or nine days to cover the forty miles. Although inland communications remained gene-rally poor and unimproved, early modern states played a major role in the improvements which did take place. For instance, from the reign of Henri IV onwards, the French state took an interest in the develop-ment of road communications and also in the improvement of internal navigation. The most spectacular example of this is, of course, the Canale des Deux Mers, built between 1668 and 1681 to link the estuary of the Gironde on the Atlantic coast with Sète on the Mediterranean. The state's immediate concern in its construction may have been mili-tary and naval (to allow ships of the Mediterranean fleet to reach the Atlantic, and vice versa, without the risky and long voyage around Spain), but it was clear to the Canale's backers, including Colbert, that the Canale also had major economic and commercial potential. Certainly by the middle of the eighteenth century, the Canale played an important part in the development of textile and other industries at centres such as Castelnau in the area around Toulouse. These industries were able to expand in the eighteenth century to meet demand from important colonial markets because of the advantages of the Canale and also of road improvements related to the development of the canal trade.[17] Elsewhere in France there was state support for projects such as the improvement of the navigation of both the Loire and the Seine and their linking by canal. In other European states governments and local authorities were beginning to improve means of communication.

However, one country above all stands apart from this slow progress and that is England. The construction of the Exeter Ship Canal during the reign of Elizabeth I remained an isolated event in England until the middle of the eighteenth century.[18] It was only around the middle years of the eighteenth century that any real start was made in England on the improvement of either water-borne or land systems of communication, and even then the improvements were largely undertaken by private initiative and finance, with little or no direct government finance or, indeed, encouragement. Consequently, they were on a very small scale and of limited practical use. The seven-foot beam which most of the English Midland canals allowed for boats compares badly with the much larger beam of craft on the deeper and wider continental canals. This backwardness of the communications system in England, and the non-governmental nature of the projecting and financing of those improvements which did take place, may have led so many British economic historians to underestimate the importance of transport improvement on the Continent in the early modern period and the role of the state in its development.

If the role of the early modern state in the development of a more efficient transport structure was important, the state also had a direct role in the development and growth of industrial production and industrial technology. The state was the most important consumer of industrial products. The demands of the state included, most significantly, a wide range of products whose production was highly specialised, technologically advanced and demanding of high capital investment. For instance, the state required a whole range of military goods such as cannons, rifles and pistols which were technologically advanced, required highly skilled and specialised means for their production, and involved high capital investment, as well as high raw material costs. The state also required a number of consumer goods, linked to the conspicuous display of the palaces and the royal courts, which again required highly specialised and highly capitalised production. The royal manufactories of later eighteenth-century France and Spain, the porcelain factories of Meissen, the state controlled and developed armaments industries in the German states and Sweden, all point to the importance of the state as a patron of and a partner in highly specialised and technologically advanced industrial production. The fact that, in many cases, the royal manufactories did not establish themselves permanently does not reduce their importance as a part of the history of the development of industry in Europe.[19] The state not merely supported the establishment of the new industries, both by direct financial contribution and by the granting of monopolies and other privileges, but in addition it provided them with a guaranteed market and also, in most cases, tried to maintain their standards by means of regulation. For instance, the establishment of official standards for artillery and small arms went a long way to encouraging tighter quality control and hence, indirectly, more standardised, more 'industrial' forms of production.

The early modern state was capable of formulating and executing specifically economic policies. In the middle and later eighteenth century the rise of the *Philosophes* and of the Enlightenment brought economic matters firmly to the centre, or at least near to the centre, of the concerns of government.[20] Even before this governments were concerned with the economy. All early modern states were preoccupied with the question of food supply: hungry populations were more likely to revolt than well-fed ones; food shortages caused the breakdown of local economies and of local law and order as populations migrated in desperation in search of food or work. From the classical period, European administrations, both local and national, had sought ways of ensuring food supplies, by purchase, by regulation of the market or by attempts to improve communications. The fact that they were successful only in part does not conceal the fact that early modern states did make considerable attempts to regulate the food market and to ensure the effective and relatively cheap distribution of food to at least urban populations. In Italy, especially in the north, city governments intervened actively in the grain market to ensure supplies at reasonable prices for the people.[21] The supply of food for Paris was a crucial concern of French governments throughout the early modern period, and the breakdown of that system in the later eighteenth century contributed to popular unrest at the time of the Revolution.[22]

Early modern states did, even before the eighteenth century, attempt from time to time to stimulate both trade and industry. The granting of monopolies to chartered companies or to groups of individual traders was clearly an attempt to give them some kind of certainty within which to operate. States, too, made more considered and more conscious attempts to encourage economic development, in particular the growth of trade (or the reduction of the domination of trade by outsiders) and the development of manufactures. The most famous of these attempts at economic policy – whose concerns were, it is true, as much military and political as they were purely economic – was the policy of J. B. Colbert in the France of Louis XIV.[23] It is increasingly clear that Colbert was not alone. The Brandenburg of Frederick William IV, the Spain of Charles II or the Portugal of Pedro III were only some of the late seventeenth-century states which sought, more or less successfully, to develop their trade and industry.[24]

Economic historians are now also re-examining the question of how far the early modern state harmed economic activity and prosperity by its actions. The issue of taxation lies at the centre of this problem, and in particular its effects on the prosperity of the great mass of the population, who were not in any way exempt from all or part of the taxation burden. There are two separate but related issues involved. The first is the level of taxation and the second is how successful the state was in collecting its revenue.

Throughout the early modern period complaints are recorded, from the privileged as well as from the unprivileged, that too much of the production of the economy was being taken away in taxation. Riots and revolts against taxation were a common feature of life in early modern Europe. It is, however, extremely difficult to calculate real levels of tax on any individual or any group in society. It is even more difficult to assess the impact of particular levels of taxation on the total economy of even quite small households with few sources of income. Early modern taxation came neither in a single simple package, nor even as a group of standard and relatively comprehensible taxes on particular commodities or activities. Over most of Europe, the historical development of the tax base had ensured that taxes which had been levied piecemeal, as a particular response to particular crises, had then become permanently entrenched in the system. Rates of taxation, the incidence of taxation and privileges and exemptions all differed from commodity to commodity and, in most European states, from place to place and from region to region. It would have been difficult for states themselves to calculate what might be expected as a return from taxation on individual commodities and individual activities. In fact, most states did not even try to do so because their taxation system was based on the practice of tax-farming. This meant that each tax was franchised to a contractor who paid a fixed sum in return for the right to collect that tax. The tax-farmer kept the taxes he collected and hoped to make a profit out of his franchise. Hence, in the early modern period, government statistics record only the prices paid by the contractors and give no indication of the taxes actually paid by the taxed to the tax-collectors. It is therefore, impossible to calculate the proportion of the total production or wealth of a state which was paid in taxes. The only other measure of the level of taxation is the proportion of the production or income of any individual or household which was taken by the state and its agents in tax. It is extremely difficult to calculate the income of any individual or household in the early modern period because of the lack of comprehensive documentary evidence. It is even more difficult to assess the impact of taxes based on consumption on any such household because the level and patterns of consumption also remain largely undocumented. It is particularly difficult to make such calculations when some part of production is for subsistence, not merely because of the problems this causes for the calculation of income, but also because of the complex ways in which a more or less subsistence pattern of production affects patterns of purchases from the commercialised, and hence taxed, part of the economy. Many discussions of the early modern economy which see it rather simply in terms of subsistence production and poverty fail to address this problem. Taxation of consumption through excise duties and sales taxes are likely to be of marginal importance in economies in which most production is for auto-consumption.

Like modern states, early modern states were not universally successful in the collection of taxes. Tax avoidance and tax evasion were as common, perhaps more common, in the early modern state as in the modern. The local and consensual nature of most early modern government made evasion easier. Certainly smuggling, to avoid internal and external customs dues, was a major problem for states and for tax-farmers and tax-collectors; in the eighteenth century the French government established an internal customs cordon across France in an attempt to prevent, or at least reduce, smuggling.[25] In addition, the local nature of collection and taxation meant that taxes could be avoided entirely legally by relatively simple means. For instance, the wine shops and bars which grew up around Paris and other great French cities in the eighteenth century in order to avoid payment of the *octroi*, the tax imposed on wines (and other goods) imported into the city, were only one example of a widespread practice.[26] Any calculation of the total level of taxation and its effect on individual family budgets ought to take into account the extent to which any individual was able to avoid paying taxes either in part or in full. It is no surprise that the economic historian will not find documentary evidence for this.

If it is impossible to calculate the incidence of state taxation on individuals or groups in any realistic way, it is also important to remember that during the early modern period the state was only one of a number of organisations and structures which were taking a share of production.

All over Europe the Church had retained the right to collect a proportion of production as tithe, and feudal overlords kept the right to collect as feudal and customary dues a share of production which was not
strictly part of an economic bargain to provide land or employment.

In both Catholic and Protestant Europe the organised Church, or
more strictly the complex of separate and competing institutions which
went to make up the organised Church, retained its right to tithe.
Historically, tithes were paid to ecclesiastical corporations or individuals.
They consisted of a fixed proportion of the crop, arable or pastoral,
produced on a specific piece of land. The traditional level of tithe
was one in ten: one sheaf in ten, one young animal in every ten born.
A great deal of the tithe-receiving right in many European states had
been alienated by the original owners and had passed into lay hands.
Tithing rights had become, and continued to be, an important saleable
commodity and one which was seen, in many parts of Europe, as being
a valuable and reasonably secure investment. The history of tithe and
its assessment and collection during the early modern period is a complex one, and one which offers many new insights into the operation of
rural economy and society, but the study of this is still in its infancy.[27]
There is clear evidence, however, for the continuing collection of tithe
in kind over much of Europe and also that the mechanisms for the collection of tithe, which were essentially local and contractual, were at
least as effective as the states' own mechanisms for the collection of
taxes. There is also good documentary evidence of growing resistance
to the collection and payment of tithe all over Europe in the eighteenth
century. In some places this took the form of anti-tithe riots and peti-
tions, but in many others resistance was expressed through litigation
and the legal process, perhaps indicating the levels of rural society
which were being most affected by tithe. These lawsuits in general
tended not to express total opposition to the principles of tithe, but
rather focused on complex arguments about the exemption of particular pieces of land from tithe, or on claims, often successful, that the
right to tithe applied only to traditional crops such as wheat and not to
the new crops, such as maize, which were being introduced. The proportion of production taken in tithe varied widely – from a twenty-fifth
in some parts of Italy to a quarter in some parts of Spain and Germany.
Evasion and avoidance were perhaps more difficult than with some
other forms of taxation, since the tithe was taken as a fixed proportion
of physical production and also because the tithe gatherer lived locally,
but nonetheless it clearly took place on a large scale. It is as difficult to

calculate the incidence of tithe as it is to calculate the incidence of taxation, and for similar reasons. In addition, unlike taxation, tithes fell on the subsistence element in production – on the food that families produced for their own consumption as well as on the commercialised consumption of households – and, as a result, the complexity of calculation, and the huge element of the unknown, are even larger for tithe.

The other form of taxation levied on production in the early modern period comprises feudal and customary dues. These are even more complex than tithe and it is even harder for the economic historian to assess the extent, nature and effect of their payment and collection. 'Feudal and customary dues' is a term which covers all non-tithe fixed and variable payments other than rents which were connected with specific pieces of land. Payment could be in kind or in service or commuted to cash. Although it is in many cases easy to confuse dues and rents, the distinction between them was important in legal terms and has become important to economic historians. Traditionally the payment of rent is seen as a characteristic of the sort of contractual relationships which are typical of a modern economy. Rent is a price and, like all other prices, is fixed by supply and demand, rather than by tradition or by the claims of a feudal overlord. Dues were seen as characteristic of an unmodernised, traditional society, where non-economic factors confused the operation of the market. Like taxes and tithes, feudal dues are outside the normal economic framework, determined not by supply and demand but by the political social or cultural demands of state, church or nobility. In theory this is fine, but it is often difficult to determine whether a charge is a feudal due or an element of rent.

In early modern Europe, feudal and customary dues were complex. Their incidence varied very widely, not merely from state to state but also within regions and often within small communities. They were not universally levied in one form. Taxes were, largely, paid in money, and tithes were largely paid in kind. Feudal and customary dues, however, were paid in a range of differing ways: in kind, in service or in money. This makes the valuation of feudal dues and attempts to calculate their effect on family budgets very difficult. For instance, how can days of service on the lord's fields be valued in a situation where the labour market was restricted and where most workers worked on their own account without any cash payment? During the period, the pattern of the collection of feudal dues changed, both in the form in which they were collected and also the rate at which they were levied. A further complexity is that, although the majority of feudal rights remained in noble hands, a substantial and growing proportion were in the hands of non-noble owners, usually wealthier townspeople or the leading non-noble landowners of rural areas who, in many cases, were paying taxes in town and countryside. The payment of feudal dues was not simply the transfer of 'commercial' wealth to anti-commercial traditional groups such as the nobility.

It can be seen that the whole question of the amount of taxation, its distribution and its overall effect on the economy, is a massively complex one and it is difficult to see how accurate information can be gathered by economic historians. The patchy documentation available allows some general observations.

Undoubtedly the pattern of taxation was not equitable and was to some extent regressive in that a disproportionate share of taxation fell on the less well-off, and in particular on the urban poor, who were forced by their situation to buy more of the goods on which taxation fell. It is also clear that this pattern was mitigated for at least some of the urban poor by subsidised food at times of difficulty, by smuggling and by tax evasion, and also by their continuing contacts with their families and relatives in the surrounding countryside who could and did provide them with subsistence goods outside the taxation framework. In the countryside taxation fell particularly heavily on the less well-to-do, although its impact diminished the more a family produced for its own consumption and the less a family was forced to rely on the market for its food and other needs. There is no evidence that in early modern Europe taxation took a definitely greater share of total production than did either tithe or feudal dues except in a few periods of very high taxation, such as the 1690s in France. It cannot be shown that the proportion of production taken by the early modern European state from most individuals or households was any higher than the proportion taken by modern states. Although general calculations are recognised to be flawed and to involve theoretical projection based on limited information known to be unquantifiably unreliable, they do suggest that the early modern state probably took a lower proportion of total national production than any modern state. Indeed, most recent calculations suggest that the proportion taken by the combination of tax, tithe and feudal dues was less than the total tax-take of modern national governments. The non-statistical evidence for a general growth of prosperity suggests that, despite recorded complaints, the level of taxation in the early modern period was usually within limits that could be accommodated by the majority of households.[28] Grumbles about taxation are commonplace in all ages and are not necessarily related to the ability of the complainants to pay those taxes. It is true that sometimes, at times of crisis, unduly severe increases in taxation required by the military or other demands of the state did make the crises deeper and longer lasting. The same can be said of the fiscal policies of some modern governments.

Finally, to complete this re-evaluation of the relationship of the early modern state to the economy, it is necessary to consider its political structure to determine whether the exercise of power did, or did not, coincide with the legal and social assumptions of vested power.

Economic historians have tended to look at the state in the early modern period with what can perhaps best be described as a 'top-down' view. The early modern state embodied centralist absolutism, which meant that what was of crucial importance were the central institutions and organs of government. The agents of that central government operated in the state to impose the decisions of government on the population and to gather information on which the government could base further policy. In adopting this viewpoint, economic historians were influenced in part by the habit of early modern governments of seeing their operations in that way, and also by unconscious assumptions in the context of the modern state. In this picture the state and its government existed as a separate entity, with its own ethos and *esprit de corps*, separate from the great mass of the population who formed the subjects or the 'governed'. The interests of this separate entity differed diametrically from those of the governed, not least when the state wished to restrict the privileges and independence of the governed or to raise taxes from them. Consequently, the state and the governed were inevitably antagonistic and their relationship was characterised by permanent and irresolvable conflict.

An economic historian who adopts the 'top-down' viewpoint is likely to make certain assumptions about the economic policies and social structure of the period. The first is that economic policy was developed and implemented on the basis of national concerns, one of which had crucially to be the defence and survival of the administrative and governmental structure itself. The second assumption is that the state was an extractive structure, which took wealth out of each region's economy and gave little or nothing back. Consequently, the early modern state was a brake on economic change and development in an economy which was regionally based. At best the state redistributed wealth between different areas and different activities but, given the nature of its demands and its expenditure, it normally slowed down or damaged economic activity, especially in the more remote and backward areas of the state.

The third assumption was that, despite its claims to power, the centralised state was weak in imposing its will on the mass of the population. The state had very limited powers of coercion and could never be certain of the continued loyalty of its agents, such as the military. Poor communications meant that its knowledge of what was happening in the provinces was imperfect.

The top-down viewpoint presents the early modern state almost as if it were a foreshadowing of nineteenth-century colonial domination, with an alien ruling group enforcing political and economic exploitation of a subject population. In the nineteenth century the European colonial state consisted of a small (European) elite who imposed their form of government on very large numbers of (Asian or African) subjects who already had their own indigenous systems of society and government. The rulers took locally produced wealth out of each colony and gave proportionally little in return. The colonial state was weak: it lacked information, it often failed to understand the societies and polities it ruled, it lacked effective coercive force. The parallels with the early modern state are instructive. It is important to note that the colonial state managed to give the appearance of great strength and great control while, at the same time, being fundamentally weak, because it relied for its operation and indeed, for its continuing existence, not upon its own power but upon the involvement and incorporation of large sections of the governed. The colonial state managed to survive, because in pursuing its aims it also incidentally served and met the demands of sufficient numbers of the governed for them to be willing to give it their support. The colonial state could only survive as long as it had the active support and involvement of the colonised.

The resemblance between the early modern state and the nineteenth-century colonial state is superficial, but the comparison illustrates dramatically that, before the intervention of twentieth-century forms of coercion, a small ruling group could not sustain government without the (tacit) consent of the governed.

The government of the early modern state usually worked: the system was not constantly breaking down in chaos. Taxes were collected, justice was administered, law and order were maintained, at least to the extent that the normal activity of the economy, production, manufacture, and local, regional, international and intercontinental trade could be carried on. Although there were revolts against government, even civil wars, they were the exception rather than the rule. There were periods when changes were imposed by a conquering elite distinguished from the governed by differences of language, custom and above all religion, as in Granada following the Christian reconquest in 1492 or in some areas of Germany during the Thirty Years War. In general, though, change was organic and gradual.

The history of early modern Europe was essentially evolutionary; as a whole it developed slowly over time rather than being a series of abrupt changes brought about by revolutionary events. Pre-existing rights and jurisdictions were usually incorporated in the political structure rather than being swept away. The early modern state had neither the manpower nor the financial strength to govern without the consent and involvement of the governed.

The top-down viewpoint leaves out of consideration the well-documented evidence that the population of early modern Europe did not merely consent to being governed by the ruling elite. They all participated in a political and economic administration which extended throughout all sectors of society.

Even the most superficial look at the way in which countries were governed before the late nineteenth century clearly indicates the level of local and 'amateur' involvement in government. Towns and cities, even the largest such as Paris and Lyon, were largely governed by bodies of citizens rather than by royal officials. In the countryside communities were largely self-governing, either through formal institutions like communes or through more informal types of communal joint action.[29] Over much of Europe taxes were collected from the taxpayers not by paid officials of government, but by local officials, often locally appointed.[30] Law and order was largely maintained on a day-to-day basis by local action, by, that is to say, the actions of the governed rather than the government. In many areas of Europe, justice on a local level continued to be administered by private or local agency rather than by the state; seigneurial justice in France, Spain and Germany was much more common at the level of small cases than was royal or princely justice.

This, then, suggests a rather different approach to the early modern state and its organisation. Viewed from the side rather than from the top, the early modern state has a rather different aspect. It now appears to be an inclusive, branching structure, involving many levels of society, local elites and local leadership as much as it involved the bureaucracy or the state centre. The early modern state was an integrative structure involving and incorporating large numbers of individuals, localities and interests rather than a structure of domination. It was diffuse in structure, rather than logical, ordered and centralised. It could be depicted accurately as an elaborate net woven of small interconnecting interests. It was only with the reforming princes of the Enlightenment in the late eighteenth century that the early modern state began to try to create a more rational structure. It should be emphasised that the reticular form of the early modern state was efficient and flexible enough to cope with the strains imposed by both crisis and prosperity. This view of the state as a reticular, inclusive structure has important implications for the role of the State in the economy.

First, far from being an abstractor of wealth, the state offered to local operators, and to the local elites in particular,[31] advantages, economic as well as social and political, which made their support for the state and its system more secure. Association with the state and with government could be a powerful conferrer of social status, and involvement with the state and its patronage networks gave some local elites greater patronage to bestow and hence greater power. There were economic advantages to be gained by contact with government. Tax collectors and other officials were paid by a share of the funds they collected; bribes and presents given to officials to obtain desired decisions could be an important element in building up local fortunes. It is clear that some proportion, and probably quite a large proportion, of the state's take from local society was not abstracted, but retained in the hands of local elites.

Second, the reticular structure of government meant that even a royal court was not entirely remote from the mass of the population. The noble courtiers had urban houses and rural estates. They often had administrative duties locally and they were accessible to local interests either in person or through their domestic and other employees.

Third, the reticular structure of government meant that the whole arena of state action extended far beyond the simple decisions of ministers and provincial governors to include the actions of local as well as national government. It becomes impossible to exclude from the range of action of the state the actions of its subordinate entities; in particular, the state must be understood to include the governments of subject towns and cities. In many parts of Europe it was municipal governments which played the leading role in, for instance, the establishment and maintenance of systems of poor relief, systems of food supply and price control, the regulation of production within the city (and indeed, if they could manage it, beyond the city walls). Beyond the cities and towns institutions of local rural self-government were involved as yet another dimension of the state. In all cases the state mechanism was used by the local leaders to further their own interests just as much as the state used them. It is difficult to see how there could be widespread conflict between rulers and ruled when so many people at all levels of society played both roles simultaneously.

Such a complex and diffuse structure, however, makes it very difficult to assess the overall effect of the early modern state on the European economy. As yet there has been insufficient study of the lower levels of government and their operation in this context to make any general statement about it. It is, however, clear that it is wrong to attempt to assess the early modern state according to assumptions that it had the same aims, the same structure and the same effects as the modern state. Although the early modern European state was moving in the direction of the sort of organisation the modern state has, it was no more than part of the way there. It may well be that the most important function of the state during the early modern period was not to act as an agent directly encouraging economic growth, but rather as one of the major pressures towards a greater monetarisation of the economy, by insisting on the payment of taxes in cash rather than in kind, and as one of the major generators of changing patterns of consumption by creating and maintaining new, non-land-based elites.

The final twist to this is that the role of the state in the modern economy is no longer seen by political economists as being anything like so clear-cut and decisive as it was perhaps 20 years ago. The failure of state economic management in the 1970s and 1980s has led to a much greater scepticism about the ability of the state to produce the effects and the development which were supposedly the great strengths of the modern state and the great failure of its early modern predecessor.

5

THE PROSPERITY OF THE SOUTH

In *The Expansion of England*, based on a series of lectures delivered in Cambridge and published in the late Victorian period,[1] Sir John Seeley expressed what was to become the central item of belief of a whole school of early modern history. Although Seeley's concerns were political and imperial, his perception of the fundamental changes in the overall structure and balance of power in Europe was profoundly important in shaping the way in which many economic historians in the century which followed the book's publication saw the development of the economy of Europe between the fifteenth and the nineteenth centuries. Their version of Seeley stated that, in the Middle Ages and the Age of the Renaissance, the centre of Europe, economically as well as politically and culturally, lay south of the Alps, in the regions surrounding the Mediterranean, that is, southern France, eastern Spain – especially Catalonia – and above all, northern and central Italy. These regions, and the trade to the Levant and Asia which they dominated, had been the key to economic growth and development in Europe since the Ancient period. Through them flowed all Europe's trade with Asia and to them flowed all the wealth which that trade generated. In particular, in the cities of the South there developed Europe's first bourgeois societies and bourgeois patterns of consumption. Around this concentration of wealth and consumption grew up industry, finance and long-distance commerce within Europe. The connections of the Mediterranean system extended throughout Northern and Western Europe, reinforced by the political and religious position of the Papal Court in Rome. The Mediterranean was truly and decisively the centre of the European economy.

At the end of the Middle Ages, it was believed, this Mediterranean domination came to an abrupt end. The centre of European commercial activity swung from the Mediterranean to the shores of the Atlantic, above all to the North Sea. If the Middle Ages had belonged to the Mediterranean, the early modern period belonged to the Atlantic. It was the cities of the North-west, above all Antwerp, Amsterdam and London, which became the new economic and commercial centres of the European world. The key to European prosperity was no longer the Levantine trade with Asia, but the oceanic trade with Asia and the Americas. The success of the northern states and cities was not simply a matter of a changing economic geography. The northerners introduced not merely new routes, but also new commercial and financial organisations and forms. These structures and institutions were recognisably modern capitalist ones, if in an early and as yet undeveloped form. The joint-stock companies, the English and Dutch East India Companies, the Dutch West India Company, the English Royal Africa Company, and the corporate banks, such as the Amsterdam Exchange Bank of 1609 and the Bank of England, were regarded as the direct ancestors of nineteenth- and twentieth-century financial and commercial institutions. It was argued that the efficiency and modernity of these new systems of commerce rapidly destroyed the commercial and financial structures of the previous age, including the great commercial fairs and the highly specialised exchange fairs of Besançon, Lyon and Piacenza, as well as the small-scale and rather 'simple' family and partnership commercial structures of the Mediterranean economy.

It was argued that the growth of northern commercial wealth led to greater urbanisation and the maritime and commercial cities of the Atlantic coast of Europe grew in population as well as prosperity. Urbanisation led to immigration from surrounding areas, and indeed from great distances, into the growing cities, causing major social and economic problems, as well as major opportunities. The new cities developed as centres of consumption and of social ostentation (although not too much, since the prudent ethics of northern Protestantism were seen as being one of the key sources of northern success), which meant that they also developed as centres of service and luxury industries. The growth of the cities meant that new means had to be found to feed their populations: so commercialised and specialised agricultural systems developed, often at some distance from the city itself. The new cities also became centres of important 'colonial' industries because the source of much of their wealth, and certainly much of their *raison d'être*, lay in their contacts with the extra-European world. They produced goods for consumption in Asia and the Americas and they also refined and processed colonial products such as sugar.

The triumph of the North was inevitably accompanied by the decline of the South. For Seeley, who was in typically Victorian terms talking about world, or at least European, political leadership, this was self-evident, and also fitted clearly within his nationalist and Protestant agenda. His argument was, however, quickly extended to the economic sphere: the rise of northern prosperity inevitably involved the loss of southern prosperity. The underlying assumption that the early modern period was one of stasis, in which change and development were only possible as a result of the redistribution of existing wealth, inevitably meant that the spectacular rise of the northern states and cities could occur only if there were a parallel and equally spectacular decline in the formerly dominant South.

This great shift, in prosperity as well as political domination, was a sudden one. Originally the defining date was 1500, the point at which, within a decade, the discovery of the Americas had given Atlantic Castile access to immense new wealth and power, and the opening of the Cape route to Asia had diverted the vastly important and valuable trade of India and the Spice Islands away from its traditional overland and Mediterranean route and into the hands of Portugal. From Seville and Lisbon the new routes ran on to Antwerp and to Northern Europe, rather than to the Mediterranean cities. By 1521 the Venetian Senate was forced to send to Lisbon for spices to provision the city's markets.[2] It became clear to later economic (and political) historians that 1500 was not the defining point. Braudel, amongst others, was able to point to Italian revival after the 1520s and to a new Golden Age of Venice in the middle and later sixteenth century. The turning point then became the 1590s, the decade which saw the first great explosion of northern Netherlandish commerce, and above all the stratospheric rise of Amsterdam.[3]

The true decline of the South was said to have begun after the 1590s. It was at its most obvious in northern and central Italy, perhaps because it was there that the prosperity of the Middle Ages and the Renaissance had been at its greatest, but it was clear everywhere. In Catalonia, the long, slow decline of Barcelona continued; elsewhere in Mediterranean Spain and in Castile evidence of the same process was clear – a drop in population, the lessening prosperity of towns and cities and the growing degradation of agriculture. In Languedoc and Provence, it was argued, the early seventeenth century ushered in a long period of decay and poverty, the origins of modern Europe's southern problem. At the same time, those areas north of the Alps which had relied closely upon their links with the Mediterranean went into a long and irreversible decline. In particular, the trading cities of central and southern Germany, such as Augsburg and Nuremberg, stagnated and failed. Their impoverishment was not solely the consequence of the decline of the Mediterranean, but their inability to recover from the shocks of the Thirty Years War could in part be ascribed to the weakening of their position caused by the changing structure of the European economy.[4]

Southern decline was regarded as being at its most spectacular in the great trading cities of northern and central Italy. Centres like Venice, Milan and Florence all suffered serious loss of population, wealth and power. Their commerce was diminished to a shadow of what it had been, their populations were reduced by disease in the mid-seventeenth century and they never fully recovered. In addition, their industries weakened or disappeared and their financial role ceased to be of more than regional significance. Most strikingly, perhaps, they were abandoned by their commercial elites who, in the course of the sixteenth, seventeenth and eighteenth centuries, committed what could only called 'treason'.[5] They made no attempt to revive the commercial, financial and industrial base of their cities and retreated to the countryside as neo-noble landlords as part of a 'refeudalisation' of the Italian rural economy.

Venice was seen as the great stereotype of this pattern of decline. Dominant in the Mediterranean in the sixteenth century, it disastrously lost its leadership to the Netherlands in the 1590s. Its Asiatic trade was in ruins by the 1620s; its population and commerce were seriously affected by the plague outbreaks of the late 1620s and the 1630s. At the same time its commercial nobility began to convert themselves into a territorial nobility, more concerned with land and with villas than with trade and the counting house. In the second half of the seventeenth century the decline continued; the Mediterranean empire was lost, trade and industry decayed further until, in the eighteenth century, Venice was little more than a theme park of decadence, dependent upon tourism rather than upon production and commerce for its surviving prosperity.[6]

The Venetian pattern was repeated in the smaller centres of Italy. Cities like Pisa, Verona and Brescia, which in their glorious, not long distant past had been populous centres of commerce and industry, entered a long period of stagnation. Population fell, industrial employment and commerce were reduced. Behind the decline lay a much more fundamental and significant shift. The smaller towns and cities could no longer be seen as centres of production and commerce servicing international markets. They were reduced to local market centres servicing their increasingly rural and increasingly impoverished hinterlands. Towns and cities were incapable of generating any growth or change, while no help could be expected from the countryside, which was lapsing further and further back into rural poverty and feudalism.

This pattern of weakening commerce, declining urbanisation and growing rural poverty could also be seen in southern Italy. Although Naples was one of the greatest cities of Europe, it was a city of poverty and hence it provided no real stimulus to the rest of the southern economy, which, in any case, was heavily dominated by merchants and capitalists from the decaying cities of northern Italy, especially Genoa.[7] In Spain and southern France similar patterns, affecting both great cities and the rural hinterland, could be identified. The only towns and areas of Southern Europe which could be said to be flourishing were those which were lucky enough to have close links with the economically dynamic North. In particular the 'free ports' of Italy, such as Livorno or Ancona, were able to develop parasitically on the backs of northern prosperity, as an extension of the North into the South, by attracting traders from the North, usually by means of state encouragement.

By the eighteenth century, just at that point when the Atlantic North of Europe was beginning to move on to the next stage of its inevitable expansion, the South, it was asserted, was irretrievably sunk into long-term decline. Lacking both the will and the means to change and grow, it was condemned to stagnation and poverty until, in the later nineteenth century – in some areas the twentieth – it was effectively colonised by Northern Europe and provided with the means (a combination of industrialisation and commercial agriculture) which finally permitted it to share in the prosperity of the North.

In short, in this Seeleyan view the inevitable rise of the Atlantic economies inescapably involved the irreversible decline of the South. The shift of the economic centre of Europe to the shores of the Atlantic and to the North Sea could happen only if, at the same time and in parallel, the former centre, the Mediterranean, declined. Because the growth of the North was spectacular and long-term, the decline of the South had to be equally spectacular and equally permanent.

Underlying such a view of the early modern period are three major assumptions which, it must be made clear, are not Seeley's, but ones which have been added to, or rather have accreted to, his arguments by later historians.

First, the idea that the rise of the North was inevitably accompanied by a parallel decline of the South depends heavily on the assumption that, during the early modern period, indeed throughout the period before industrialisation, the pool of resource, the volume of usable wealth in Europe, was essentially fixed. There were periods of growth, but they were inevitably followed by periods of decline, which were as great as, or greater than, the preceding growth. Population could only grow to a Malthusian maximum and then fall back; until the middle of the eighteenth century, European population could not have expanded beyond its thirteenth-century maxima. In such a situation, if Amsterdam were to expand rapidly and dynamically, it could only do so if some other city declined to a similar, or greater, extent.

The second assumption upon which this Seeleyan interpretation depends is that, in any economy, prosperity is synonymous with change and growth. It is an assumption which underlies much economic history, of the modern period as well as of earlier periods. Its corollary is that any economy which is not changing and growing, no matter what base level it is at, is in a more parlous state and is less prosperous than an economy which is growing.[8] This assumption has its origins and its force in the idea that what is significant about the early modern economy were those elements in it which can be seen as being the antecedents of the Industrial Revolution of the nineteenth century.

The third great assumption upon which the Seeleyan construct depends is that the only possibility of growth and hence increasing prosperity came from outside, from the wealth which Europe was able to plunder from the non-European world. The diversion of Europe's trade with Asia to the northern ports and the development of new economies in the Americas, again centred on the North Atlantic ports, were crucially important to the development of northern domination and also as stimulators to changes in the northern economies which, in the eighteenth century, were to lead to industrialisation. The most important elements in that external contact were the Asiatic trade and the trade with the growing North American colonies. The trade with Central and South America was seen as being of lesser significance either in scale or in its effects.

This picture of northern progress and southern decline which has been so central to most discussions of early modern European history is based on a series of assumptions which do not derive from the facts such as they are known, but rather from a series of intellectual constructs imposed from outside. Seeley's own Victorian construct was clear; he sought to demonstrate the superiority of 'modern', 'capitalist'[9] Protestant England over 'backward', 'pre-capitalist', Catholic Southern Europe. The construct of his successors is also clear, although not so overtly expressed. They saw the economic history of early modern Europe as no more than a part of a great structure of European and world economic development, which was to lead inevitably to particular patterns of development in production, labour and consumption in late eighteenth-century England which, in turn, would spread to much of continental Western Europe in the nineteenth century. The backward, old-fashioned South had to decline to allow for the dynamic growth of the North. It simply was not possible for the older economic historians to accept that two differing models of prosperity, one with 'growth' and one without, could have existed side by side. The idea of northern prosperity and southern decline does have some evidence to support it, but it is often difficult to escape the impression that evidence has been found to support a pre-existing theory rather than the theory being built up from the available evidence.

The idea of an increasingly backward and increasingly impoverished South, effectively doomed to failure by the success of the North, has had many attractions for the political and social elites of many southern European countries in the nineteenth and twentieth centuries. For example, it was much easier to blame the problem of the *mezzogiorno* in Italy on a long-run and inevitable working-out of inescapable economic laws than on the failings of local elites or of national policies.

The whole question of the decline of the South and the rise of the North is complicated by the basic issue of definition; what is meant by the North and by the South? Earlier historians tended to define them on the basis of the answer they required, that is to say that the North comprised those areas of Europe which experienced growth and change and the South comprised those which did not.

Those areas which had been the major centres of urban and commercial development in the later Middle Ages around the Mediterranean must be included in the South. Hence Italy, Languedoc and Provence in France, Catalonia, Aragon and Valencia in Spain are all very clearly southern in this sense.[10] The rest of Iberia, however, is extremely difficult to categorise. In many ways its pattern of urban development links it to the Mediterranean South and certainly its agricultural systems are essentially southern in both crops and organisation; Andalucia could hardly be more southern. On the other hand, in the early modern period the commercial and industrial links of much of Iberia were very clearly Atlantic and therefore in some ways northern. Portugal is a good example: its major economic (and political) concerns were in the New World and Asia or lay in the increasing demand from Northern Europe, especially England, for wine.[11] Again, although Andalucia's agriculture was clearly 'southern', it also belonged to the North in that much of its sixteenth-century prosperity (which continued and revived in the seventeenth and eighteenth centuries) was based directly or indirectly on the wealth of America, either through the wealth generated in Seville and Cadiz or through the growing commercial agriculture of the Guadalquivir Valley, which supplied food and other goods to Spanish America.[12] Even Castile was much more closely linked commercially and financially to the Atlantic North than it was to the Mediterranean South. This had been so even in the later Middle Ages, when the sheep-ranching of Old and New Castile and the mining industry of the Basque Country had been dependent upon northern European markets. The Atlantic nature of Castile and of the whole of western Spain increased in the early modern period. The wealth derived from America was not limited to Andalucia: a great deal accrued to the crown of Castile and much private conquistador wealth was repatriated to Extremadura and La Mancha.[13] Growing northern prosperity also increased demand for wine and for the salt of Galicia. Iberia belonged simultaneously to both the Mediterranean South and the Atlantic North.

Southern France equally does not fit convincingly or easily in one or the other camp. There can be little doubt that Provence and Mediterranean Languedoc, with their highly developed urban structures, complex industrial patterns and clear involvement in Mediterranean commerce and finance, belonged to the South. Equally, given the importance of Lyon as both a commercial and a financial centre in the sixteenth century and later, the city and the Rhône valley downstream from it must be southern, although its trade was increasingly with the North (both the Netherlands and Bordeaux) and even, by the eighteenth century, with the Americas.[14] Geographically much of the southern Massif Central is inescapably southern, but much of its developing industry in the sixteenth century, and its reviving industry in the eighteenth, was closely linked with Bordeaux and hence with the Atlantic North and West.[15] In the same way, inland Languedoc and the Toulousain clearly belonged geographically and in agricultural terms to the Mediterranean South, but much of their commerce and industry was directed, particularly after the opening of the Canal des Deux Mers, to Bordeaux and the Atlantic.[16]

The position of Germany in the North/South categorisation is even more complex than that of France or Spain. There are two major and related problems which prevent any full discussion of the early modern German economy. The first is that, with the exception of the rather specialised, and also rather politically and emotionally supercharged, issue of the short- and long-term effects of the Thirty Years War on the German economy, there has been very little recent work on this period. The second is that it has suited historians (essentially for political and nationalist reasons) to portray the period between the Reformation and Unification as being a dead one in German history, a period of decline and stagnation, in which little of major interest could have happened, except possibly a marked deterioration and retrogression of agriculture and agrarian relations. This, in its turn, has led to a tendency to say that since the German economy was in decline and apparently resistant to change it must have been an essentially southern one.

Much of southern Germany, in particular Bavaria, the Tyrol, much of Austria, eastern Swabia, Franconia and even parts of Saxony were very closely linked in the sixteenth century with the cities of the Mediterranean. Further away from the Alps, however, the picture becomes much more blurred. The Rhineland was closely linked with the Mediterranean because of its importance as a trade route, but by the same token it was closely linked to the economies of the North Sea. It is difficult to allot cities like Cologne or Frankfurt am Main to one group or the other.[17] Even though northern Germany clearly belongs geographically and in economic type to the northern economies, its role in the general economy of the North was as a supplier of agricultural products and of migrant labour, rather than as an active participant in dynamic economic growth and change. Eastern Germany, Poland and western Russia present a further problem. These regions can either be seen either as colonial extensions of the northern European economies or as a third economic region and type.

The South can be seen as reaching the North Sea. The great commercial centres of the sixteenth century in the southern Netherlands, Antwerp, Brussels, Ghent and Bruges, owed much of their wealth and prosperity to their links with the Mediterranean. In many ways they were as vital a part of the southern economy as were Venice and Genoa themselves. Hamburg, one of the great commercial cities of the period, and the one about which least is known, was undoubtedly northern, involved in the trade of the Baltic and, increasingly, the trade of the Atlantic, but much of its commercial hinterland lay in areas which have just been allocated to the southern economy.[18] The division between North and South was not by any means clear-cut.

What is increasingly obvious is that what is being described is not the difference between two geographical regions, however loosely defined, but rather the perceived difference between two economic systems. The two economic systems are defined, implicitly if not explicitly, in just those terms of 'progress' and 'stagnation' which have been discussed earlier. The South was old-fashioned, stagnant, declining, inward-looking, the North was modern and modernising, progressive and outward-looking.

There can be very little doubt that southern Europe was prosperous in the fifteenth and sixteenth centuries. The key to that prosperity was its great cities, which were characteristic of the southern economy. Levels of urbanisation were high, both in terms of the populations of individual cities and also of the proportion of the total population living in urban centres.[19] The cities were both the main centres of industrial production and the major centres of consumption. Southern society was largely, but not entirely, dominated by its urban elites rather than by territorial aristocrats.

At the apex of the economic system were the great cities. Most of these, like Venice, Milan, Genoa, Florence, Marseilles, Barcelona and Lyon, were commercial and financial centres, but two of the greatest of them, Rome and Naples, were much more administrative centres and centres of services and consumption. All the southern cities were larger than any but the very largest of northern cities in the sixteenth century and, as a consequence, were also major attractors of migrants, not merely from their immediate hinterlands but from much further afield.

Two sorts of economic activity distinguished the great southern cities. They were, above all, nodes of commerce, trading over huge distances. The cities of the Mediterranean were the great entry points into Europe for goods produced elsewhere, especially in Asia, and they were also the great distributors of those goods and goods of their own production to the rest of Europe. Mediterranean trade moved over the passes of the Alps, up the Rhône valley to Germany, where a whole series of commercial centres related to Mediterranean trade, or to supplying the demand generated by southern prosperity, developed.

Commerce was only a part of the system, since the wealth of the South had helped to generate a whole financial structure. The bankers of Italy and Catalonia were central to much development in the north of Europe. The techniques they evolved were crucially important in the development of northern financial institutions and practices in the seventeenth and eighteenth centuries. Although southern finance and banking were advanced, they did retain (and were to retain throughout the early modern period) one crucial feature which distinguished them from the most advanced forms of northern finance in the seventeenth and eighteenth centuries. Despite the early appearance of civically supported joint-stock banks in Genoa and Venice in the later sixteenth centuries, both banking and commercial and industrial finance in the South continued to be organised on an individual basis, or on the basis of small partnerships, rather than on the larger, joint-stock basis which was to develop in the North.[20]

Although the great cities were the most typical feature of the southern system, they were not the only urban centres. What distinguished the pattern of the South from that of the North in the sixteenth century and for the next 200 years was not merely the existence of great cities but also the existence below them in the urban hierarchy of a large number of lesser cities and towns which were still much larger than all but the greatest towns in the North. Only a few areas of the geographical South, most strikingly the Kingdom of Naples, departed from this pattern.[21] These smaller cities and towns were themselves commercial centres. In many cases they traded not on a local or regional level, but on a European scale. Cities like Toledo, Brescia or Verona were not amongst the largest of commercial centres but they were centres from which trade went to all parts of Europe, and whose city elites were passionately concerned with commercial intelligence from the whole of the continent. Like the great cities, these smaller towns and cities were also centres of industrial production, often of technologically advanced or expensive goods. Also like the great cities, the lesser urban centres were jealous of the sources of their prosperity. Industry was confined by law within the walls of the city and skilled artisans were prevented from moving away, either to the countryside or to competitors.

The density of population implicit in this amount of economic activity necessitated highly complex systems of food production and food distribution. The importance of this issue in the southern cities can be seen in the financial and organisational lengths urban elites were willing to go to ensure a secure and affordable supply of food in the cities. Most southern cities were forced to import large quantities of food from a considerable distance, as indeed they had been doing since the time of the Roman Empire. In the fifteenth and sixteenth centuries, for instance, Venice and Florence obtained much of the grain which fed the populace from the eastern Mediterranean. Genoa, because of its geographical position, was perhaps more than any other city dependent upon food imports. It imported grain from the western Mediterranean basin, from eastern Spain and Corsica, but above all from Sicily and the Kingdom of Naples, whose agricultural economies became, in many ways, no more than colonial extensions of the Genoese economy.

If the Italian cities were unable to feed themselves from their own territories, this did not mean that those territories were undeveloped, nor that they remained as some kind of agricultural backwater. The study of southern agriculture in the early modern period has been prejudiced in the past by the agrarian disasters of the nineteenth century, when much of southern Europe went through a period of severe agricultural depression, aggravated but not caused by the general agricultural depression of the later nineteenth century. It has been assumed that the nineteenth-century decline was the product of a much earlier weakness in southern agriculture. All the evidence points not to the weakness but to the strength of southern agriculture, not only in the sixteenth century but also in the seventeenth and eighteenth centuries. It could hardly have been otherwise; there had to be some firm agricultural base for the towns and cities of the South to develop as they did. Sixteenth-century southern agriculture is, in many ways, distinguished by its relative advance and sophistication compared with that of the North. Over much of the South, agriculture had become commercialised at an early period so that grain and other crops were produced specifically for urban consumption and 'capitalist' farming developed at an early period. Southern agriculture was also, within the limits of its age and the geographical and climatic constraints with which it had to deal, technologically advanced, both in the sense of using machinery (for instance for irrigation or drainage) and also in the sense of adopting new crops, new rotations and new methods of stock breeding. After all, many of the 'new' agricultural techniques introduced in the Netherlands and England in the seventeenth and even eighteenth centuries were in fact imports from the South.

In one respect, however, southern agriculture was not 'modern'. Unlike the agriculture of some parts of Northern Europe, especially in the eighteenth century, which has provided the paradigm for patterns of agricultural development into this century, often with disastrous results, southern agriculture was not specialised. This lack of specialisation can be seen in two ways. First, over much of the South, although the great mass of agricultural production was for market, few producers ceased completely to produce also for their own consumption. This was possible because of the second form of non-specialisation. Southern agriculture had been centred, for millennia, around the pattern called, in Italian, *coltura mista*. In *coltura mista*, the farmer produced many different crops, rather than concentrating on a single one. This diversity of production was often applied to single plots of land as well as to the holding as a whole. This pattern, which appears in many ways so backward, so 'un-modern', compared with the specialisation of twentieth-century agriculture, or indeed of some eighteenth-century English, Dutch or northern French agriculture has, in fact, a very sound economic justification. In a world in which production is precarious, where yields may vary sharply, and where access to markets can be difficult, and where therefore security of return is at a premium, it makes far more sense to spread the risk of cultivation and harvest over a range of crops rather than to rely on the success of a single one, whose failure would lead to total disaster.

Southern agriculture typifies very clearly the importance of stability and risk-reduction in early modern economic activity. *Coltura mista*, and its variants throughout the South, avoided the risks of overdependence on single crops and single markets. Southern commerce, too, was clearly based on risk-spreading and diversification. Lack of specialisation did not mean a lack of prosperity. By the sixteenth century, the southern system had delivered high levels (high, that is, for its date) of prosperity to southern populations. That prosperity was extremely unequally spread and undoubtedly there were pockets of impoverishment. The southern economy might not have been changing rapidly or dynamically, although it was not totally static, but this was a result of its high level of development and performance, rather than of its stagnation.

A risk-reducing strategy did not mean that the South had been free from crisis. The history of the southern economy throughout its great age of prosperity in the later Middle Ages was punctuated by a series of major crises. One had struck in the years around 1500 and had coincided with, but was not caused by, the opening up of the Cape route to Asia by the Portuguese and the discovery of America. The end of the sixteenth century and the beginning of the seventeenth saw such another crisis. Again, this crisis coincided with a major series of events which were important in the traditional view of early modern economic history, in this case the most rapid period of Dutch overseas expansion and the great shift of the Asiatic trade from the Mediterranean to the

North. Traditionally historians assumed that this coincidence explained the crisis and they saw it as the decisive turning-point, after which the South, unable to compete with the modern and capitalist North, slipped further and further into decadence and decline.

The first half of the seventeenth century was a period of major difficulty for the southern European economy, as indeed it was for the whole of the European economy, even including the Northern Netherlands during the period 1627–50.[22] Urban and total populations were at best stagnant and generally declined. The traditional international commerce of the southern cities was in severe, in some cases terminal, crisis and many of the South's urban industries suffered very severe recession. Poverty, and in particular urban poverty, increased sharply and imposed further pressures on already weakened urban budgets. High taxation weakened consumption and placed strains on the social and economic structure. In the countryside the economy became, for a period, more introverted, more concerned with auto-consumption than with supplying the market.

As with all economic crises at all periods, the causes of the crisis in the southern economy were complex and the new problems generated for the South by the rise of the North are much less central than the traditional interpretations suggest. There seem to have been essentially three elements in the crisis, two of which had been common to most, if not all, previous southern crises. It should also be noted that several of these factors also affected the northern economies, especially in the second quarter of the seventeenth century.

The first major element was population pressure. In the South, as in the North, population had been growing strongly, if erratically, since the great post-Black Death trough in the middle years of the fifteenth century, and that population growth had been one of the factors contributing to the growth and prosperity of Europe in the sixteenth century. The Malthusian trap inevitably shut. As population levels grew, so did the pressure of people on resources. In southern Europe as well as in the North those resources were not absolutely fixed. In the South unused marginal land was still available for much of the sixteenth century and the supply of land was also being increased by drainage and irrigation.[23] Above all the South, with its highly developed commercial and internal transportation systems, was able to import food from areas such as the Black Sea littoral and North Africa, where population pressure was much less. But by the last decades of the sixteenth century even these resources were insufficient to prevent crisis.

In part this was simply a consequence of numbers. An increasing population pushed cultivation into more and more marginal land where yields were low and soil fertility rapidly exhausted. For instance, wheat cultivation was carried well above the 2000-metre contour in the Alpine foothills in the last years of the sixteenth century and the first years of the seventeenth.[24] The extension of cultivation into marginal land also led to overcropping and deforestation in many parts of the South, which in turn led to soil erosion and dust-bowling. Deforestation also led to severe shortages of wood, for building, for building ships, for making tools and implements, for furniture and domestic articles and not least for firewood and charcoal, throughout much of the South. In addition, whether as a result of overcropping and overgrazing, or of climatic deterioration or of political change (and it was almost certainly a complex mixture of all of these), many of Southern Europe's main supply areas for food went into crisis from the mid-sixteenth century onwards. Production in Sicily and North Africa, and also possibly in the eastern parts of the Kingdom of Naples, declined sharply from mid-century on. At the same time supplies from the Black Sea and Anatolia reduced sharply. The causes of this decline may have been climatic (the result of growing aridity, especially in Anatolia), or the result of agricultural change (in particular the growing importance of grazing in Anatolia), or the result of commercial or political activity (the diversion of Black Sea grain to Russia and the Baltic in response to growing demand there, or the forced diversion of the exports of Moldavia and Wallachia [the modern Romania] to Turkey to feed the rapidly expanding population of Istanbul).[25]

In the South, the last decades of the sixteenth century and the first years of the seventeenth were characterised by many of the symptoms of the onset of Malthusian crisis. Subsistence crises, commercial crises and outbreaks of epidemic disease all slowed the pace of the economy and of population growth. The years 1590–95 were especially difficult for much of the South (as they were for much of Europe), and were especially significant since they were to bring northern competition, and northern finance, even more strongly into the Mediterranean basin.[26] The timing of the actual Malthusian downturn is often very difficult to identify and it happened at different times in different parts of the South. In Spain and southern Italy the major downturn appears to have happened in the last years of the sixteenth century. In northern Italy and much of Germany the 1630s seem to have been crucial and in central Italy it may well not have been until the 1650s that a major downswing occurred. It is not possible to be very precise about the extent of these population declines because most of the evidence which is available relates to urban populations which were, in any case, peculiarly fluctuating and unstable.

The epidemics and subsistence crises which were an integral part of the Malthusian trap seriously affected trade. In times of plague, whether actual or rumoured, trade was stopped, or seriously limited by quarantine and embargo regulations intended to stop or restrict the spread of disease.[27] Subsistence crisis did not merely reduce the purchasing power of the population but also affected the movement of trade, especially to the southern cities which, with their highly developed and highly sophisticated systems of food subsidy and distribution, became natural targets for the hungry. Equally naturally, the cities tried to protect themselves from the crippling costs of escalating poor relief by closing their gates, against trade as well as against the poor. A reduction in population also meant falling demand for industrial goods and for services, as well as falling market demand for food. As a consequence the prosperity of the towns and cities declined and there were fewer urban opportunities for rural families. In much of Southern Europe the immediate response to this economic crisis seems to have been introversion. There was a refocusing of productive activity, especially in agriculture, away from commercialisation and the market and towards greater self-sufficiency and auto-consumption. Southern agriculture, with its complex mix of activities, was much more able to do this, and much more able to do it without drastic social and economic change than a more specialised system would have been.[28]

The second major element in the crisis in the southern economy was political crisis. It is extremely difficult to separate the political factors from the Malthusian crisis but, despite the manifold weaknesses of the early modern state and the diffuseness of the political structure, political and state action (or inaction) crucially affected the economy. The most obvious form of political crisis which could hit a region and its economy is war. Southern Europe was relatively free from the direct experience of war during this period. The one great exception, the Thirty Years War in Germany, did have major effects throughout the South, but outside Germany its effects were indirect rather than direct.

Warfare in the South in the sixteenth and seventeenth centuries was confined largely to the Balkans and to the seas. It must not be forgotten that early modern Europe was still under pressure from the expanding Ottoman Empire. In the sixteenth century the Turk was a real threat to the security of Europe, and Turkish military and commercial expansion in the eastern and central Mediterranean and North Africa was at least as real a threat to the prosperity and supremacy of the cities of the Mediterranean South as was the expansion of Northern Europe. In the sixteenth century Ottoman expansion and Ottoman policy in the Levant and Iraq were far more important components in the history of European–Asian trade than was the Cape trade and its problems and potential. Although the Turkish threat declined in the early seventeenth century, the vulnerability of Europe's eastern borders was again revealed in the second half of the seventeenth century. During the period of the Köprülü Grand Viziers (1656–1702) resurgent Ottoman imperialism brought Turkish troops to the gates of Vienna. Although with hindsight the Turkish defeat before Vienna in 1683 and the Turkish humiliation in the Treaty of Karlovitz in 1699 marked the end of the Turkish threat in the East, that was by no means immediately obvious. The cost and the pressures of resisting the Turkish threat fell very heavily on the powers of the Mediterranean, especially upon the Italian cities, particularly Venice, at a time when they were already weakened by other crises.

So, it was the indirect effects of distant war, rather than the direct consequences of destructive local wars, that played a major role in the crisis of the South. A region which was heavily dependent upon long-distance trade, and upon the security of long-distance financial relations, was likely to be seriously affected by warfare at a distance. The great wars of Northern Europe (the French Wars of Religion, the Dutch Revolt, the Thirty Years War) all had major effects on the southern economy. While they stimulated some kinds of demand, in particular for the military goods in which industries in the South were specialists, this increase was no compensation for the economic and commercial disruption of the wars. They created new and dangerous threats to the security of long-distance trade: markets were closed; the costs of insurance increased. Warfare also involved, particularly in the seventeenth century, considerable short-term destruction of wealth. The massively destructive tactics employed by the belligerents in the Thirty Years War led to falling demand for just those relatively expensive goods which were the main components of southern commerce. The South, too, had to suffer the effects of wars outside Europe other than the Turkish threat to Europe's south-eastern frontier. In particular, the long-distance overland commerce of the southern cities with Asia exposed them to the effects of Levantine and Asiatic warfare. In the late sixteenth and early

seventeenth centuries, just when northern, in particular Dutch, competition for the Asiatic trade was becoming serious, the Italian cities were
forced to cope with the disruptive effects of the Second Turko-Persian
War of 1621–28 on their trade with the Indian Ocean.[29]

Another aspect of warfare and political crisis which played a major
role in the late sixteenth-/early seventeenth-century crisis in the South
was its cost and the problems of meeting that cost. Even though wars
were not waged in the south of Europe, the accidents of European politics meant that in the later sixteenth century, just at a time when other
problems were arising for the southern economy, a disproportionate, or
at least a larger, share of the financing of war fell on the South. Spain's
position as the leading power in Europe in the sixteenth century
involved her in a series of expensive wars in the North, most importantly the long and bitter struggle with the northern Netherlands.
The Netherlands, north and south, had been major contributors to the
financing of the Spanish Empire before the 1570s and the war was a
double blow to Spain's finances: not merely did the war increase expenditure massively, it also removed a major part of the Empire's income.
To some extent that loss was covered by the importation of bullion – gold
until the 1540s and, after the 1550s, silver – from Spain's American
colonies. However, from the 1620s onwards even this flow reduced; the
actions of the Dutch in capturing the bullion fleets, although spectacular, were less important than the decline in both production and export
in Mexico and Peru, which began after 1610.[30] Increasingly more and
more of the cost of empire and political leadership fell on Spain itself,
and above all on Castile. Elsewhere, the instability of Europe meant
that military preparedness had to be increased, costs expanded and
taxes put up. In Germany too, both before and after 1618, the costs of
war, both potential and actual, led to major increases in taxation.[31]

Unreformed taxation systems meant that increased taxation was
imposed chiefly on consumption. This ensured it fell most heavily on
the less wealthy sections of society and hence had a disproportionate
effect on the consumption of industrial goods and the sort of imported
luxury or semi-luxury goods which were the main stock-in-trade of the
southern cities. Taxes were also levied on goods, including foodstuffs,
as they entered market centres for sale, discouraging producers from
taking their goods to market and hence increasing the introversion of
the rural economy further.

The only major alternatives to increased taxation which governments
had to help meet the costs of war were manipulation of the currency

and borrowing. Despite its huge imports of silver from America, even after the decline which set in the 1620s, the Spanish government regularly debased its coinage. The monarchy gained short-term advantage from the bullion it removed from the coinage, but the economy suffered the longer-term, seriously damaging effects of inflation. In Germany, too, the years around 1618 were years of major currency debasement and inflation. European governments mainly turned to borrowing to offset the direct and indirect costs of war and diplomacy. Some of this borrowing was internal, when the state and its officials pressured its more wealthy subjects to lend to the state, but a great deal, and much of the largest borrowing, was external. In the late sixteenth and early seventeenth centuries, states turned to the great bankers and financiers of Europe to provide the credit, and above all the cash they needed to allow them to continue their wars. The economic and financial geography of late sixteenth-century Europe meant that most of those great bankers were southern Europeans and that their banks and financial empires were essentially individual and personal. In the short-term many of the financiers did very well out of their government loans, gaining commercial as well as financial privileges and in many cases, also social advancement.[32] But in the long term borrowing made the financial position of the indebted states more precarious and made their bankruptcy more inevitable, with disastrous consequences for their lenders. The inability of the states to pay their debts, or even the interest on them, was to be a major cause of the failure of a number of the great banking houses of the South in the early and mid-seventeenth centuries, most famously the final collapse of the Fugger of Augsburg. The failure of the bankers was not merely a personal disaster. The financial uncertainty which their bankruptcies produced drove up interest rates which had already been increased by the massive demands of the states themselves. This made financial and commercial investment appear much less attractive than would otherwise have been the case.

External war was not the only way in which political crisis could affect the economy. Internal political disorder could also have major economic consequences. For instance, the Wars of Religion, the Huguenot revolts of the 1620s and the Frondes in France and the revolts in Catalonia and Naples all created conditions of social and economic instability and difficulty. In addition other political actions by governments could have important economic effects. For example, Richelieu's campaigns against the Huguenots in south-western France acted as a damper on the economy because they were particularly important in the textile industry. The expulsion of the Moriscos from Spain in the first decades of the seventeenth century was not the absolutely cata-strophic event of the traditional northern liberal and Protestant view-point, but it did have major negative effects on the economy, especially in the Kingdom of Valencia.[33]

The third major element in the crisis of the South in the later six-teenth and early seventeenth centuries was the role of northern compe-tition. It was much less important than either population pressure or politics. In many ways the North benefited from the crisis in the south-ern economy and possibly made it worse, rather than playing much of a role in its creation. The success of the North weakened the commer-cial and financial position of the southern cities and the countryside which depended upon them at a time when the southern cities could no longer rely on the proceeds of the Asiatic trade to buffer their prosperity against the problems of Europe. In addition, at least for a time, the subsistence crisis forced the southern cities into a dependence on the northern ones, especially Baltic supplies of wheat and rye. In that sense the South became subordinate to, and controlled by, the North but that dependence on northern food supplies was relatively short-lived.

It is by no means clear that this crisis was, or had to be, the final defining crisis of southern prosperity. Although the crisis weakened the southern economy – as had so many earlier crises – it left its fundamen-tal structures and those of southern society in place. The causes of the crisis lay much more within the structure of the southern economy as it had existed and as it continued to exist than in outside pressure from a completely new and inevitably conquering economic system. One of the central features of the crisis was a Malthusian downturn and, like all Malthusian downturns, it contained within itself the seeds of revival and new prosperity. Population decline resulted in a reduction of pres-sure on land, and hence at least a partial resolution of subsistence crisis. Increased agricultural prosperity led to increasing consumption and, since the South still retained much of Europe's specialised indus-trial capacity, industrial revival. A southern revival, albeit with differ-ences from the previous situation, was to be expected.

Historians have in recent years realised that there is convincing evidence that, far from being the definitive and terminal collapse of the economy, the crisis of the early seventeenth century was followed in the South by a period of prosperity which lasted for perhaps a century, beginning around 1675, and ended only with the arrival of the general European economic crisis of the 1770s and 1780s. That southern prosperity was general, but it was not universal. In early modern Europe an unequal distribution of income and wealth meant that, even in the most prosperous areas and in times of greatest prosperity, a proportion of the population lived in great poverty and destitution. Equally, not all areas of the South were prosperous. For instance, the sharecroppers of Altopascio in Tuscany were grindingly poor;[34] but they should not be seen automatically as typical of southern agriculture. Furthermore, in the South as in the North, the fluctuations of the economy, international and continental as well as regional, and the fluctuations of the weather and seasons, produced times of slump as well as times of boom. Taken overall, however, the South seems to have been remarkably prosperous in the late seventeenth and eighteenth centuries, especially for a region which had supposedly been consigned to the economic scrapheap of history.

Even in the period of crisis there were periods of relative recovery and some areas were much less seriously affected than others. Throughout the South, and its extension northwards into Germany, from about 1675 onwards there are very clear signs of returning prosperity. Urban populations in the great cities and the lesser centres began to grow again. The long-distance commerce of the cities never fully recovered in the sense that they never regained their former role in the trade with Asia. Nonetheless many towns and cities revived with new roles. They became centres of Mediterranean commerce, including playing a role in the Levantine trade, no longer for Indian or Chinese goods, but for the luxury productions of Iran, Iraq and the Middle East. As, especially in the eighteenth century, trade with the Americas became increasingly important, southern cities like Barcelona and Marseilles also became involved in the wider Atlantic trade.[35] The southern cities also regained and developed their roles as centres of regional trade and finance. Traders and governments now went to Amsterdam or London to raise capital but the financial structures and expertise of the South had not disappeared, and they again concentrated on their original core business of finance within the southern economy. The loss of an international financial role can even be seen as a bonus rather than a catastrophe. In the early modern period international finance, and in particular state finance was, and was to remain, the most risky of all forms of finance, and in losing its role in it the South may well have increased rather than decreased its stability and long-term prosperity.

The late seventeenth and eighteenth centuries also saw a major revival in the South in the industrial sphere, supposedly the area in which the North displayed its superiority over the South most clearly. Patterns of production differed in that new products had appeared and, most significantly, the location of industry had changed. The process by which industrial production shifted from the tightly organised and regulated towns and cities to the more 'open' countryside had begun before the great crisis, but the crisis speeded it up. In many parts of the South, the development of rural industry was accompanied by the development of new products. For example, the production of old types of textiles continued in the cities as before and were restricted by guild regulations. Rural industry produced new, more fashionable fabrics, often against a background of urban guild complaints about the intrinsically low quality of the goods being produced. The rise of rural industry was a symptom of change in industrial organisation and also in production. It is evidence of the flexibility of the southern economic system.

If the rise of rural industry emphasises the economic flexibility of the South even after the great crisis, it also demonstrates clearly the continuing nature of its social structure. In the South this process of so-called 'proto-industrialisation' in no way marks a major change in the social or economic organisation of the countryside. The system of risk-spreading had meant that the economic portfolio of most families already included a wide range of economic activities; so adding industrial production to it was no major change. The high level of rural migration into towns and cities, and the equally high level of return migration to the countryside, meant that whatever the theoretical legal, economic or cultural distinctions between town and country, their inhabitants did not belong to exclusive separate spheres but in fact merged and mingled continually. Most of the industrial workers of the southern towns and cities in the age before the great crisis were rural people who had migrated into the city to work, and at some time in their lives they would probably return to the countryside. For southern families in the early modern period there was intrinsically no distinction between urban production and rural production.

Southern industry in the late seventeenth and eighteenth centuries was not just flexible, it was technologically innovative, arguably considerably more so than northern industry, at least until the 1750s and 1760s. For instance, the development of machine-based production in the silk industry in Lyon in the eighteenth century and the development of technology in the Languedoc textile industry and in the royal manufactories of Spain are symptoms of a dynamic and developing industrial sector, and not of one in terminal decline.[36] The development of new industries, such as the iron smelting and founding industries in the Corrèze valley,[37] or the machine production of salt in southern Languedoc, again point to industrial growth. Even in southern and central Germany there is evidence of industrial growth and change.

Although clear statistical evidence is lacking, it can be argued that until the middle of the eighteenth century, and possibly until the end of the century, Europe's industrial heartland still lay in the South rather than the North. It was in the South rather than the North that the bulk of industrial production, certainly of industrial production, for more than local consumption was centred. Equally it can be argued that, until the later eighteenth century, it was southern rather than northern industry which was developing most rapidly and changing most dynamically. In many ways the South looked nearer to industrial revolution than the North.

Industrial prosperity and development were matched by the recovery of agriculture, and by the revival of commercial and market-orientated agriculture. The new pattern of international commerce meant that the South could no longer rely on imported food in large quantities to feed its cities. An increasing proportion of the food consumed was produced locally and urban centres again became consumers of the production of their hinterlands rather than receiving grain from far afield. Some areas continued to specialise in the production of grain for regional commerce. For instance, in southern Italy Puglia continued to be a major exporter of grain to Genoa and now also supplied other Mediterranean cities. Naples, however, imported its grain from Sicily even though Puglian grain was cheaper, more abundant and kept better than Sicilian grain. This was partly because it was easier to import grain from Sicily by sea to Naples than it was to bring it by road (or by sea) from Puglia but it was also a consequence of the unwillingness of the Neapolitan population to eat Puglian grain because it was widely regarded as inferior to Sicilian grain.[38] This apparent irrationality indicates, yet again, the importance of fashion and perception in the early modern economy as in the modern. It also suggests that the population of Naples was hardly desperately short of food. In Sicily, too, the seventeenth and eighteenth centuries saw a major agricultural revival, with a growth of rural repopulation and the establishment of new, larger-scale wheat farms. So successful was this expansion that, by the eighteenth century, the problem in many parts of Sicily seems not to have been scarcity of production, but rather overproduction.[39]

Elsewhere in the South new crops appeared. For instance, in the Veneto the seventeenth and eighteenth centuries saw a major increase in rice production.[40] Rice has very specific requirements for its cultivation and meeting them necessarily involved capital investment and technological development. The scale of the irrigation and drainage works, and of the hydraulic work to rivers and watercourses which were necessary to allow the development of large-scale rice production, were considerable and involved large sums of capital and considerable technical skill. They were certainly on a sufficient scale to worry the Venetian government into instituting tight regulation of the works.[41] Other less demanding new crops such as maize were widely grown. This was a developing and changing agriculture and one which was able to assimilate change within its old structure rather than being revolutionised by it.

The evidence points to reviving and continuing prosperity for the South. That prosperity left its mark in a number of ways. The physical environment was improved: towns and cities were rebuilt, rural housing was improved. Consumption seems to have increased every bit as much in the South as in the North and the same changes occur in distribution and retailing. For instance, fixed shops appeared and cafés opened even in small towns and villages. Just as in the North, in the eighteenth century, inventories of the possessions of the relatively less well-off indicate both an increase in the number of possessions and also a shift towards more fashionable and convenient goods. This holds true for the industrial and service workers of Lyon studied by Maurice Garden and for the Tuscan agriculturalists studied by Paolo Malanima.[42]

Traditional historians found it easy to see the South in the seventeenth and eighteenth centuries as no more than a kind of informal economic colony of the North, as a parasite upon northern growth. In fact documentary evidence shows that the dependence of the South on the North which had developed with the subsistence crises of the late sixteenth century lessened in the course of the seventeenth and eighteenth centuries. In part this was the result of the re-expansion of southern agriculture and the growing ability of the South to feed itself. In addition, the South increasingly, if never completely, freed itself from a dependence on the North for its contacts with the non-European world, in particular the Americas. Especially in the eighteenth century, ports like Barcelona and Marseilles, through which the production of southern industry intended for American (especially South American) consumption passed, developed important return trades in sugar and other tropical goods.[43] In addition, the southern ports revived their commerce with the ports of the Levant, trading no longer in the spices of Asia, but in the production of the Middle East and Turkey.[44]

It can even be argued that parts of the Atlantic economy were, to some extent, dependent upon southern prosperity for their growth. Two of the great Atlantic commercial centres, Bordeaux and Hamburg, were essentially outlets for, and suppliers to, areas which clearly belong to the South – Languedoc and southern and central Germany. While it would be wrong to suggest that both cities had economies which were entirely based on the South (Hamburg had its important Baltic and Scandinavian trades, Bordeaux a colonial re-export trade as well as a trade to central and northern France), nonetheless their trading role did crucially involve dealing with hinterlands which were in both cases essentially southern. The growing prosperity of both cities in the seventeenth and eighteenth centuries (in the case of Hamburg, until it was cut off effectively from its southern and central German hinterlands by Prussian tariff policy after 1763)[45] demonstrates both the continuing complexity of the relationship between North and South right through the eighteenth century, and indicates very strongly how prosperous were the southern hinterlands of these great 'northern' cities.

It is clear that the crisis of the late sixteenth and early seventeenth centuries was not a terminal one for southern prosperity. Whatever may have happened politically and diplomatically, the centre of the European economy did not shift decisively northwards after the death of Philip II. The crisis caused problems for the South, some of which were long-term, and the response to the crisis involved some restructuring of the economic system, but the system survived. After 1675 the southern economy began again to deliver prosperity to the South, a prosperity which was to continue until the 1770s and 1780s when, along with the whole of Europe, the South entered what was perhaps the longest period of economic difficulty since the late sixteenth century. It will never be known whether that crisis did what the earlier crisis had failed to do and destroyed the essential structures of the southern economy, since it was followed immediately by the Napoleonic Wars, which brought profound political and cultural crisis.

Southern prosperity was based less on specialisation than on a spread of economic activity, and with it a spread of risk. This refusal to concentrate may, in the long term, have meant that the South was less able to innovate and to restructure, but it also meant that the need to do so was much less. The southern economy was much less likely to develop bottlenecks, the points of constriction in production and growth which were to play such an important role in the generation of technological change in other regions of Europe. This did not mean that the South was not prosperous, but simply that it did not 'grow' as rapidly as other areas. It was unlikely statistically that the South would grow as rapidly as parts of the North did during industrialisation since it started from a higher base. The fact that it did not need to change and was able to solve its own problems within its own system suggests that it was in many ways more prosperous and certainly, in early modern terms, more successful than the North.

6

THE PROSPERITY OF THE NORTH

It is no easier to define those areas which belong to the North than it is to define those of the South. Certain areas, such as the Baltic, Scandinavia and the British Isles, are clearly northern because of their relative backwardness in and before the sixteenth century. Northern Germany, in particular the Baltic and North Sea littoral, dominated in the Middle Ages by the Hanseatic cities, was equally northern, although the boundary between 'north' and 'south' within Germany is and always has been uncertain and fluctuating. France north of the Loire undoubtedly belongs to the North, despite the importance of its southern commerce and its production for southern markets in, for instance, Champagne, in the sixteenth century and later. The area between the Loire and the Garonne is an awkward boundary zone, in some ways looking northwards for markets, but also looking to the South for many of its institutions.

The position of Atlantic seaports like Bordeaux or Hamburg which looked to southern hinterlands for their markets has already been referred to, but the very heartland of the great shift of the economic, commercial and political centre of Europe from South to North, the Netherlands, are also difficult to categorise. In the fifteenth and the sixteenth centuries, before any suggestion of structural shift, their concerns were divided between North and South. The southern Netherlands, in particular Brabant and Flanders, were the financial and commercial centre of the North, but were also the most important northern extension of the southern economy because they were the mart and entrepôt through which northern and southern goods were exchanged. In this role they can be described as northern colonial centres of the South which related the commercial metropolis of the

138

South to the dependent backward economies of the North. On the other hand, the north-western Netherlands, Holland and Zeeland, were much more clearly northern and Atlantic, concerned with the bulk trades of the Baltic and the North Sea, in particular fish and timber, and with the goods of the Atlantic seaboard, in particular the salt and wines of Spain and Portugal.[1] Even in the sixteenth century this simple division of the Netherlands was breaking down. After 1500 Antwerp became the major market for imports from the New World and, briefly, for those from Asia, a refocusing towards a northern, Atlantic future rather than a southern one. After the Dutch Revolt and the Sack of Antwerp in 1584, the South, in the form of capital and commercial contact and expertise developed in the southern Netherlands cities, moved to the northern Netherlands, above all to Amsterdam. In what Jonathan Israel has called the first Golden Age, much of the capital and much of the knowledge and innovation upon which Dutch greatness was based was of southern origin.

The essential artificiality of the traditional distinction between North and South is striking. The conclusion is inescapable that the distinction is one drawn because it fits comfortably within a predetermined pattern of development rather than for any other reason. It is an interpretation which relies heavily on concentrating on certain sectors only of the northern economy, rather than looking at the whole. It relies upon comparing unlike with unlike: upon comparing the leading sectors of the northern economy either with the whole of the Southern economy or, more usually, with the most backward and stressed areas of the South.

Before and during the sixteenth century the evidence shows that the economy of the north of Europe was backward. It was little more than a relatively primitive colonial area supplying primary products, such as raw wool, iron and fish, and some very basic manufactured goods, such as woollen cloth, to the prosperous South. At this time there are very striking contrasts between North and South. Despite contemporaries' fears of imminent overpopulation, in England and elsewhere it is clear that, despite some pockets of relatively dense population, the North was sparsely populated, whether the point of comparison is the contemporary population of the South or later population levels in the North. Not merely was population small, but it was predominantly rural. In the early modern period, even in southern Europe, levels of urbanisation nowhere approached those of the nineteenth and twentieth centuries, but over much of the North they were extremely low. A small proportion of the population lived in towns, and the towns of the

North, with a few exceptions, were very small: many northern towns were smaller than most southern villages. Most of these small northern towns were in essence service and market centres for their rural hinterlands, rather than having longer-distance commercial significance.

Northern agriculture was also relatively backward before and during the sixteenth century. Yields were low, so production was extensive, dependent on the large areas of land available rather than on technological or organisational sophistication for its success. Such innovation as had taken place centred round reorganisation for the better production of industrial raw materials, in particular wool, rather than involving more efficient food production. Despite the development of commercial production to feed the growing cities of the North such as London or Paris in the sixteenth century, much of northern agriculture was focused on the production of food for auto-consumption, or for consumption very locally, rather than on the commercial production of surpluses for market. The survival of feudal tenures with payments in services and in kind in much of the North, and the very diffused nature of the social and political structures of the region, define a much more introverted and 'backward' agricultural system than typified the South.

If northern agriculture in the sixteenth century and before was essentially backward and introverted like that of a modern economic colony, in many ways the whole northern economy filled this colonial role. The normal economic function of the North was to supply food, raw materials or basic manufactures to the South. The most prosperous trades of the North were essentially those in raw materials: wool, metals and wood, or in food, especially grain and fish, which were consumed in the more advanced South. Even where the North produced manufactures, such as woollen textiles, they were either of a lower quality than those of the South or were exported southwards for finishing. In return for these primary or near-primary exports, the North imported luxury and manufactured goods of high value from the South. The colonial nature of the North was also clear in the financial relationships of the region with the southern centres of finance and banking.

Another characteristic of the economy of the North in the sixteenth century and before is high levels of poverty, related to the high levels of economic insecurity and precariousness. Any pre-modern economy dependent primarily upon agricultural production and upon local agriculture for its food supplies was inevitably unstable and precarious because it was controlled by the vagaries of changeable, unpredictable and unreliable weather. Climate did not only play a role in the success or failure of the harvest, but also played a major role in determining what those harvests could be. It is no longer possible to believe that no advances had been made in crop types and varieties since the Roman period. However, medieval and early modern varieties of food grains such as rye and wheat were much less productive than modern varieties, and they were also much more susceptible to both climatic variation and to disease. Crop failure was always a threat, but in the North it was both more likely and more destructive in its effects. The extensive nature of northern production also imposed severe limits on per capita production in an age without mechanisation. Much of the agricultural development of the early modern period was concerned as much with solving these problems as in making possible a more commercialised and progressive agricultural sector. The 'contribution of agriculture to economic development' in the period was an accidental spin-off from this, rather than a conscious part of the development of a capitalist or modern economy.

The picture of the North which emerges at the middle or end of the sixteenth century is one of relative backwardness and introversion, of a colonial economy rather than one which was inevitably to become the powerhouse of European, and indeed world economic advance. Nonetheless, by the late eighteenth century, the North had undoubtedly made major advances, both in economic organisation and in prosperity.

At the centre of the northern expansion after the sixteenth century lay the development and growth of its great cities, above all the great commercial port cities of the Atlantic and North Sea littoral: Amsterdam, London, Bordeaux, Nantes and Hamburg. The success of these cities was based upon international and regional commerce and upon finance, as that of the great southern cities had been. Northern cities such as Amsterdam or London became entrepôts for the goods of much of the world just as Venice or Genoa had been. Spices, textiles and other luxury goods from Asia, sugar, cotton and tobacco from the Americas, furs, timber and other goods from northern Europe, salt and wine from southern Europe, all passed through them on their way to consumers elsewhere. Like the great cities of the South, the northern cities developed industries related to their long-distance commerce, processing and refining the produce they imported before re-exporting it. In some cases, such as Amsterdam, the spread of trade-related industry was wider than the city itself. The great urban centres of the Randstad in South Holland developed, in part, into centres processing the colonial produce imported through Amsterdam.[2] Virtually all of the towns involved in the colonial processing trades were not new creations, but older towns which had shifted their patterns of production. Like the southern cities, the northern cities underwent rapid population growth based on migration from a wide area. In addition, the northern commercial cities became important centres of international finance for commerce, industry and for states.

Outside the great cities the proportion of the northern population living in towns increased throughout the early modern period, albeit slowly.[3] Even at the end of the eighteenth century the urban population of Northern Europe was much smaller than that of the South, strikingly so, if a few heavily urbanised areas in the western Netherlands and southern England are excluded. Northern towns remained generally smaller in size and fewer in number than those of Southern Europe. The picture of urban growth was not universal; just as in the South, many northern towns, especially in northern France and western Germany, were stagnant in population terms or declined over the period.

Between the sixteenth century and the end of the seventeenth the population of Northern Europe grew at a slow rate, and with some periods of stagnation, if not actual decline. In the seventeenth century growth seems to have been especially slow, except in the western areas of the northern Netherlands and some parts of England. It was not until the eighteenth century that in the North, as in the South, population grew most rapidly and most consistently. Even in the eighteenth century, there were periods, such as the 1730s and the 1770s and 1780s, when population growth slowed, or even stopped. Much of this population growth was rural rather than urban and in many parts of northern Europe, the eighteenth century saw a decline in the proportion of the population which was urban, rather than an increase. What was important about the population growth of the eighteenth century was that, despite checks, particularly in the last three decades of the century, it did not stop. Northern Europe seemed, in the eighteenth century, to have broken out of the Malthusian trap, ironically just at the point that the Rev. Dr Malthus was discovering it. Even in the South the evidence points to an eighteenth-century expansion which was, by the end of the century, to take total population to unprecedented levels.[4]

According to the traditional historiography, this unparalleled growth of the northern European economy was caused by three things: the development of intercontinental commerce, the development of industry and changes in agriculture and agricultural production.

First, it was long-distance, and in particular, intercontinental, commerce which created the wealth of the great northern commercial entrepôts. This wealth, in its turn, by a process of diffusion, be it the Keynesian multiplier effect or the 'trickle-down effect', stimulated increasing wealth throughout the whole of the northern economy, hence generating consumption and leading to higher demand for industrial production and also for food. It might be going too far to argue, as Eric Williams did as long ago as 1954,[5] that the northern Industrial Revolution was based on the proceeds of the eighteenth-century African slave trade. Nonetheless, historians recently have come to realise that the prosperity of the North came not from its intrinsic geographical advantages, nor from its cultural superiority, nor from the superiority of its economic and financial organisation, but from the geographical and historical accident that the trade of the Atlantic and the trade with Asia via the Cape of Good Hope were most conveniently carried on from the ports of the Atlantic littoral of Europe.

Second, industry and industrial organisation were, of course, to become the very centre of northern dominance in the nineteenth and twentieth centuries. Industrial revolution and the pattern of economic and social relationships which went with it were the very core of the traditional interpretation of the early modern period, and what was important in it were those factors and those elements which led to or were part of the development of the new industrial system. There can be little doubt that northern industry did begin to change in the early modern period. In the western Netherlands, in England and in the area around Bordeaux or Hamburg,[6] new industries appeared, new both in their scale and also in their methods of production. The production of, for instance, sugar, paper and glass developed not merely in amount of production but also in the scale of the productive units. Elsewhere, for example in the West Riding of Yorkshire or parts of Normandy, new and much larger-scale manufactories of woollen and other textiles developed, which produced not merely more cloth, but also new types of cloth to cater for a European market which was becoming more demanding and more fashion-conscious. Particularly after the middle years of the eighteenth century, the production of textiles, silk as well as wool and cotton, was increasingly mechanised and new manufacturing towns and villages began to appear.

It is rather too easy to get carried away by enthusiasm for this 'early industrial revolution' in the North. There certainly were changes in the scale and organisation of industry, but even at the end of the eighteenth century, and even in England, most northern industry still operated in traditional, unrevolutionised ways. The expansion in textile production in England and France in the later years of the eighteenth century was largely a consequence of the expansion of traditional forms of production rather than the development of new ones. It was domestic craft outworkers rather than factory hands who brought about the increased production of the eighteenth century. 'Proto-industrialisation' had developed as much in the North as in the South, and its grand title cannot conceal the fact that it was a traditional form of production, linked into the pattern of the farming year, seasonally fluctuating, rather than some revolutionary step, socially or economically. The dependence of early mechanised industry throughout Europe on water power meant that the new industries, like the old, were essentially tied to the fluctuation of the climate and to dispersal rather than concentration. In many senses it was not to be until the large-scale use of steam power in industry in the 1830s and later that the Industrial Revolution can be said to have truly begun.

The picture of northern industry was not one of universal growth and prosperity. Just as the rest of the economy was subject to fluctuations, some based on the changing seasons and harvests, others based on the normal patterns of boom and slump in trade, so too the industries of the North fluctuated. For some industries in both the seventeenth and eighteenth centuries, the period was one of decline and disappearance: for instance, the textile industries of parts of Picardy or parts of the Rhineland, some of the textile industries of the Randstad or of East Anglia, the shipbuilding industry of the North Holland and West Frisian ports,[7] all suffered long-run decline and final extinction.

Third, the development of Northern agriculture was not uniform. Some areas, such as the south-east of England, the eastern Netherlands, and the Hohenlohe plateau in south-western Germany, developed prosperous agricultural systems, based on the supply of grain or meat and dairy products to the growing urban centres. In other areas, such as the great wheat-producing areas of the Ile de France and Champagne, where commercial production had been important since the Middle Ages, the process of specialisation and commercialisation continued. In these areas and elsewhere changes in patterns of land use and tenure tended to concentrate holdings and the profits of agriculture into fewer hands. In the eighteenth century, and before in some areas, this may well have led to the creation of a much larger pool of rural poverty and hence of a pool of cheaper labour which could be taken up by the new industries of the late eighteenth century and the nineteenth century.

Northern agriculture did introduce new techniques and new crops in the seventeenth and eighteenth centuries (contrary to popular belief, continental Europe was much more swift to do this than was England), but most of the changes in agriculture were in organisation rather than in production methods. The details of these changes are hugely complicated and vary from country to country, indeed from region to region. Throughout the North these changes in agriculture were as frequently brought about by traditional means as by modern ones. In England, where feudal practice had been replaced by contract, written or unwritten, as early as the fifteenth and sixteenth centuries, the chosen methods were in a sense modern and involved the changing of contracts or the use of legislation. In contrast, in many parts of the Continent, in northern France, for instance, or in the Hohenlohe, existing feudal structures and procedures were used to bring about the changes.[8] Agricultural change was certainly possible within the old system. It was not necessary to revolutionise the system to develop new patterns of production.

Some parts of northern agriculture were profoundly changed, but it should be noted that over much of the North the process of agricultural change was slow, possibly even non-existent. Perhaps this was to be expected. Around the periphery, in northern and western Scotland, possibly in most of Scotland, the north of England and Wales, in Ireland and much of Scandinavia, change was very slow. But the same is also true for many areas of the heartlands of the North, in France and Germany. This is not to say that these areas had ever had a purely self-sufficient agricultural system, but merely that the pace and amount of change to more market-orientated production were slow. In some cases low levels of development occurred because of the distance of the areas from markets. In other cases, such as the Paris basin immediately around the city, or the agriculture of many areas of the southern Netherlands, the slowness of agricultural change is rather a consequence of the high levels of production and commercialisation they had reached at an early stage.

It is inappropriate to take the most 'progressive' examples of northern agriculture and designate them as typical of the whole of the northern economy. It is even more misleading to compare those leading sectors of the northern economy with the whole of the southern economy, or with the depressed sectors of the southern economy, and seek thereby to demonstrate the success of the North and the failure of the South. This comparing of unlikes has all too frequently led to the economy of the prosperous northern cities, or of the most advanced agricultural areas of the North being contrasted with declining southern cities or with areas of agricultural decline like the Tuscan plains. To do so is to use the evidence forensically, to establish the case for a particular historiographical, social or political construct rather than to examine the evidence critically. The traditional historiography of the rise of the North and the decline of the South is carried on in terms of symbols. Amsterdam or London symbolise the North and all it stands for, the triumph of modernity and the creation of a new pattern of prosperity, while Naples or perhaps Altopascio symbolise the decline, backwardness and poverty of the South. When historians or economists start arguing in symbols, there is every reason to be suspicious.

This symbolic nature of much of the argument is very clear in the discussion of the process by which the North rose, and in particular of what are seen as the crucial decades of the shift of the economic centre of Europe from the Mediterranean to the North Sea, between 1590 and 1620. In the traditional historiography the shift, symbolised by the rise of Amsterdam, took place bewilderingly rapidly. Despite the great crisis of the 1550s, Antwerp, and with it the whole southern nexus in the North, remained dominant into the 1560s and the 1570s. The sack of Antwerp in 1581 and the Dutch closure of the Schledte in 1584 marked the end of the South. By 1620, perhaps even by the foundation of the Amsterdam Exchange Bank in 1609, the North was in full control and the South was in terminal decline. In a period of no more than a quarter of a century, economic and commercial patterns which had been built into the whole structure of the European economy virtually since the time of the Roman Empire were overturned. Such a revolution needs some explanation. The traditional historian had no real difficulty with this: the rise of the North was inevitable because of its economic and financial superiority and of the capitalist system which it represented.[9] Therefore the period of the transition was no more than the fortuitous coming-together of a series of conditions which allowed 'an idea whose time had come' to triumph.

The period of the transition, 1590–1620, was a period of crisis, of subsistence crisis and of crisis in Europe's trade with the non-European world, especially Asia. The 1590s in particular was a decade of major subsistence crisis, or rather of a series of subsistence crises, which affected both Northern and Southern Europe. The nature of these crises has been discussed earlier, in relation to the South. As far as the North was concerned, although it too was affected by crisis, the food shortages created a major opportunity. Virtually the only sources of grain available in Europe in the early 1590s were around the Baltic, in Sweden, Poland and western Russia. These areas were largely the preserve of northern European traders, both the Hanseatic cities and the fish and timber merchants of the northern Netherlands. The Dutch in particular were in a position to take advantage of this opportunity because they had relatively efficient bulk-carrying ships capable of undertaking the long voyages through the treacherous waters of the Bay of Biscay and the Atlantic necessary to carry grain into the western Mediterranean. The profits from the grain trade provided a major boost to the Dutch cities, chiefly but not solely Amsterdam, at a time when their economies were in difficulties in the aftermath of the worst fighting of the War of Independence. In addition, the presence in southern ports of large numbers of Dutch ships, already with the advantages of low operating costs, but which had also covered much of the cost of their voyages by the profits of the grain trade at a time of shortage, meant that they were able to undercut local carriers for return loads to the North. In this way they further increased their profits, and perhaps marginally reduced the costs of southern goods in the North.

Even though this series of subsistence crises marked what was to be an important turning-point in the history of Mediterranean food supplies, it is difficult to isolate any elements which, at the time, distinguished it from any previous subsistence crisis in the Mediterranean. It is clear that, in the medium term, the crisis of the 1590s and subsequent crises in the early seventeenth century did not lead to a growing dependence of the South upon northern grain supplies. Instead there was a readjustment of supplies and production in the South and a continuing, or returning, dependence on southern supplies. Indeed, by the later seventeenth century, many areas of the South were again exporting grain, not merely to Western Europe but also further afield.[10] Other periods of crisis, like that of the 1690s, again led some southern cities to look northwards for their grain supplies, but this entirely commercial and pragmatic search for the best bargain did not mean or involve southern economic subjection. The contribution of the subsistence crisis of the late sixteenth and early seventeenth centuries to the 'rise of the North' should be seen as providing a temporary boost to profits and hence to potential investment, particularly in the northern Netherlands, at a time when the combined effects of expensive and dangerous warfare and general economic and subsistence crisis threatened serious economic and commercial disaster.

The effects of the subsistence crisis seem indeed to have been greater within the northern and Atlantic economy rather than in its relationship with the South. In particular the 1590s and the first decades of the seventeenth century saw Dutch ships and Dutch traders dominating much of the trade of Europe's Atlantic seaboard, from Portugal and Galicia, northwards along the French Atlantic coast and also to the northern German coast and into the Baltic; eastern England also experienced major Dutch commercial incursions.[11] This expansion was in part because of the subsistence crisis but it was also made possible by the commercial and political weakness of most of the other northern and Atlantic powers and states in the years around the end of the sixteenth century. The most dynamic of the commercial powers of a North which was still essentially backward took advantage of the weakness of the other northern powers to establish its commercial and shipping hegemony over them. The causes of this success were as much fortuitous or political as they were to do with superior maritime technology or economic progress.

The other feature of the great shift between 1590 and 1620 was the capture of Europe's trade with the non-European world by the northern trading states and the consequent decline of the prosperity of the South. The success of the northerners, especially of the Dutch, in the late sixteenth and more particularly the early seventeenth centuries in gaining a stranglehold on the trade with Asia was in part a consequence of the maritime, commercial and financial advantages they had. But it was also a consequence of difficulties, chiefly political and fiscal, within the complex trading patterns of the overland trade, a type of crisis which was both typical and recurrent. A similar crisis in the late fifteenth and early sixteenth centuries had led to similar consequences for European trade in the short term. There was no immediate reason to believe that the crisis around 1600 was any different. But this time the combination of unusually protracted political difficulties in Asia and the Middle East with the commercial expertise of the Dutch, especially the advantages their new type of financial organisation gave them, resulted in change. Even so, in many ways the real domination of extra-European trade by the North considerably postdates this so-called period of transition.

It would be wrong to portray the rise of the northern Netherlands in the period after 1590 as anything less than an economic miracle, or to fail to recognise in some of the changes in financial and commercial organisation which occurred there, especially in the late sixteenth and early seventeenth centuries, very clear signs of the appearance of the ancestors of many nineteenth- and twentieth-century financial structures. According to older historians, it is above all in the appearance of these new 'capitalist' systems of finance that the originality of the North and its 'progressive economy' lie. In particular it was the joint-stock company which was to conquer the world in the name of the northern economy and of an emerging and inevitably successful capitalism.

The North was differentiated from the South by the appearance of joint-stock financing, which allowed northern institutions and hence northern commerce and industry to operate on a larger scale, with more complex organisation and with greater stability. As joint-stock companies evolved they developed a rationale and a series of aims which were more openly and clearly 'entrepreneurial' and 'capitalist' than the mixed motives of individual traders or partners (like those of southern trade and industry), who were liable to compromise their commercial or industrial aims by concentrating on extraneous matters like personal social advancement or personal security. The long-run perspective of the joint-stock companies gave them the ability, almost the imperative, to consider trade and profit in the long run rather than being concerned with immediate profit and quick returns. Paradoxically, by being less profit-focused, the companies were able to maximise profit over the long term and, coincidentally, to squeeze out most of their smaller-scale competitors.

It is true that in both England and, more particularly, in the northern Netherlands in the years after 1590, new methods did develop on an *ad hoc* basis to draw in finance for commerce, in particular for long-distance commerce, on a larger scale and on a more permanent basis than previously. The origins of joint-stock financing in the Netherlands in particular are reasonably clear and lie in the fifteenth century, if not earlier. In the relatively poor northern Netherlands, finance for the building of ships and for the extension of commerce was difficult to raise. The North lacked numbers of very wealthy merchants and financiers able to risk large sums either on voyages or on the building of new ships. To get round this problem the system of *rederij* developed in the northern Netherlands. The *rederij* was a form of partnership which allowed many more investors in a ship or a venture than did its more traditional southern equivalent, the *commenda*. The *rederij* effectively allowed many or most of the partners to be sleeping partners, investing money and sharing both the potential risk and the potential profits of the venture without needing specialised knowledge of the trade and without running the risk of physical involvement in a voyage. By spreading risk it made investment in commerce safer and hence more attractive for many relatively well-to-do people, including land-owners and members of the nobility. Its final great advantage was that, since most investors were only marginally involved, they were not reliant on the return from their investment for the bulk of their income and hence were more willing to leave their capital invested over a longer term.

This longer-term investment was especially important in long-distance trade, such as that with Asia. Trading with Asia, overland as well as round the Cape, was always a slow process. The voyage from Europe to the Spice Islands in Indonesia could easily take more than a year and the return journey was obviously at least as long. The new joint-stock financing structure which the Dutch and the English were using meant that the returns on trade with Asia were even slower than they were in the overland trade. Both the Dutch and the English had already tried to infiltrate the overland trade (significantly, with little success) in the late sixteenth and early seventeenth centuries. In the overland trade individual traders were involved only in single stages of the trade; that is, spices bought in India were not taken to Europe by a single trader, but were the subject of a series of intermediate exchanges. The European traders of Venice or Genoa bought their spices and other eastern commodities in the entrepôts of the Levant rather than in India or Indonesia. Hence the interval between invest-ment, when the goods were bought, and return, when the spices or other goods reached Europe, was relatively short. The Dutch and the English, on the other hand, intended to sail directly to Asia, cutting out the middlemen. This had obvious economic and political advantages, but it did have the major disadvantage of introducing a much greater delay between investment and return as well as increasing the risk. Risky, long-term investment was unlikely to attract those who wanted to invest large sums of money securely. Hence an extended version of *rederij* was a pragmatic solution to a commonplace problem. It can be seen as a northern and 'modern' example of risk reduction and spread-ing. Joint-stock finance grew out of the traditional system to deal with its problems and did not represent in itself any great shift in economic culture. In the early modern period, the joint-stock companies were of potential rather than of actual importance outside their specialised areas of activity.

Although the potential of the joint-stock companies was great, it would be wrong to exaggerate their importance in the seventeenth and eighteenth centuries. It would be wrong to see them as prime examples of the newly developing commercial capitalism. They are only the distant evolutionary ancestors of new forms of commercial and industrial activity. Joint-stock financing was limited, even in the northern Netherlands and England, to a few, very specialised activities, connected with potentially high-risk, long-distance trade.[12] Very little joint-stock finance was involved in internal trade and even less in industry. The establishment and continuation of joint-stock companies were very much political rather than economic. Joint-stock companies could only be established with state approval and were always subject to intense state regulation, which tended to increase rather than decrease as the seventeenth and eighteenth centuries progressed. The catastrophes of the South Sea Bubble and of the Law scandal in France in the years around 1720 meant that, in the eighteenth century, regulation of joint-stock financing grew massively to the point at which in England it became virtually impossible. At the same time, the massive losses which the collapse of the schemes had caused for investors reduced the trust which people were willing to place in joint-stock financing. By the eighteenth century joint-stock financing, rather than being the first indication of a new world, appeared to contemporaries to be a relic from an earlier age.

Even in those areas where joint-stock financing was established and, as importantly, where it survived, it is difficult to see the joint-stock companies as being essentially modern, commercial operations. Just as their origins had been in part political, the great joint-stock companies continued to be involved heavily in the political sphere, especially in the Netherlands. This affected their financial power, and their ability to act in the distant areas where they operated as quasi-governments pursuing their own foreign policies. This aspect is perhaps most clearly seen in the history of the Dutch West India Company, which began life as a political rather than an economic project and whose activities during the first 30 years of its existence were dominated by the foreign policy of its Directors which was, for much of the period, in opposition to that of the Dutch Republic.[13]

It is also rather misleading to describe the great chartered trading companies of the northern Netherlands or England in the seventeenth and eighteenth centuries as typical joint-stock companies, especially after the earliest stages of their development. They were joint-stock companies in the formal sense that their charters vested the proprietorship of the companies in shareholders who had put up a proportion of the joint capital of the company and who were able to sell their shares to others. In the case of both the English and Dutch East India Companies in the seventeenth century, sales of large numbers of shares had to be approved by the Boards of Directors and, in the case of the Dutch Company, by a series of other committees whose function was to maintain the political as well as commercial stability and balance of the company. The shareholders drew a return from their investment in the form of dividends related to the commercial outturn of the company.[14] All this looks very much like the prototype of a modern venture-capital joint-stock company.

However, after the early years of the companies, the bulk of the new capital they raised to expand their trade (or indeed to tide them over difficult periods) was raised not by the issuing of new joint stock but by the sale of bonds. The bondholders were much more numerous, and received a much greater share of the proceeds of the companies than did the shareholders. In part, the growing reliance of the companies on bonds was a result of their political nature. Shareownership gave rights within the political structure of the company. Consequently, the Directors, and the states, which had in most cases to approve any increase in share capital, sought to restrict the dilution of share capital to protect their own political as well as commercial dominance. If bonds were attractive politically and commercially to the Directors, they were also more attractive to investors than stock. Bonds offered a fixed and guaranteed rate of return on a capital investment which was, at least in theory, secure. Investors were not looking for an opportunity to engage, even by proxy, in entrepreneurship and venture, as a way of becoming involved in a modern capitalist, or even proto-capitalist, economy, but rather for a secure form of investment with as little risk as possible. The companies were, in effect, financially as well as commercially, mini-states, in which people could invest with some hope of security, probably more than they could hope for from virtually any seventeenth- or eighteenth-century European state. This was hardly a 'shareholding revolution' nor yet a revolution in economic attitudes. In the North as in the South, most investors, even in the great companies, were seeking stability and security rather than being prepared to take risks in the hope of high returns from growth and change.

The rise of joint-stock banking in the North in the seventeenth and eighteenth centuries had similar characteristics. The few joint-stock banks were established largely by state or city governments, chiefly for their own political or fiscal ends rather than, as in the nineteenth century, for commercial or investment purposes.[15] Outside the great chartered companies and the official industrial companies which were established in France and Spain in the later eighteenth century, virtually all commercial and industrial finance was organised on a strictly personal and individual basis and continued to be so until well into the nineteenth century. Banks did develop, but they were personal, dependent upon the financial probity and acumen of individuals or families to exactly the same extent as the Medici or Fugger banks had been before them.

There is little to suggest that a financial and capitalist revolution of a continental or even world scale had taken place in the early seventeenth century in the northern Netherlands or elsewhere in the north of Europe. Changes there certainly had been, but they were to remain on the margin of Europe's financial development until the late eighteenth and nineteenth centuries. It is reasonable to argue that the financial developments which have been discussed here have gained an exaggerated importance through being seen with hindsight from the point of view of the nineteenth century, where undoubtedly joint-stock finance did become important. Historians have seen in these financial developments the origins of later developments, and therefore they have decided that they must have been of profound importance in the earlier period. In fact they were of no more than of marginal and very specialised importance in the economy as a whole. What is significant over virtually the whole of the North, as over most of the South, is the continued vitality of old systems and patterns rather than the development of new ones.

What is also striking about the economy of Northern and North-western Europe, even in the eighteenth century, is how patchy the advance which is supposedly so typical of the North was. Some areas, especially those closely linked to the great commercial centres and to administrative and consumption centres like Paris, did undergo considerable growth and change. Some industrial areas such as the West Riding of Yorkshire and parts of Normandy also grew and changed. Over much of the North, however, change and progress are much more difficult to identify. There is little evidence that the rural economy of much of northern France or of western Germany changed, except possibly in the direction of greater economic differentiation and of greater mass poverty.

Throughout the North there is evidence that economic advance involved the growth of poverty, and especially of rural poverty. The changes in rural organisation which occurred involved a reduction in the demand for labour and greater seasonality of employment, and hence resulted in a reduction in income for many workers. At the same time, decline of long-standing forms of rural community and sociability which the changes in agricultural organisation involved, reduced the safety net which communal action had provided for the less fortunate members of rural society. The economically forced migration of increasing numbers of the lower groups in rural society to the expanding towns did little to help. Large numbers of migrants overwhelmed the labour market, and at the same time reduced the ability of town and city governments to provide support for the destitute and increased urban social and health problems.

Traditionally it was easy to equate the changes which were beginning to take place in the northern economy with, on the one hand, increasing prosperity and improving conditions, and on the other with a prudent realisation of the advantages of growth over stasis and stability. An entrepreneurial world was emerging which had realised that the future lay in new methods and forms of production and trade which were to liberate people from the constraints of the traditional economy. But, as has been indicated, there is little evidence before the later nineteenth century, and certainly not in the eighteenth century, that for the mass of the population, urban or rural, the changes produced any real advance. Indeed, there is rather more evidence of a decline than an advance. Compared with their southern contemporaries, eighteenth-century northern Europeans, taken overall, seem to have lived more impoverished and more insecure lives.

To the traditional historian the day-to-day stability of individual life had no great importance, because what mattered in the rise of the North was the long-term view of the economic, social and cultural process which economic and social historians have come, by habit as much as anything else, to call industrialisation. Those living in the past, of course, knew nothing of the long historical perspective. Families taking day-to-day decisions were much more concerned with questions of survival and security than they were with growth, change or progress, not least because such concepts were not part of their mental map. It is more appropriate to attempt to assess the changes which occurred in the North to see how far they met contemporary strategic criteria rather than how far they contributed to expectations and assumptions pushed back on to the past by the present. This is not merely some arid academic exercise. Contemporary perceptions of the nature of change and its consequences were crucially important in determining the response of everyone in a society, rich as well as poor, entrepreneur as well as feckless beggar, to the opportunities and risks of any new course of action.

In the precarious agriculturally-based economies of early modern Europe, security and the reduction of risk were high on everyone's agenda, much higher in most cases than any question of improvement or growth. Risk-avoidance and risk-reduction strategies were crucially important. In the South a combination of climatic advantages and high levels of urbanisation had made the general development of highly effective strategies possible. The picture in the North was rather different; throughout the early modern period, the Northern European economic and agricultural system was one beset by unusually high levels of instability and risk. In part this was a consequence of geographic and climatic factors. The more temperate, but also more unpredictable climate of Northern Europe meant that crop yields were much more uncertain, much more prone to disaster than those of the South. Furthermore, those same climatic and geographical factors meant that the range of crops which could be grown successfully was smaller. The sparseness of population and the difficulties of communication and in particular of bulk transport meant that, over most of the region, commercial production was more restricted, and also that in times of crisis it was extremely difficult to solve subsistence problems by moving food from region to region. Instead, people moved as refugees from calamity in their home areas in search of food and employment.[16] The problem of crisis migration always seems to have been a much more severe one north of the Alps. In the seventeenth and eighteenth centuries the poor of the North looked for salvation to the countries and economies south of the Alps, even to Naples.[17] Risk was high in the North and the changes of the seventeenth and eighteenth centuries in many ways increased that risk. It is important to be clear, however, that northerners tried, just as southerners did, to restrict the effects of risk as far as possible. Risk spreading was less possible in the North than in the South, but it still remained the preferred strategy of the great majority of the population of the North, urban as well as rural, well into the nineteenth century.

Perhaps the major factor in stimulating much of the change which took place in the North was crisis. Agriculture changed in response to crisis demand; much of the technological change in industry was generated by internal crisis. The changes, however, did not reduce risk but actually increased it, both overall and more particularly for many individuals. The changes themselves were risky. The traditional idea of the inevitability of economic change in the North in the eighteenth century produces the completely erroneous assumption that since the changes which were occurring were part of an unstoppable historical tide, they were not risky or a gamble. In fact the changes which took place were, and were seen at the time, as being very risky. To abandon, or even to modify extensively well-established and proven ways of doing things in an essentially precarious economy must always involve taking a major risk, and it is a gamble which could easily have literally fatal consequences for the participants. It must be emphasised that not all changes, and not all instigators or adopters of change, were success-ful. It is probably truer to say that the majority, perhaps even the great majority, of innovators failed with catastrophic consequences for them-selves and those dependent on them. Posterity tends to remember only those who were lucky and succeeded against the odds and does not realise that these were exceptional and not the norm.

Not merely was the introduction of change in itself risky, but in addi-tion many of the changes made in the northern economy increased rather than reduced risk both for the capitalist and for the agricultural or industrial workers. For instance, mechanisation offered great oppor-tunities for commercial success, but it also involved much greater finan-cial exposure because of the capital cost of the machinery, and much greater risk as a consequence of commercial downturn, since greater productivity meant larger stocks in trade and the need to hold greater stocks of raw materials. The development of long-distance commerce exposed the traders, and all those directly or indirectly dependent upon them, to the insecurity of markets and regions over which they had little control or influence. The changes in agriculture led to greater specialisa-tion and commercialisation of production, but specialisation also meant that the insurance provided against crop failure by multiple cropping was removed. Even the development, in town or countryside, of indus-trial employment can be seen as a further increase in risk. The newly urbanised industrial worker became dependent upon a single form of employment in a centre where the largest proportion of available employment was in that single industry which was in its nature unstable and fluctuating. The loss of industrial employment meant almost cer-tainly total unemployment, with no real hope of alternatives. It is striking that in the more traditional cities of the North, such as Paris, the poor seem to have avoided occupational specialisation as far as possible.[18] Even in the countryside, the spread of rural industry, which could have been a valuable addition to a range of employment, lost that role in the North. The organisational and technological changes going on in agriculture had the effect of creating a large pool of rural unemployed or underemployed, for whom domestic industrial employment offered not an additional source of revenue but their sole income and an extremely uncertain one.

It is striking that despite, or perhaps because of, its economic advance, the North was more seriously affected by economic and subsistence crisis in the seventeenth and eighteenth centuries than was the South. In particular the great European depressions of the 1690s, 1730s, 1770s and 1780s were much more severe in Northern Europe, in particular in France and western Germany, than they were in Southern Europe. The greatest famine, perhaps the only true famine, of the early modern period, that of the early 1770s, affected not the supposedly declining and backward South, but rather the supposedly advancing and developing North.[19] It is not easy to see the North as triumphant, as the economic winner. Even in the late eighteenth century, the economy of the South had much more to recommend it and provided a much more stable and prosperous way of life, with a range of choice and opportunity for the individual, than did the North.

It would not be difficult to replace the old 'triumphant' North with an alternative picture of Northern Europe in the seventeenth and eighteenth centuries in terms of a modern Third-World economy. There were large differences between rich and poor and almost certainly, in the eighteenth century, those differences were widening. Northern agriculture was moving into a classic Third-World colonial pattern, increasingly monocultural, increasingly dependent upon distant and more developed consumers for its markets. Like any Third-World agriculture, it was crucially dependent upon the prosperity of its consumers for its own prosperity, and like any Third-World economy, relatively small fluctuations in the economy of its consumers had disproportionate effects on its own. The changes which had produced this monocultural structure had, along with growing population, served to increase the pool of poverty-stricken rural workers who had few prospects in their own home areas, either for agricultural employment or for any form of alternative source of income. They had few choices. They could remain in poverty in the countryside, eking out a very basic subsistence in times of relative prosperity and joining a sea of refugees in times of crisis. The alternative was to move to urban centres, there to provide either a cheap labour force for new industries, themselves highly risky and precarious, or an addition to the pool of urban poverty, at least in the towns finding a much greater range of small employments and hence an increased hope of survival.

Such a picture is as exaggerated and distorted as the old image because it leaves out a great deal which is of importance. It does, however, remind us of a number of important things. The portrayal of the economy of Northern, and especially North-western Europe in the seventeenth and eighteenth centuries as being modern and developing, representing a clear stage on the way to the economy of modern Europe is, in a number of obvious senses, true. The modern economy of Europe did grow out of the northern economy, the Industrial Revolution did happen in England and many of the features and developments of the northern economy in the seventeenth and eighteenth centuries were the precursors of later development. Nonetheless, it is misleading to see the final 'victory' of northern growth and of northern methods as being inherent or inevitable, even in the eighteenth century. As has already been said, the success of the North was based not on rock-solid foundations of economic truth, but rather on a series of successful, but nonetheless highly risky gambles. This should lead to a reassessment of the individuals and groups who took those gambles and brought them off. The idea that the success of the Industrial Revolution was inevitable, that it was 'an idea whose time has come', grossly undervalues the foresight, courage and often downright recklessness of the innovators and entrepreneurs who brought it about. Without them the 'modern' economy of the nineteenth and twentieth centuries might well not have developed, but they certainly did not know what the outcome in the short term would be, never mind the long term.

One reason why the modern economy might not have developed from the economy of early modern northern Europe was because there existed, in southern Europe, a very different model of an economy and of economic development. This was an economic system based on risk minimisation and stability rather than on change and growth. In the traditional historiography the contest between the two was unequal and the result was predetermined. Change and growth were fated to replace stasis and stability. Indeed, there was no contest since, from the early seventeenth century onwards, the North was outstripping the South which, after about 1620 and 1630, sank into a kind of picturesque poverty from which it rose only in the later nineteenth or even twentieth centuries as a consequence of the export of northern know-how, northern methods and northern capital to Europe's southern problem area. It is clear, however, that the South continued to be prosperous, that its economic system continued to deliver prosperity to its towns and rural areas until the late eighteenth century, and indeed there are some grounds for saying that, at least until 1770, overall levels of prosperity in the South were as high or higher than those in the North. Certainly, by all the traditional measures of economic advance, levels of urbanisation, commercialisation, industrial activity and industrial production and possibly agricultural production and innovation, the South remained in advance of the North until well on in the eighteenth century.

The problem, of course, has been that there has been a fundamental confusion between change and growth on the one hand and actual levels of performance on the other. It is a common failing of economic historians, schooled in Marxian and neo-Marxian modes of thought, to see growth as being of paramount importance in the history of any economy. Growth is what matters either in terms of the health of economies or, by a rather dubious transfer, in terms of the prosperity or wellbeing of populations. It is a statistical truism that rapid rates of growth are much easier to achieve when an economy starts from a low base and sets off to catch more developed economies. The more developed an economy, the lower its growth rates and the less significant overall any change or innovation are going to be. Although the more developed economy has lower growth rates, it does not mean that it is necessarily less prosperous than the more rapidly growing less-developed economy, nor does it necessarily mean that its population suffers greater poverty. This over-concentration on change has distorted many interpretations of the economic situation of Europe in the early modern period, just as it continues to distort interpretations of the economies of the modern world. It is made worse in the case of early modern Europe by two other factors. The first is that it is in this period that traditional historians are looking for what they consider the most significant of all changes, that is, for the changes which would lead on to the central event of their interpretation, industrialisation. Perhaps inevitably, this has led them to overestimate the importance of changes, which, it could be argued, were marginal to much of the system, and to understimate or ignore those things which were stable in the system and which, it could be argued, were much more important to early modern people and to their strategies. The second distorting factor is related to the first. The aim of individuals in the southern economy was not to inaugurate change but was the management of change so as to increase stability and reduce risk. In these circumstances, comparisons of rates of growth and change are even more misleading. In some senses the southern economy would have been less rather than more successful had its rates of growth and change been higher.

There is also a deeper level at which the traditional approach is misleading. It sets up the two models as being in competition and seeks to explain development in terms of the victory of one system over the other. There are a number of major fallacies in such a picture.

The first is that the distinction between North and South was a clear and universal one. It is, however, clear that throughout the early modern period there were as many, perhaps more, areas in which North and South were the same, rather than sharply distinguished. Above all, this was the case in their concern for and planning towards security through diversity, rather than growth through specialisation. The ideals of mixed farming, and varied patterns of employment for families, were as strong throughout much of the North as they were in the South, and this concern was to survive at least through the first stages of industrialisation in the North. The issue was one of the availability and non-availability of means for diversification rather than the importance of diversification. The North had, for climatic reasons, and also perhaps because of its much less complex patterns of land tenure, fewer opportunities for diversification than did the South, but if anything, that made diversification more rather than less important as a goal. In both North and South families sought to spread risk rather than to take it.

Second, the creation of a model in which the systems are in conflict and in which, in the end, one or the other had to 'win', blurs what seems to be the most important element in this history. At the end of the eighteenth century, in a very real sense, both systems had 'won'; both had for decades been delivering unprecedented levels of prosperity for their populations. These were alternative, and successful ways of delivering prosperity rather than one failed and one successful one.

Third, the idea of two systems in confrontation removes the possibility of their co-evolution, of a historical situation in which two systems living together in relative stability, develop, in part, of course, in their own terms but also in part in response to changes in the other. Changes in the southern economy in the late Middle Ages had crucial importance for the development of northern economic activity; the Mediterranean subsistence crises of the late sixteenth century led to important changes in the North. Again, the development of the North's colonial contacts led to the development of new industrial and agricultural activity in the South, and the development of northern prosperity in the seventeenth and eighteenth centuries led to the development of new service industries in Italy and southern France designed to cater for the rich northern tourist.

It is important to conclude by emphasising that throughout the early modern period the two systems were, in fact, closely similar in many respects and that they existed comfortably together. The idea of conflict and competition between them is a modern invention. Until the end of the eighteenth century it was impossible to designate 'winners' and 'losers'.

7

EUROPE'S PLACE IN THE WORLD

The early modern period has been traditionally seen by Europeans as the first great age in which Europe reached out beyond its geographical boundaries to trade with and ultimately colonise the non-European world. For many historians it was this very expansionism which distinguished the early modern period from what went before. The great explosion of Portuguese and Castilian (or Castilian-sponsored) exploration and then conquest which began in the mid-fifteenth century was seen as the point at which Europe, which had been under pressure from outside for the previous millennium, finally took the initiative and began to expand. This expansion altered the cultural and psychological profile of the continent and led to economic change, especially in the Atlantic regions, which were most conveniently placed geographically to benefit from extra-European maritime contact.

Until the mid-fifteenth century, Europeans had been satisfied to obtain the huge range of goods they received from outside Europe largely through the means of Asian or African traders. The silks, spices and carpets of the East were brought to Europe, or at least to the margin of Europe in the Levant, by Asiatic traders. The gold of West Africa, which was so vital to the establishment of gold-based currencies in Western and Southern Europe in the later Middle Ages, came to Europe through African or Arab traders;[1] Europe did not seek any direct contact with producers or even with the original traders, but was willing to be the consumer at the end of a long chain of trade.

In Iberia from the middle of the fifteenth century onwards there developed a desire, perhaps a need, to contact more directly areas of production, first of African gold and then of Asiatic spices.[2] The origins of this change were political or religious rather than economic,

162

but behind it lay a pressure to greater economic efficiency, to cutting out the middleman and trading directly, and therefore more profitably, with the producer. The Portuguese rounded Cape Verde in the 1440s and the Cape of Good Hope in the 1490s in pursuit of a Christian mission, but also in search of profits and, by extension, power. Traditional historians saw in European expansion the inherent tendency of expanding and developing economies to expand imperially as well as commercially.

This pattern was repeated in Spanish expansion into the Americas after 1492. Whatever Columbus's motives actually were (and there will always be dispute over them and over the motives of the Catholic Kings of Spain in choosing, however reluctantly, to support and sponsor him), there was little doubt in traditional historiography that underlying it all was the working-out of an inevitable European imperative to colonial expansion and territorial conquest. The profound advantages of Europe, economically and politically, over extra-European peoples and systems predetermined the outcome.

By the end of the sixteenth century, when the first wave of European empires – those of Spain and Portugal in the New World and the Portuguese empire in Asia and the East Coast of Africa – had become established, Europe's relationship with the non-European world moved on to its next inevitable stage. Traditional historians considered that the rise of the powers of Northern Europe, especially the Northern Netherlands and England, to commercial and financial dominance was inevitably accompanied by their growing involvement in the extra-European world. They replaced older Southern European colonial powers, especially the Portuguese in the Far East, and they created new colonies of settlement in the Caribbean and, on the eastern seaboard of North America, the colonies which were to develop into the United States and Canada. Around these Caribbean and North American colonies was to grow up a whole new series of trading structures, the Atlantic economies. Traditional historians thought this whole process grew essentially out of the imperial imperative which was built into the system of trade, finance and commerce which had developed in Europe.

The great region of expansion in the seventeenth century was the Americas, and the Atlantic economies continued to expand dynamically, perhaps even more dynamically, in the eighteenth century. However, it was in Asia, above all in India, that the great events of the eighteenth century were to be played out. The eighteenth century saw the rise of the English East India Company, first to commercial dominance in coastal India and then, after 1757, to the role of territorial ruler. Although the conquest of Bengal was, in some ways, a surprise and certainly a divergence from existing company policy, nonetheless it could be seen with hindsight as inevitable, as the expected outcome of the development of the new commercial system of Northern Europe. Certainly, the traditional historians saw the success of the company as the inevitable outcome of any conflict between a developed, modern power such as England and a declining, backward, 'Third World' country.

A number of assumptions underlie this traditional interpretation of European expansion in the early modern period. The first is that expansion beyond the traditional commercial frontiers of Europe was a necessary consequence of economic change within Europe. The second assumption was that European commercial expansion necessarily and inevitably involved what would come to be called colonial expansion, that is to say the creation of areas of political conquest and political control. Once Europe had established a commercial presence in, for instance, India or Indonesia, it was only a matter of time before that commercial presence was converted into political control, first of the commercial centres themselves but ultimately of the areas of production. This assumption, of a necessary territorial imperative linked to commercial expansion, is one which pervades not merely studies of 'the expansion of Europe' in the early modern period but is also very common amongst European historians of expansion in the nineteenth century. Here again a nineteenth-century outcome is seen as inevitable, and therefore the earlier stages of that process are perceived as equally inevitable. Third, again based on the reading-back of nineteenth- and twentieth-century situations into the past, there is the assumption that in the relations between Europe and the non-European world from the fifteenth century onwards, it was Europe which was the developed region and the non-European world the underdeveloped one. In a conflict between modernity, progress and development on the one hand, and backwardness and underdevelopment on the other, modernity must, inevitably, triumph.

Viewed from a less Eurocentric, and a less nineteenth- and twentieth-century-centric point of view, all these assumptions appear, at the very least, debatable, and in many cases, downright wrong.

The picture of the dynamic Europe of the early modern period thrusting out to conquer the world needs very considerable modification. In the 1440s and the 1450s, when the first major Portuguese voyages of exploration and expansion were moving around Africa, the armies of the Ottomans were conquering the last remnants of the Byzantine Empire and advancing into the Balkans. In the same period the Almoravid rulers of Morocco were expanding to threaten Portugal's position in North Africa and even posing a threat to Portugal itself. It has been argued convincingly that the original cause of Portuguese concern with a possible coastal route to West Africa in the mid-fifteenth century was the desperate need to regain access to the gold supplies from the mines of Bambuk which had been cut by Moroccan expansion, that it was a response to extra-European pressure, rather than the expansiveness of a newly confident and powerful Europe. In the 1490s, the period when the Castilians were beginning to establish their control in the New World (and incidentally were completing the military process of the Reconquest with the conquest of Granada), the Ottomans under Selim I and Suleyman I were completing the conquest of the Western Balkans. In the late 1520s, when the Spaniards under Pizarro were beginning their conquest of the Inca Empire, the Turks were besieging Vienna. At the time of the foundation of the Dutch and English East India Companies, the Habsburgs were paying tribute to the Sultan for their lands in Austria and Hungary. It was not until the 1680s, the decade in which Pennsylvania was established, that the Ottomans recognised the loss of any territory in Europe as being permanent; in 1683 the Turks were again at the gates of Vienna. Even in the mid-eighteenth century, the Ottoman Empire was still regaining territory in the Balkans. It is very difficult to see early modern Europe as being simply expansive. It was also still under serious threat from the East, especially in the sixteenth century and again during the Köprülü period in the later seventeenth century. The presumed confidence of Europe's Atlantic expansion has to be seen against this background of continuing and serious pressure from the East. For most Europeans in the seventeenth century, the threat from the East was of far greater importance and immediacy than the prospects of oceanic expansion.

In the nineteenth and twentieth centuries Europeans became more and more convinced of their manifest destiny to dominate the world, at first commercially and then politically. Their conviction of the rightness and inevitability of the path they were following led them to write history in terms of its outcome rather than in terms of the much more complex patterns of actuality. Their view of the role of Europe in the extra-European world before the nineteenth century was distorted by their conviction that what happened in Europe, and what happened to Europeans beyond Europe, was of overriding significance not merely in Europe's own history, but also in the history of the non-European world. They believed that when the Europeans arrived they were able to transform the political, economic and cultural patterns of the non-European world, if not overnight, certainly very rapidly.

It is clear that the effects of the Europeans beyond Europe in the early modern period were extremely varied in their importance and were largely determined by the existing social, political and economic structures of the non-European world. In a world context Europe was politically small and insignificant. In Central and South America in the sixteenth century, in Indonesia in the seventeenth or in India in the eighteenth, Europeans managed to establish political domination as a consequence of the weakness or disunity of the states and peoples they conquered rather than because of the strength of Europe. The few hundred followers of Cortés or Pizarro, the Dutch East India Company's fleet and the English East India Company's army were small in comparison with the armies and navies of the powers they were dealing with. They would not have been able to conquer provinces or empires without the help they were given by the disunity and internal weakness of those empires themselves. They were lucky in the timing of their enterprises. The Europeans came not as decisive conquerors but rather as small but important players in already existing and unstable situations. The empires and dominations they established were, like all European colonial expansion in the nineteenth century, dependent for survival and certainly for continuing administrative survival upon the acquiescence of traditional elites and power structures. The only areas where the dependence of European empires on the continuation and support of existing power structures did not apply was in the Americas.

In North America the European settlers came into contact with few powerful traditional structures before the late eighteenth century. The Atlantic seaboard had to transplant patterns of society and administration from Europe, since there were no existing structures which could be relied on. As a consequence the development of the North American colonies was relatively slow and was dominated, both economically and psychologically, by the continuing pioneer element, that is to say by a large subsistence sector which succeeded a first stage in which expansion was dominated by trapping and the fur trade. Strikingly, where Europeans in North America did come into contact with powerful traditional structures, in the St Lawrence and upper Hudson Valleys, this shift to pioneer agriculture was much longer delayed than elsewhere. The Five Nations Confederacy and its connections allowed Europeans to trade fur, which was increasingly hunted out on the eastern seaboard itself in the Great Plains and the Great Lakes regions, and so a successful and profitable trade continued through the seventeenth and eighteenth centuries. The power of the Confederacy also prevented the establishment of European settlements any larger than the factories and surrounding fields. The history of Canada under French rule has often been seen as a missed opportunity, as an example of an intolerant government's refusal to allow religious dissenters (in this case Huguenots) to establish themselves in the colony and hence move its development on from a stage of primitive extraction to one of settled agriculture and commerce, so that Canada could follow the pattern which was so successful in the English colonies further south. This is to misunderstand the nature of Canada's economy in the seventeenth and eighteenth centuries. It confuses settlement with success and primitive extraction with failure, and also misrepresents the necessary relationship between a small-scale, weak European presence on the one hand and a powerful non-European state or people on the other. Just because the Five Nations Confederacy was not a modern, or pre-modern state does not mean it was not powerful. It was certainly too powerful to be trifled with by a few European adventurers or missionaries.[3]

The importance of the European colonisation of North America was not apparent until the eighteenth century. In the early modern period it was the expansion of Europe, especially Iberia, into Middle and South America which was important. Until late in the eighteenth century there were more Europeans or people of European descent in Iberian America and the Caribbean than there were in North America. The economic effects of Latin American expansion, both in terms of the value and importance of exports and of the stimulation of industrial and commercial growth and change in Europe, were greater than those of the expansion of the North American economies until the end of the eighteenth century.

It would appear that in Central and South America Europe had conquered and colonised important and wealthy non-European states and empires. The initial startling success of Cortés and Pizarro owed much to luck and chance as well as to the unstable political situations in both the Aztec and Inca empires in the early sixteenth century. But even more important was a factor over which the Spaniards had no more control than the indigenous states, the spread of disease and the associated demographic catastrophe. The indigenous populations had little if any immunity to European diseases and in less than a century after the conquest, the Amerindian population of Mexico had fallen by more than 90 per cent and that of Peru by at least 80 per cent.[4] The first conquistadors in Mexico and Peru had aimed to take over existing systems of labour service and revenue such as the Inca *mita* system of forced communal labour which, under Spanish rule, became a form of labour tribute exacted on a communal basis. However, the demographic catastrophe weakened traditional society and economy in Spanish and Portuguese America to such an extent that the conquerors were forced by circumstances to develop new economic and social structures. In the Caribbean and in Brazil similar problems, demographic decline and very small-scale political organisations, forced the colonisers to establish their own structures rather than to take over existing ones. It should be clear that this was essentially a second-best rather than a preferred course of action.

Even in the Americas the effects of European expansion in the early modern period should not be seen in terms of a confident and triumphant continent imposing its political and economic will on non-European societies. Instead it consisted of the settlement, and at times very hesitant settlement, of Europeans in a continent which was very sparsely populated in the North and became depopulated in the South. It is also significant that many of the societies and economies which they sought to set up or to continue were essentially pre-modern, even medieval, rather than modern. The society which the conquistadors sought to establish in Iberian America was in essence medieval, an extension of Iberian feudalism. The exploitation of the silver mines of Mexico and Peru was organised through state monopolies and through forced labour.[5] In North America it is all too easy to allow the later economic and social development of the colonies to mask the fact that the underlying social and economic ideals of many of them, from Virginia to the Puritan colonies of New England, were essentially pre-modern, the creation of godly commonwealths or of versions of English society purged of recent deteriorations. At least until the later eighteenth century, the economies of the new North American colonies were dominated by production for auto-consumption or by the production for export of raw materials, often using slave labour. A great deal of the early European population of the Americas did not come from the 'modern' groups in the metropolitan societies, but rather from much more traditional and traditionally minded people who saw in the new continent the chance to preserve their way of life. The drive to American conquest and settlement in Spain came not from the developing bourgeoisie of Seville or Barcelona, but from the declining but fiercely proud and impoverished nobility of Extremadura and La Mancha, who were not seeking new economic or social modes but rather ways of maintaining old ones. In the North, too, it is difficult to find much evidence before the eighteenth century of a capitalist drive to establish colonies of settlement. The settlers and the investors in most of the English colonies, and many in the Dutch Nieuw Amsterdam colony, came to establish essentially rural economies and societies, based upon great estates or on small farms or in small communities, rather than to establish new and dynamic structures. In the early modern period, North America was settled largely by reactionary migrants who wished to establish in the American colonies societies and economies which returned to what they saw as the essentials of pre-modern European society.

The nature of Europe's relationships with the Americas was determined by the presence or absence of existing social and political systems. Where those pre-existing societies were strong, Europe had to come to terms with them. In Asia the limitations of European influence and power were even more obvious. The political powers of Asia, not only the great empires such as Mughal India, Ming or Qing China or Tokugawa Japan, but also many of the smaller powers, such as the sultanates of Java and the Moluccas or the states of Sri Lanka, were immeasurably greater and more powerful than any European state and certainly more powerful than any European trader or trading company. In much of Asia Europe could trade only with the active support or consent of the ruling power. Europe's territorial gains in Asia were not made in the territories of the great powers but rather where they were dealing with small-scale local rulers who were militarily weak. Europe was indescribably marginal to much of Asia and to many of its concerns. Even at the very end of the eighteenth century both Japan and China were able to cut themselves off from contact with Europe. European demand and European trade were significant in some areas of Asia, and in the eighteenth century in particular, specialised forms of production, such as the production of porcelain for the European market, sprang up to service European demand, but these new trades and industries were still marginal to the major concerns of the economies of which they formed part. Europe's effect on Asia was small, certainly before the 1750s or 1760s. European capitalism certainly did not colonise, or even begin colonising much of Asia before 1800, and it is hardly surprising that this should be so.

It is chiefly because Europe's contact with Asia was carried on by merchant capitalists that the effect of Europe on Asia in the early modern period was as small as it was. The great expansion of European contact with Asia in the seventeenth and eighteenth centuries was not carried on by government or states but rather by companies of merchants. Even in the sixteenth century the *Carriera da India*, the main instrument of Portuguese expansion and contact in Asia, was organised rather more on commercial than on governmental lines. Although the *Carriera* and, on a much grander scale, the Dutch and English East India Companies were ultimately to become great territorial powers and were to lose their primarily commercial role, that great transition from trade to control came at the very end of the early modern period, and when it came it caused major problems both for the commercial organisations and also for their metropolitan states. Even in the late eighteenth century the great chartered companies were trying desperately to avoid their new role. For instance, the English East India Company only took over financial and fiscal control of the Bengal state when it became clear that all other possible agencies had failed.

It is only in the context of the commercial nature of European contact with Asia that that contact can be fully understood. It is not simply a question of understanding the strategic aims of European merchants but also of understanding the economic relationship between the two continents and the existing structure of Asian trade.

Unlike the trade with the Americas, Europe's trade with Asia was a very old one. In the medieval period, the trade with Asia had been a major element in the power and significance of the Italian trading cities. Venice, Genoa, Pisa, Lucca, Florence and many others had engaged in trade with Asia either through the trading centres of the Levant such as Alexandria, Cairo, Jaffa, Beirut, Damascus, Aleppo, or, when that route became too difficult, via the great overland route, the *Via Tartarica*. This linked the Italian bases on the Black Sea with the great trading and producing centres of northern China and Central Asia, and it was the route along which came not only the goods of China, but also bubonic plague in the early years of the fourteenth century. The early modern development of new sea routes to Asia, and of new ways of organising that trade on the European side, must be seen within the context of a long-run trading system, rather than in terms of the creation of new ones.

If the trade with Asia was an old one, it was also one which had very particular economic and organisational characteristics. Central to these was the relative level of development of Europe and Asia throughout the medieval period and, indeed, for much of the early modern period. As inheritors of a colonial past, modern Europeans have had a tendency to see their relationship with the non-European world as being an unequal one in which Europe plays the leading role. They also tend to assume that Europe played the same role of the developed economy in earlier periods as it was to do in the nineteenth and twentieth centuries, and that the non-European world had the role of being backward and relatively underdeveloped. There can be an unconscious assumption that European contact with Asia in the early modern period was a kind of 'civilising mission' in which European commercial, financial and technological superiority would lead inevitably to European domination and control, first commercial and economic, but finally political.

This interpretation of the relationship with Asia is emphatically wrong. It totally misunderstands the relative economic positions of the two continents, at least until the last years of the eighteenth century, and the nature of their relationship. This misunderstanding makes it virtually impossible to understand the problems which Europeans faced in trading with Asia and the complexity of the solutions which were necessary to resolve them. It also makes it much more difficult to comprehend the history of the competition between the European traders and companies in Asia.

Europeans were marginal in the trade of Asia even at the end of the eighteenth century. European penetration was very small within the great empires of Asia, with their highly complex and highly developed systems of production and internal trade. It could be argued that problems of transport played some part in this because distances inside India or China were huge and the movement of goods was slow. However, in both states relatively low-value goods were moved over long distances, but the great mass of these goods were produced internally for internal consumption. European goods could not and did not compete in Asian mass markets on either quality or price. The great empires were able to protect their own interests by preventing large inflows of European goods, partially by tariffs and partially by direct prohibition. They were opened to European trade and goods only by political decision or internal political failure, and not as a result of the economic pressure of European expansion. It was the collapse of Mughal power and then of many of the unstable Mughal successor states which opened up India to British manufactures in the late eighteenth century.

It was the internal collapse of the Qing empire after the death of Chien Lung which allowed China to be opened – and then only by gunboats – to large-scale European trade. It was internal collapse and revolution which opened Japan in the 1850s and 1860s.

Even outside the great Asian states European trade constituted only a small part of the totality of Asian trade. The seventeenth and eighteenth centuries saw a continuing expansion of European demand for Asiatic goods, which almost certainly increased the importance of Europe as a consumer of Asian goods, but even at the end of the eighteenth century, the greater part of Asian production, be it textiles, ceramics or spices, was traded and consumed within the Asian regional economy. Although Europeans played an increasingly important role in this trade within Asia and although, in the case of Japan, they were to be granted a monopoly of external trade following the closure of the country in 1644, nonetheless they still remained only one of many elements in Asiatic trade. For instance, the role of the Gujaratis or of the Omani Arabs in the trade of the Indian Ocean in the seventeenth and eighteenth centuries, or the continuing importance of Asiatic centres like Johor or Achin in the trade of Indonesia and East Asia, indicate very clearly that Europeans, even at the very end of the early modern period, and even in the areas which were most central to their economic and commercial interests, were by no means able to monopolise or even dominate the trade of Asia.[6]

Asia had much which Europe desired, but Europe had very little to offer in return which Asia could not produce for itself at least as well and as cheaply as Europe could. It was Asia which was the developed area and Europe the underdeveloped, certainly until the mid-eighteenth century and arguably until the early nineteenth. Throughout the early modern period, as had been the case in the Middle Ages, Europe found it difficult to pay for its imports from Asia in any way other than in cash or, more importantly, in bullion. Braudel referred some fifty years ago to the great eastward tide of silver which flowed from the mines of Spanish America, across the Atlantic to Europe and then on to Asia to pay for Europe's Asiatic imports.[7] It is difficult to see how Europe's trade with Asia could have expanded in the way it did, in the seventeenth century in particular, without the influx of American silver and without the chance that silver, in relatively plentiful supply in Europe, was in short supply and therefore of higher value in Asia. Silver increased in value merely by being exported to Asia, and the profits from that chance provided to some considerable extent the margin upon which the expansion of European trade in Asia became possible.

This export of bullion, the paying for goods in money rather than by the exchange of other goods, is typical of the relationship between developed and underdeveloped countries, and it was Europe which was underdeveloped. The unbalanced nature of the trade was of concern to contemporary states as well as to modern economic historians. The early history of the Dutch and English East India Companies is punctuated by attempts by the Dutch and English states to reduce or prevent the export of bullion to the East, an export which was seen as weakening their financial and economic positions. For the companies, the need to transport large quantities of bullion from Europe to finance their trade in Asia became a major burden, both commercially and organisationally, and was to be a major factor in their decision to seek profits not merely from the intercontinental trade but also from engaging in trade within Asia. It has been calculated that between 1602 and 1650, the Dutch East India Company exported a total of 445 million florins' worth of bullion to Asia.[8] A great deal of the Dutch East India Company's European trade in the later seventeenth and eighteenth centuries was to be financed not from exports of goods or bullion from Europe but from the profits of their inter-Asian trade.

The Europeans were able to engage successfully in the Asian trade not because of the economic or commercial advantages that being European gave them, but because of their involvement in Asiatic trading systems and because of their ability to work those systems effeively, so competing with Asian traders on their own terms and in their own areas.

The structure of Asiatic trade was essentially pre-modern. Trade was largely carried on on an individual basis and finance was personal rather than in any way institutionalised; so that if borrowing were necessary, it tended to be confined to tight family or communal units. The Asiatic trader tended to involve almost all of his capital in any individual venture – indeed, in most cases he had little choice but to do so. The costs of engaging in the trade were high and usually precluded any other form of investment. Risk was built centrally into the system; the trader risked his goods simply by moving them about by land or by sea. The most important form of risk was that inherent in trading in markets where there were huge numbers of relatively equally matched traders and where prices were liable to sudden sharp fluctuation, either because of actual gluts and shortages or because of rumour. Asian traders, like all pre-nineteenth-century traders, operated in a world where the basic knowledge on which modern traders formulate their strategies was only very partially available. There was no rapid and sure method of communication to provide information about supply or demand or about political and climatic factors. Each trader had to base each decision upon intuition, experience and general knowledge, rather than on fact. The slowness and uncertainty of communication affected the physical movement of the goods from point of purchase to point of sale. For instance, it could take several weeks or several months to move goods from Indonesia to the west coast of India, and market conditions could and did change completely during the period of transit. What had been a good bargain, based upon the expectation of good market conditions when the goods were bought, could easily change into disaster by the time the goods reached the port or market in which they were sold. The Asiatic trader could not usually wait for conditions to improve for more than a few days or weeks. This fact was well known to purchasers, who frequently put off buying for as long as possible in an attempt to force the trader to accept a lower price rather than run the risk of total loss, since his income, indeed his survival, depended upon realising the value of his goods as soon as possible, and certainly before the end of the trading season. The structure and problems of Asiatic trade in the early modern period were in essence very similar to those of European trade.

It was into this highly risky system that the Europeans came in the sixteenth and early seventeenth centuries, and it is important to realise that it was a system with which European traders were as familiar as were the Asians. When they came to Asia via the long and dangerous Cape route, they were engaging in trade which was even more risky than the internal trade of Asia. It was risky in the sense that the long sea route was more dangerous than the coasting routes of Asia. Furthermore, unlike the Asian traders, who normally were involved in only one of a series of intermediate exchanges between the areas of original production and the areas of final consumption, the Europeans were taking the whole physical risk themselves in a single stage. Insurance helped, but this was still a physically and financially extremely risky undertaking. The Europeans also introduced a new element of risk for themselves by transferring the trade between Asia and Europe to sea voyages. The gap between the departure of a voyage from Europe and its final return could be as much as two years. In that period economic and commercial conditions in Europe could easily have changed fundamentally and hence the commercial decisions taken before or during the voyage could only be based on guesswork and hope.[9]

The one advantage the Europeans, and particularly the great companies of the seventeenth and eighteenth centuries, had over Asiatic traders was in their organisation and their financial structure. If the European companies came to play a major role in certain sectors of Asiatic trade, it was because of their organisational and financial structures, not because of better technology nor because of the superiority of European goods, either in quality or method of production.

First, the Dutch and English East India Companies had a much larger capital base than any individual Asiatic trader, even at the beginning of their development in the last years of the sixteenth century and the first decades of the seventeenth. In the small-scale local market system which characterised both the spice trade of Indonesia and the export trade of the West Coast of India, their larger capital base gave them great advantages. They were able to dominate, if not monopolise, supply markets and hence, especially in Indonesia, to dictate prices. Large profits from the early voyages attracted more capital, and more capital meant that the companies' trading advantages could be extended. By the 1630s, if not earlier in the case of Indonesia, the Dutch East India Company was able to establish a dominating, though not monopolistic, commercial position for itself. While the English Company was never to have the same commercial dominance in peninsular India, which was its main sphere of activity, nonetheless it was able to operate as the largest single buyer.

Second, long-term financing allowed the European companies to take a much longer-term view of profits and returns than could the Asiatic traders. The huge amounts of capital which were necessary to get into the Asiatic trade, and the long gap between investment and return enforced by the slowness of the oceanic navigation from the point of production to the point of final sale, meant that the companies had to seek longer-term finance than was the case in other forms of trade. The companies were increasingly able to play a major role in setting supply prices and were also able to control the selling prices of spices, textiles and ceramics in Europe. After the first few years of their existence, they aimed to stabilise returns, so as to make possible the regular payment of interest on their capital, which was chiefly held in the form of bonds. This changed the overall pattern of the trade, above all of that with Europe, but also within Asia. Although the risks of trade remained the same for the small-scale traders, the great peaks of profit on which they had relied in the past were removed by the smoothing effects of the companies and their policies. Catastrophic losses were still possible, but the great peaks of profit which had been there to balance them out no longer existed. The rise of the companies led to a final realignment of the long-distance trade with Europe to the Cape route in the early years of the seventeenth century, and it began a long shift in patterns of maritime trade in Asia which was to continue into the nineteenth and twentieth centuries.

It must be emphasised, however, that the European companies could not monopolise the trade of Asia. Their partial dependence upon the profits of the inter-Asian trade for the capital necessary to carry on their European trade meant that the companies were integrated into the existing trade of Asia rather than being its dominators and controllers. The leading role of the European companies was not solely a consequence of the superiority of their economic and financial organisation. The Dutch Company, in particular, since it was dealing with relatively weak and small-scale rulers in Indonesia, used traditional Asiatic methods, such as force and the threat of force, to impose its will on both Asiatic producers and European competitors. The English Company was dealing with states which were too powerful to be intimidated by a few foreigners and their ships, even in the period of confusion in western and southern India which followed Shivaji's creation of the Maratha state and Aurangzebe's wars in the south. The Company did attempt to pressurise the small-scale rulers and governors of coastal towns and regions into granting them monopolies of trade or trading privileges or extra-territorial rights.[10]

The success of the companies in Asia before the middle of the eighteenth century, and arguably not even then, cannot be explained by any inherent superiority of European goods or European organisation. The European presence in Asia, although it had some importance in areas like Indonesia and, in different ways, in Japan, remained essentially marginal to the major issues and trends of the Asian economy. Rather than coming into Asian trade as its inevitable dominator, borne on by a wave of economic inevitability, the Europeans came to Asia as marginal players in an already highly complex and highly developed commercial and industrial economy and were able to operate there largely as part of that structure. Until the end of the early modern period Europe came to Asia as the relatively underdeveloped partner, seeking the industrial products and high-value luxury goods it was unable to produce for itself. There is certainly no evidence of vital and successful

European industry or capitalism overwhelming and defeating backward Asian organisation.

In the Americas European influence and expansion had a considerable and a destructive impact on non-European societies and cultures. In Asia Europe was the underdeveloped and marginal player in a much more advanced and much more massive economic system where European influence was relatively small. In Africa, and in particular West Africa, growing European contact and demand led to considerable economic and social change within African economies and African political systems without direct European involvement. Despite the crucial importance of Africa and its trade to the whole of the developing Atlantic economies during the early modern period, Europeans neither established nor sought extensive political control or sovereignty. Instead, a partnership between Europe and Africa developed and became, for at least two centuries, the central feature of contact and trade between the two continents. It was the breakdown of that partnership in the late nineteenth century which led to the first expansion of European political control in areas like Ghana and Nigeria.

The trade in slaves was central to the development of the European Atlantic economies. After the elimination of the native populations of the Caribbean islands and the mainland of the Americas by disease in the early and middle sixteenth century it was clear that the Americas could only be exploited if a large supply of cheap labour could be provided. This became more and more important as new crops, in particular tobacco and sugar, were developed on the Caribbean islands and on the South American mainland, especially in Brazil. Not merely had there to be a supply of labour but, since experience showed that the life expectancy of manual workers in the tropics was low, there had to be a constant supply of new labour; perhaps 10 or 15 per cent of the labour force had to be replaced each year. Expansion of production – and tobacco and sugar were both boom crops in the early modern period – required even greater increases in the labour force each year.

Europeans had been taking slaves directly from the coast of West Africa since the middle of the fifteenth century. The Portuguese and, to a lesser extent, the Spaniards had collected slaves on the Senegambian coast and also further west to work their developing sugar plantations on the Cape Verde islands, and on São Tomé and Principe. In these early days the slaves were 'harvested' by direct raiding on coastal villages by European raiding parties. The development of demand from the other side of the Atlantic, especially in the later sixteenth century and in the two centuries which followed, however, made such a system too inefficient and too insecure to meet the requirements of the American plantations. Coastal raiding had to be replaced by more secure ways of recruitment, and the former concentration of the trade on the relatively narrow and sparsely populated coastal regions of the Senegambia had to be replaced by other areas which had access to greater and more certain supplies. This implied a movement westwards and southwards, to the West African coast between modern Ghana and the modern Cameroon and also to the coast of modern Angola.

In these areas the Europeans did not set out to establish their own trading structures, that is to say they did not seek to establish the mechanisms of their 'economic and commercial superiority'. Europeans had many disadvantages as traders in the slave areas of Africa. African climatic and health conditions were such as to make life on the coast and in the interior hazardous for Europeans. In the seventeenth century the average life expectancy of a European trader on the Slave Coast was less than six months, and that life expectancy could be expected to decline the further into the interior the Europeans went. It is worth pointing out that so strong was the subsequent belief that Europeans could not survive in West Africa that it was not until Mungo Park's great voyage into the interior in the last years of the eighteenth century that Europeans attempted to penetrate what was, for them, an economically crucial area, despite what was by then almost two hundred years of close contact.

Even had the Europeans wished to do so they would have found pushing into the interior politically difficult. Even where, as for instance at Whydah in present-day Dahomey, they were dealing with a 'weak' state, the Europeans lacked the military power to coerce the rulers. Behind the coast lay a series of much more powerful African states, for instance Dahomey, Ashanti in modern Ghana and Benin in modern Nigeria, which were clearly too militarily powerful to be coerced and for whom access to the interior was too important to be ceded to the Europeans.

The Europeans did not come into a continent which was totally without forms of trade or exchange and create them from scratch. They established contact where they did, because at those points they had access to and contact with pre-existing trading systems and traders. Indigenous African trading systems were complex and difficult for outsiders to operate, especially when what was being done was to insert into traditional systems new demands, for very large numbers of slaves, and offer new goods, such as European manufactures or firearms. The fragmented nature of African societies and of African cultural and economic systems meant that long-distance trade presented special and complex difficulties. Europeans would have needed much time and skill to deal with these intricacies and time was something European traders in Africa did not have, driven as they were by the heady mix of fear of disease, the dangers and risks of the long oceanic passage to the Americas and the pressures of a clamorous market in the Americas.

The high period of the Atlantic slave trade ran from the early to middle years of the seventeenth century to the era of the War of American Independence and depended on a system of close partnership between Europeans and Africans. The Europeans concerned themselves exclusively with the purchase of slaves at the slave-trading ports of West Africa and their shipment to the Americas. The supply of slaves to the ports was exclusively in the hands of African traders and of African trading systems. Although the slave trade was crucial to the Atlantic economy, and hence in some ways to the whole of the developing European economy, the supply of its basic commodity was in the hands of non-Europeans and, furthermore, the Europeans were not merely willing but eager to allow this to happen.[11]

All European traders, English and Dutch on the upper West Coast, Portuguese in Angola, formed partnerships with African traders and African states. Some of them, like the Kongo or the Ngola, who were the main partners of the Portuguese, were already traders linked with the interior through networks which had existed for some centuries. Some, like the Dahomeyans or the Ashanti, established new contacts and new structures related to European demand.[12] Much of the new wealth which flowed into African polities accrued to states rather than to individuals, so that much of the effect of the expansion of trade was concentrated on the states. The slave trade in West Africa in fact strengthened existing African political units and made it more rather than less difficult for Europeans to challenge the existing political and commercial structures, even had they wanted to.

The slave trade shows a very different picture of the relationship between Europe and the non-European world from that of a dynamic Europe, overwhelming by its sheer economic force the more backward trading and economic systems of the non-European world. Europe depended on Africa to develop its American empires. It was the African states which set up and ran the complex and sophisticated organisations necessary to meet European demands. The exigencies of the American slave economy required not merely that slaves should be available, but that they should be available in the requisite numbers (and, until the last years of the eighteenth century, that was an increasing number), at the right places (that is to say, at the relatively few points in the West African coast where trade was safely possible for Europeans), at the right time (since trade was dependent upon the fluctuations of the wind systems), at the right price and with sufficient security of delivery for the plantation owners to be able to plan on the basis of continuing and expanding supplies. Complex systems were built up which were able to guarantee that these European demands were met and it is important to recognise that all these were achieved by African traders and African rulers, rather than upon Europeans.[13] African rulers were well aware of their ability to damage the profits of European traders and also of the desperation which slave traders displayed should the supply of slaves be interrupted. Throughout the seventeenth and eighteenth centuries they were to use their power to drive up prices in the coastal ports by withholding, or threatening to withhold, their slaves from the markets. Had African rulers refused to supply Europeans with slaves, the whole transatlantic slave trade would have collapsed and early modern Europe would have been powerless to restore it. Ironically, the great losers from Europe's final abolition of the slave trade were the African states and rulers who had come to depend on it.

The picture which emerges of Europe's relationship with the non-European world during the early modern period is clearly not one of a triumphant and modernising economy expanding across the world and overwhelming the existing systems of economy and trade. Equally, it is not a picture of a backward, undeveloped world in which European industry and manufacturing had an unstoppable advantage. Instead, the situation was highly complex. Europe did have some advantages over other economies, for instance in commercial organisation; on the other hand it was backward economically compared with Asia. Sometimes Europe did have powerful effects, but, as in Central and South America, those effects were often purely accidental and were counterproductive to European interests. In most cases Europe was weak and essentially marginal, both politically and economically, as a player on the world stage. Europeans were usually dependent upon traders and rulers from the areas in which they were dealing for their survival and prosperity. Even in an area regarded by nineteenth-century Europeans as primitive and backward, such as Africa, Europeans were dependent on a partnership with local traders for one of the fundamental trades of the whole European early modern commercial and economic system.

With hindsight it is easy to say that developments in the early modern period were the foundation of the great European expansion, economic and cultural as well as political, of the nineteenth and twentieth centuries; that the roots of European world domination must lie in the commercial developments of the seventeenth and eighteenth centuries. In fact the relationship between early modern expansion and what came afterwards is debatable. In many ways the great colonisers and imperialists of the nineteenth century were to repudiate the patterns and methods of early modern expansion, often preferring impose their own ideas rather than work in partnership within existing economic and political structures. Even where there is a connection between early modern and later expansion, it has to be recognised that during the early modern period Europe's relationships with the non-European world were complex rather than simple and they were certainly more equal than they were to become in the nineteenth and twentieth centuries. Most importantly, the attitude of Europeans in the early modern period to other cultures was less arrogant, more open-minded and more ready to learn from them than it was to be later on.

Europe's contact with different cultures and other economies did not only have effects for the non-European world, as was the assumption of the nineteenth century. Europe itself was widely affected by the consequences of those contacts and in this context it is important to remember that the effects of overseas expansion were not limited to a few states. It has always been clear that, for the great 'expansionist' powers of the seventeenth and eighteenth centuries, the United Netherlands and England (in this context it would be more correct to say Britain), overseas trade and contact had important economic consequences. These were, however, by no means the only European states to play a role in overseas expansion, nor the only ones to be affected by it. In the sixteenth century Spain and Portugal had been more important players, while in the seventeenth and eighteenth centuries France, although it was finally to lose its major colonial role in the later eighteenth century, was as important as either England or the Netherlands. Other European states such as Sweden, Prussia, the Austrian Netherlands and Denmark were also involved in extra-European expansion. Nor were the effects of the widening of horizons limited to those states which were directly involved. 'Colonial' industries and trades also developed in ports like Hamburg, which were not formally involved in trade with extra-European areas.[14] The effects of extra-European trade and contact were very widely spread all across maritime Western Europe and their influence extended far into the interior.

Perhaps the most immediately obvious way in which overseas expansion affected Europe was in the development of the migration of Europeans to new regions of the world, especially to the New World. One of the prime factors which had led the European states to develop an interest in overseas colonisation rather than just commercial expansion had been the perceived problem of overpopulation. From the sixteenth century onwards governments had their attention drawn to a series of problems which they thought were caused by too great a number of people. The growth of poverty and landlessness, the problems of and increasing number of impoverished nobles and the cadet members of rich noble or elite families, the increased levels of crime, disorder and immorality, all these were seen as being consequences of too large a population. From the early years of the sixteenth century onwards, governments and private projectors saw settlement overseas as a way of solving serious domestic problems, while at the same time extending the power and influence of the state over a much wider area. In the seventeenth and eighteenth centuries states became involved in plans to export their problem people to other parts of the globe. For some sectors of society an enthusiasm for emigration seems to have been genuine. In particular, the gentry and the minor nobility of Europe thought that colonial settlement, especially in the Americas, offered new opportunities to find a role acceptable to them which offered the possibility of appropriate prosperity and status. The same type of colonial enthusiasm was shown by the poor nobility of western Spain who formed the backbone of the conquistadors, and who were to continue to be disproportionately represented amongst both settlers and administrators in the Spanish-American Empire, by the junior members of English gentry families who were to form so much of the first generation of settlers in Virginia or later in the Carolinas and Georgia, or of the early settlers and proprietors of Barbados, by the scions of poor noble families who were to be an important element in the first successful establishment of the French colony in Canada, and by the members of Regent families who were to establish the Patroon estates in Dutch New York. It is important, however, to recognise what the nature of that enthusiasm was. What all these 'elite' settlers had in common was a desire to replicate in the Americas the social forms and largely the economic modes of the Old World, but to replicate them so as to enhance their personal status and prosperity in a way that was not open to them in Europe. Here was no new social spirit or economic force.

If some sectors of the elite were enthusiastic about colonial expansion and settlement, most of the population seems to have been rather less so, certainly before the eighteenth century. This would be surprising if the traditional picture of the early modern economy were accurate, because a supposedly desperate and impoverished population should have been eager to leave the Old World. After all, the American colonies offered everyone an opportunity for employment and prosperity, with unlimited access to land, that commodity which was believed to be central to the whole economic and social structure. The Americas offered the possibility of enough free or cheap land for all possible settlers. The Barbados projectors made exactly that specific offer: any Englishman who was willing to go to work in the new colony for a minimum of seven years was offered not merely free passage to the island, but also free freehold land on the island, and more land than they could have dreamed of in England.[15] The unwillingness of the poor and the landless in England and elsewhere in Europe to take up these opportunities with enthusiasm should perhaps cause economic historians some doubts as to the centrality of land in the social and economic structure of the early modern period. It certainly caused major problems for the colonial projectors and was one of the factors which led them to seek other supplies of labour, especially in Africa. America in particular attracted people chiefly from marginal areas of Europe, where the risk and uncertainty of life in the new colonies was not noticeably larger than in their home areas. The Scots-Irish who migrated to the middle colonies (New York, Delaware, New Jersey and Pennsylvania) and New England in the late seventeenth and eighteenth centuries, the Germans and Swedes who moved to the middle colonies in the same period, all came from areas of marginal prosperity and high-risk agriculture, rather than from areas of greater prosperity and security. Even the prospect of making a personal fortune trading in the wealth of Asia was not enough to attract many Europeans to settle overseas.

In the early modern period, migration from Europe for colonial settlement was of limited appeal. In some regions experiencing economic hardship it was of considerable local importance, but migration overseas played a major role in only one country in the eighteenth century, and that was Portugal. The great expansion and prosperity of the Brazilian economy, and the extension of settlement in the south of the country in the later seventeenth and eighteenth centuries, especially after the discovery of major gold deposits in the southern province of Minas Gerães in the 1690s, were to completely restructure Portugal's empire and economy. By the end of the eighteenth century Brazil had almost certainly a larger population of Portuguese origin than metropolitan Portugal, and certainly the colony was by that stage much wealthier than the metropolis. That expansion was related to major migration of population from all social and economic sectors and regions of Portugal, and was to be completed by the migration of the court to Rio following the Napoleonic invasion in the 1790s.[16]

Colonial migration was less than the projectors of colonies hoped, for the effects of colonial expansion and trade on production and industry in metropolitan Europe were very considerable. Colonial expansion helped with problems of unemployment and poverty in Europe, not by exporting surplus population but by creating new colonially related forms of employment in Europe. The most obvious was the establishment of industries based on the processing and finishing of colonial or Asiatic goods for the European market. Colonial goods, in particular sugar and tobacco, were amongst the great boom goods of the early modern period, and moved from being unknown or rare luxuries at the beginning of the period to being items of general mass consumption by its end. This huge increase in demand led to massive development of industrial processes to maintain supply. Sugar refining, and its related industries such as the production of spirits, expanded, especially in maritime areas around the ports through which the raw materials were imported. In the eighteenth century the northern Netherlands had major sugar-refining centres not merely in and around Amsterdam, but also around other centres like Middelburg, whose declining economies were often revived or at least helped by the employment and trade which the new colonial-based industry brought. It was not merely the amount of raw materials which was being processed which was of significance. By their very nature the industrial processes which were related to colonial expansion tended to be complex and capital-intensive. As a consequence the colonial-based industries tended to operate as much larger units, employing much larger labour forces than the average for the period, and they also involved much more complex equipment and machinery. Furthermore, the processes themselves were not simple and were potentially dangerous. The explosion of a sugar refinery could, and did, prove fatal for large numbers of people, not merely in the factory itself but also in the surrounding neighbourhood. The expansion of the colonial-based industries also led to the development of new skills and new patterns of management and control, not least to ensure that accidents were at least minimised and that the loss of investment which a catastrophic breakdown involved was reduced. The colonial trades were as important for the changes in organisation and management methods they introduced into Europe as for the sheer volume of production and employment they generated.

The development of the colonial-based industries can be seen as an early step by Europe in the direction of industrial development, so beginning the reversal of Europe's under-developed relationship with much of the rest of the world. The development of industries to replace extra-European goods with those produced within Europe is even more obviously a part of the reversal. The shift in European perceptions from the medieval situation in which the luxury goods of Asia appeared so miraculous, so extraordinary that it was impossible to compete with them, except possibly to produce crude and derivative replicas, to one in which it was believed possible to emulate and even surpass Asia, was one of the most fundamental changes in Europe's self-image. It was one of the crucial prerequisites for the development of the entrepreneurial mindset of the eighteenth century. From the sixteenth century onwards Europeans were trying to replace Asian goods, and in particular Asian manufactured goods, with goods produced in Europe. The great success in this was the development of the European silk industry, in particular in Italy and Lyon, but also in the Netherlands and England in the eighteenth century. Europe also began to produce carpets and ceramics to compete with Asian production. By the middle to late eighteenth century there had been one major change in that European-produced porcelain was selling at similar levels to Asiatic items at the luxury end of the market, while China and to a lesser extent Japan were supplying the less expensive part of the trade.

By the eighteenth century the colonies themselves, in particular the North American ones, were beginning to establish their own industrial production. In some cases this was designed to reduce the need for imports from Europe by setting up industries to produce goods for sale in the colonies, which was a major concern of metropolitan governments in England and Spain. In other cases, some European industry was transferred to the Americas in order to solve long-standing problems over shortages of raw materials in Europe. Outstanding in this respect is the development of shipbuilding in New England and the transfer of some yards and their capital across the Atlantic. Shipowners and shipbuilders looked to have their vessels constructed near to the areas where the raw materials, in particular timber, were to be found, and by the eighteenth century this meant across the Atlantic. This transfer of shipbuilding to North America was only a continuance of a process which had been going on since the sixteenth century. As the supplies of usable timber in the European heartland were used up, so the shipbuilding industry had increasingly moved to the periphery of the continent; in the seventeenth century, for instance, more and more of the shipbuilding of the northern Netherlands had been moved to Scandinavia, in particular to Sweden, so as to be close to the supplies of timber.[17]

The colonies were drawing away some European industries, but their developing markets provided ample opportunities for European industry. What is striking about the involvement of European industry in supplying colonial, and in particular American, markets, is just how widespread it was. It was not until after the early modern period that the English colonies of the eastern seaboard of North America were to become much the most important area economically as well as politically. Until at least the middle of the eighteenth century, and probably until the early nineteenth century, it was the markets of Latin America and the Caribbean which were of greatest importance. They had much larger populations and their economies were much more geared to the consumption of imported manufactures. The continuing pioneer nature of much of the North American economy into the eighteenth century, and the difficulties of communications with an essentially dispersed population, meant that North America was perforce much more self-sufficient than were either Latin America or the Caribbean.

In the early years of settlement, especially on the Caribbean islands and in Mexico, the American colonies imported food from Europe. As new types of economy became established on the American mainland the demand for food from Europe fell sharply, although the large-scale development of sugar monoculture on islands like Barbados in the seventeenth century meant that they were again forced to import food.[18] There were also major imports of manufactured goods, in particular textiles, but also of iron and steel and other base metals. Mexico and Peru were also for a time massive importers of mercury from the mines of Huencavelica in Spain which was used for the extraction of silver from its ore. The Latin American demand for food, in particular for wheat and for fruit, led to major development in the sixteenth century in the Guadalquivir Valley in southern Spain.[19] In this area, naturally focusing on Seville, an already well-developed and commercialised agricultural system expanded further to supply the new expatriate needs. This stage of dependence on Europe was relatively short-lived. The economic changes in the Americas which resulted from the loss of the native population saw an increasing amount of European food, in particular wheat, being produced in the Americas. In both Mexico and Peru the middle years of the sixteenth century saw intensive native production of maize and potatoes being replaced by more extensive wheat production. Even the second great shift, from extensive arable production to cattle ranching, which occurred in the later part of the sixteenth century, particularly in Mexico, and which set the pattern for the history of Spanish America until the later eighteenth century, did not mean the disappearance of wheat production in the Americas and a return to European imports.[20] Similarly, although the early colonies in North America required imports of food to tide them over their early crises, they soon became self-sufficient and, in the eighteenth century, they were to become exporters of grain to Europe.

In the long term, the colonies, in Asia as well as in the Americas, were much more important to Europe as importers of manufactured goods from Europe. Mexico began to develop textile and metal-goods production from the early years of the seventeenth century, and some of the English colonies in North America were to become major industrial producers, for instance of iron goods, in the eighteenth century, but they were unable to meet the demand from the expanding colonial markets which required large quantities of manufactured goods.[21] Consequently industrial production in Europe expanded to supply those markets. It must again be emphasised that it was not just the 'colonial powers', such as England and the Netherlands, which experienced such development. In both France and Spain in the seventeenth and eighteenth centuries new industries sprang up to exploit colonial markets, or old industries expanded to supply them.[22] This colonial-based industrial expansion was not limited to maritime or Atlantic regions, although perhaps the majority was based there. In France, for instance, the declining textile industries of the Massif Central and the Cévennes were revived in the seventeenth and eighteenth centuries by demand not merely from French America but even more from Spanish and Portuguese America.[23] In the late seventeenth and eighteenth centuries, new textile industries developed in and around Barcelona to supply American demand.[24] It seems likely that the effects of American colonial demand on European industry were much greater and much more widespread than was once thought.

Extra-European expansion brought Europe one thing above all, and that was wealth. Although for some individuals or groups the colonies offered new opportunities for economic, social or religious liberation, what was of paramount importance to European investors in extra-European trade and settlement, and to the European governments which supported them, or at least did not oppose them, was the immediate prospect of income and capital accumulation in Europe. The wealth of the East and West Indies came into metropolitan Europe in a number of ways. The most obvious way was through the profits which accrued to the companies and to the states from the trade and the taxation of trade. In the sixteenth century, for states like Spain and Portugal the proceeds of expansion were great and of major importance economically and politically in Europe. The bullion of the Indies was a major element in the financing of Spain's European greatness in the sixteenth century, while the finances of sixteenth-century Portugal rested very heavily on the proceeds of Asiatic trade. In the seventeenth and eighteenth centuries, the great mass of the profits from overseas trade accrued not to the state, which nonetheless took its share of the proceeds in taxation, but to the great companies and their stock and bond holders. The wealth of the Indies was in many senses new wealth; certainly it cannot be seen as simply a redistribution of wealth already in existence within Europe. That in itself was important. Equally important was the way in which that new wealth was treated in Europe. The companies did retain part of their profit to finance future trade and expansion, but a great deal of their profit was paid out in dividends or interest to their stock and bond holders. The relatively wide spread of share and bond holding ensured that the proceeds of the East India trade in particular were dispersed across the economy and so played a significant role in generating increased consumption in Europe, which stimulated production. It would of course be wrong to suggest that it was only the companies which made profits from the East India trades and that only they imported that wealth into Europe. The companies' servants, as well as private European traders, also became wealthy in the Indies. No European of any standing would have gone to the East without the reasonable prospect of personal enrichment. They too brought their wealth back to Europe to spend. The nabob was as common a figure as the rich, returned Barbados or Jamaica sugar planter in eighteenth-century Europe.

In the seventeenth and eighteenth centuries the West India trade was less dominated by great companies and their profits than was the

East India trade. Companies such as the Dutch West India Company or the English Royal Africa Company did engage in the West India trade, but they were considerably less profitable than the East India Companies. In the developing Atlantic economies it was private rather than corporate traders and producers who were important. For instance, the slave traders of Bristol, Liverpool and Bordeaux made personal fortunes, some of which were reinvested in the trade, but much of which were diverted into other forms of consumption within the European economy. The settlers in the New World too, be they the Spanish landed elite in Mexico and Peru or the sugar planters of Barbados and Jamaica, also grew wealthy, and they repatriated some part of the wealth they had gained in the New World. There was a tendency, however, for this repatriation of wealth to decline in the Iberian states as the Spanish and Portuguese colonies developed their own social patterns and as their elites became more separated from the elites of their metropolitan bases.[25] In much the same way, the proportion of new wealth generated in the English North American colonies which was returned to England diminished as the commercial and territorial elites of the colonies increasingly developed a separate 'colonial' identity and saw their main field of social endeavour as lying in the colonies themselves. The Byrds, the Jeffersons, the Roosevelts, the Lodges or the Cabots saw little reason to divert wealth from the colonies to Europe, since increasingly it was in America that they sought social status and social display.

The Caribbean was, for the northern powers, the most important and the most valuable of the American colonial areas in the seventeenth and eighteenth centuries and it was from here that the repatriation of personal wealth was most important. The plantation elites of the sugar islands largely considered themselves as Englishmen, Frenchmen or Dutchmen in exile, who lived in the Caribbean for long enough to establish or to repair their fortunes, but then intended to return home to enjoy that wealth in Europe. Large amounts of new wealth were imported into Europe from the Caribbean, in particular in the eighteenth century, so much so, indeed, that as long ago as 1954 Eric Williams argued that it was this Caribbean wealth which provided the first major stimulus for both investment and consumption in the development of the Industrial Revolution. It is certainly the case that the inflow of Caribbean wealth must have played a role in the development of new wealth and of new patterns of consumption in Europe in the eighteenth century.

The new wealth which contact with the non-European world brought to Europe spread throughout the rest of the economy. Indeed, that is one of the most striking features of overseas expansion in the early modern period. Previously much of the wealth generated by extra-European trade had circulated only within the trading community. The wealth which Venice or Genoa accumulated from their trade with Asia was largely used to finance further trade in the same sector. Each individual merchant would try to hoard some of his Asiatic profits as security for future times of difficulty. Proportionally only a very small part of his wealth would enter the general economy, by being spent by him and his family on day-to-day living expenses, and would only have an impact locally. The new companies brought far greater amounts of wealth to Europe than had the medieval merchants, and their structure meant that the proceeds from trade spread across Europe and influenced patterns of consumption and production much more widely. The structure of the companies' finances offered a relatively high level of security of income to investors, especially to bondholders. After the early buccaneering days of the companies, profits were held high and above all steady, and the servicing of the funded debt was maintained. Until the eighteenth century, and then only in a few cases, East India Company shares and bonds were a much more secure form of investment than any form of government stock or loan. This relative security of a sustained level of return had many important consequences. For instance, it ensured that the increase in wealth was relatively stable and permanent, rather than being erratic and unpredictable. In its turn this ensured that increases in consumption related to Asiatic wealth were likely to be permanent rather than ephemeral. Consequently, investment in industrial processes or in infrastructure improvements to service that consumption were likely to have a sustained rather than a short-term return, and hence investors were more likely to provide fixed capital for them. The relative security of a sustained level of return also had effects on patterns of spending: when returns are believed to be relatively secure, the need to build up reserves against a time of loss is reduced (it never disappeared totally). So the bond and share holders were likely to spend a substantial proportion of their income on goods and services for their own immediate pleasure or consumption. This ensured that the new wealth coming from the Far East, or to a lesser extent from the Americas, was spread throughout the whole European economy, since more of it was spent on consumption and a lesser proportion was saved or reinvested in trade.

It had not, however, only been to seek for trade that Europeans had begun to reach out beyond Europe. The prime aim was to seek wealth, not in the shape of the return to trade but at least in part to find wealth in its purest and most immediate form, precious metals, above all gold and silver. They were successful and found both these metals in large quantities, and the consequences of those discoveries have constituted one of the most controversial issues for economic historians.

Precious metals were the basis of the monetary system of all European states throughout the early modern period; coin, which was money, had the value its metallic content gave to it. Consequently, there should have been direct relationship between the supply of precious metals, their price, the value of the coinage in circulation and overall price levels in the economy. A massive inflow of precious metals should have reduced the intrinsic value of the currency and hence have led to monetary inflation. In the sixteenth century a great flood of bullion, at first gold and then, after 1550, silver, came from the Americas to Europe, and this coincided with a long-run period of inflation, an inflation which lasted longest and was most severe in Spain itself. The great flow of American silver slowed down after 1610 and declined after about 1630.[26] Although imports of bullion did revive somewhat after 1650, it was not until the 1690s that extra-European bullion again flowed into Europe on a large scale, in this case gold from the mines of southern Brazil. The seventeenth and eighteenth centuries saw, over most of Europe, a period of stable currency and stable prices. This was the period when new methods of minting came into wider use which made the metal content and weight of the coinage more secure. That in turn made possible the slow movement towards a system in which coins were exchanged for their symbolic nominal 'face' value (which from the late eighteenth century was increasingly stamped on them) rather than on the basis of their intrinsic metallic value.

The relationship between currency values and the supply of precious metal in the early modern period in Europe is a highly complex one, but a number of features stand out. The first is that the supply of precious metals is only one factor in determining currency values and hence prices. The supply of precious metals, which in this system determines the supply of good-quality coinage, would have a major effect on price levels only if metal supply were the only factor which changed. However, a growing economy, or one in which goods are being exchanged for money, more frequently increases the demand for coinage and that affects the relationship between metal supply and prices. In a growing economy, if the supply of coin is fixed, prices fall because coins are in demand and in short supply so their value increases and they can be changed for more goods than before. Increasing the supply of good coinage in those circumstances does not necessarily lead to inflation. If it matches the demand for coin, it will stabilise prices at their former level; if it is insufficient, prices will still fall.

Second, the quality of the money in circulation is another factor in determining currency values and prices. One of the favourite short-term ways in which sixteenth- and early seventeenth-century governments sought to generate income was by debasing the coinage, reducing its precious metal content. This practice increased prices because more of the debased coins were needed to make up the same bullion content as before.

Third, much of the bullion, especially silver, which came to Europe was exported to the East, particularly in the seventeenth and eighteenth centuries, as the basic payment for Asiatic goods. Without that silver, trade with Asia would have been much more restricted and the increase in wealth which came from the Asian trade would have been reduced. Indeed, it can be argued that the timing of the increase in silver supplies in the sixteenth century (which reduced the price of silver against gold even further) provided one of the crucial trade advantages which allowed the European companies to compete effectively in Asia at the time they were establishing themselves there. Asian-derived wealth increased demand in Europe and consequently the rate at which goods were exchanged. This increased the demand for money, and so reduced the potentially inflationary effects of the bullion imports.

There is no general agreement among economic historians over what the exact effects of bullion imports were in the European economy, but some conclusions can be drawn. The history of European money and of bullion exports during the early modern period indicates that the picture of a growing and developing economy is likely to be correct. Huge imports of bullion in the sixteenth century did cause inflation and currency confusion. However, given the scale of the imports, that inflation was slow, which indicates that the growth of the economy and the development of monetarised, commercialised production was almost keeping pace with that cash influx at a time when population was rising and when governments were taking advantage of the situation to increase the amount of money in circulation by debasing it. After the sixteenth century, with a few explicable exceptions such as Spain and Germany during the Thirty Years War, currencies were largely stable, as were prices, despite a continuing inflow of bullion from Brazil and elsewhere in the Americas, from Africa and also from Asia. By the end of the eighteenth century many European states were beginning to experience severe shortages of coin, indicating that the economy had grown much faster than the supply of bullion and coin.

It is clear that extra-European settlement and trade were increasingly important to Europe in the early modern period. It is difficult to evaluate the nature of that importance in the context of its own age. Viewed from the late twentieth century it is eminently clear that Europe's expansion beyond its borders, and in particular its expansion across the Atlantic, were to be of crucial historical importance. With hindsight it was perhaps the most important single development of the early modern period. After all, the early modern period saw the first settlement and development of the economies and societies of North America which would be so significant in world history of the twentieth century. Again, the development of extra-European trade in the early modern period can be seen with hindsight as a prelude to Europe's becoming the dominant world economic force of the nineteenth and early twentieth centuries. It is only too easy to project our knowledge of this later development back into the early modern period and to consider that extra-European settlement and trade must have been of central importance to Europe's own economic, social and political history during the sixteenth, seventeenth and eighteenth centuries.

For some European regions, for instance parts of England or of Holland and Zeeland, extra-European trade and production were of considerable importance; individual fortunes were made and new industries grew up to serve overseas trade, either to process imports or to produce goods for extra-European markets. Elsewhere in Europe, too, extra-European-related production and trade were much in evidence. Furthermore, wealth derived from overseas was particularly conspicuous in Europe. Returned traders and settlers were distinguishable by complexion and by habit; they were also noticeable because of the ways they chose to spend their new wealth. The great companies which organised the trade with Asia had a high profile because of their great wealth, because of the access to wealth they offered and also because of the great political interest they attracted. The new industries connected with overseas trade also attracted attention to themselves, particularly the processing industries, because they were on a large scale and relatively capital-intensive. They were also very noticeable when things went wrong: the explosion of a sugar refinery could not easily be ignored. This high visibility almost certainly has led historians, as it may have led some contemporaries, to overestimate the importance of the extra-European trades and sectors in the general European economy. Even for England and the northern Netherlands, colonial trade and investment were only a relatively small part of their overall economic activity. Despite the success of the Dutch East India Company, it is clear that, at least in the early and middle seventeenth century, the old 'mother-trade', the trade with the Baltic, was much more important to the Netherlands, in terms of labour and capital employed, total volume and value of goods imported and exported and also in net contribution to overall national wealth.[27] In England, too, even in the eighteenth century, the extra-European trade was of less importance to the whole economy than more traditional trade in Europe.

The contribution of extra-European expansion to the European economy should not be overestimated, but it was not unimportant. The early modern European economy was developing new patterns of consumption based upon new assumptions about disposable wealth, new spending habits and new lifestyles. The overseas trades and colonial settlements played an important part in this expansion of consumer demand. They supplied new luxuries such as tobacco, sugar, tea and coffee, and did this so successfully that, by the eighteenth century, they had become mass-consumption goods. Overseas trade also supplied new manufactured goods, ceramics and textiles at prices increasingly affordable by many. Furthermore the wealth which came from the Americas and Asia came in ways which encouraged its holders to spend and consume rather than to store or reinvest. The addition of this new wealth to the European economy acted as a 'pump-primer', spreading the new wealth widely and encouraging consumption on a wider and wider scale. Finally, what could have been one of the most disastrous consequences of extra-European expansion, the increase in the supply of bullion and hence in inflation, became, in the growing and developing economy of late seventeenth- and eighteenth-century Europe, one of the most beneficent. The inflow of bullion meant that the expansion of the economy, and in particular the extension of a commercialised and monetarised economy, was not greatly hampered by a shortage of money.

It is also important not to exaggerate Europe's impact on the non-European world in the early modern period. On the North American seaboard, European settlers displaced the native peoples (who either died of European diseases or migrated further into the interior), and then established their own essentially conservative versions of European society with no reference to the cultures which had preceded them. In Latin America the impact of the Europeans was even more drastic, but that impact was not the consequence of European economic or cultural superiority, nor was it intended. It was the tragic result of the lack of immunity to European disease amongst the Amerindian populations. Where Europeans came into contact with powerful and well-established states, as in Asia or on the West Coast of Africa, their impact was relatively small. In both Asia and Africa, the Europeans, until the end of the eighteenth century, could operate only through partnerships with traditional states and traditional traders. Of course, new demands and new patterns of trade did have an effect on the non-European partners as well as on the Europeans, but that effect has to be studied within the context of traditional Asian or African societies, polities and economies. Neither in Asia nor in Africa was there any question of new systems being introduced by Europeans in the early modern period.

It would be easy to see this reliance on traditional trade and on traditional partners as a sign of European weakness, and in a sense it was. Early modern Europe was not strong enough politically, militarily or economically to overthrow the well-established powers of the non-European world. However, to define early modern European practice as weakness is to make the erroneous assumption that the natural, indeed inevitable, outcome of contact between Europe and the non-European world was an extension of European domination. In fact, as is most clearly seen on the Slave Coast of Africa, partnership was not a second-best option but was the way that Europeans preferred to deal with difficult, complex and risky economic and political situations. European traders were looking for the profits from trade and not for political rule and control. Unlike their nineteenth-century successors, early modern Europeans were able to respect the traditional ways of their Asian and African partners, partly because they were not vastly different from European ways of doing things, partly because they did not have an arrogant assumption of European superiority.

Much of the European expansion in the early modern period fits closely into 'pre-modern' and 'pre-capitalist' patterns. European traders went to Asia or to Africa to find ways into trading patterns rather than to revolutionise them or to replace them. Settlers went to the Americas to re-create in the New World idealised forms of European society which had ceased to exist in the old, rather than to create new and dynamic social and economic systems. Even when some sectors of the North American colonies had begun to develop in new ways, the great mass of the colonial economies remained in the old patterns. Above all, the history of European expansion before 1800 contains no indication of any territorial or imperial imperative, of any need to dominate and control the extra-European world. Nor is there any indication of an inherent European superiority, commercial, industrial or technological. Despite what later historians have suggested, in the early modern period Europe was not a dominating force in the world.

CONCLUSION

In the traditional historiography the end of the early modern period of economic history came very suddenly as the political and social system collapsed. Between 1780 and 1800 a whole political and social structure which had appeared rock-solid and secure collapsed into ruins. Beginning with the reforms of Joseph II in the Habsburg Empire in the 1780s, but really accelerating with the end of the Absolute Monarchy in France from the summer of 1789 onwards, the pre-modern world seemed to come to an end with startling suddenness and, it must be said, with startling ease. By 1815 there can be little doubt that the modern period had started; by that date, the political and social map of Europe had been irrevocably changed and the Age of Industry had begun.

For the economic historian such a simple scheme seems problematic. The great events which are seen as marking the end of the early modern period are almost entirely political and symbolic rather than economically real. The great keynote change, if anything can be so identified, should be the resolution of what, by that stage, was the French National Assembly to abolish feudal privilege and the feudal system in general, passed at Versailles on the night of 4/5 August 1789. Here, if anything, was the great transition; the old world of privilege and feudalism giving place to a new world of equality, social openness and entrepreneurship. In fact a great deal of the social history of much of France over the next decades was taken up by working out the consequences of this grand statement. The resolution of 4/5 August did not in reality mark the end of a system but merely a stage in its modification.

It is difficult to see the events of the last decade of the eighteenth century and the first 15 years of the nineteenth as marking any very sharp or significant change in the economic patterns of Europe, except in some areas such as many parts of Germany or northern Italy, where there was a considerable short-term setback. Outside England new patterns of industrial organisation and development had hardly appeared before 1800. In most parts of Europe those new patterns

197

were not to develop even on a relatively minor scale until the 1830s at the earliest, and in most cases not until the 1850s or later. Even in England, the 'triumph of industrialisation' can hardly be said to have been clear or complete by 1815, even if by industrialisation is meant no more than the relatively simple and basic water-based mechanisation which was typical of British industry before the 1830s. In many ways it was the depression in trade and industry which followed the Napoleonic Wars which made the domination of new-style industrialisation in England certain, and it was the introduction of steam power in the 1830s which introduced the bases of the new urban and factory-based society.

Even in England, it was only in the mid-nineteenth century that the population became more urban than rural. It was not until the last third of the century that manufacturing industry overtook agriculture as the largest non-service employer of labour, and it was not until after the First World War that it overtook domestic service as the largest single employment sector in the British economy. In continental economies that process of the conquest of the economy by industry was even slower, and in some economies, like that of France, it did not occur until after the Second World War.

It is also worth pointing out that in most European economies the period of 'industrialisation', or at least the period of confident industrial expansion, untainted with the knowledge of the riskiness of the process and the dangers of its collapse, was a very short one, running from the late 1860s or the 1870s through to 1914. Three or four decades of depression and patchy growth followed before the brief revival of the post-Second World War period of rapid growth and confidence which was to come to an end in the 1970s and 1980s. Compared with the early modern period, and compared with its relative stability, the industrial period has been short and disturbed, characterised by boom and bust, delivering widespread unrelieved poverty as often as prosperity.

During the early industrialisation process, and in particular during the expansion of industrial production in England, the increase in supply and in consumption of industrially produced goods strengthened rather than weakened early modern patterns of consumption and of choice as agricultural workers added employment in the new industries to their portfolio of activity. In nineteenth-century rural France the break-up of the feudal estates and the new rights which were guaranteed to the peasantry by the Revolution and the Napoleonic Code gave rural families much greater freedom of action. The expansion of new forms of employment and income (such as the army, the development of industry in the Département du Nord and elsewhere, the expansion of the cities, and the rise of new industries such as the railways) and the extension of market opportunities (through the expansion of transportation systems and through the abolition, albeit partial, of internal barriers to the movement of goods) increased the range of choice available. This enabled many rural families to continue to base their economic lives on early modern strategies rather than being forced into following more 'modern' ones. The survival of the peasant societies of much of central and southern France and also of many parts of Spain and Italy should be seen not as an example of the backwardness and conservatism of traditional peasant societies (which in these areas is almost entirely a myth), but rather as a clear sign of the continuing vitality of early modern modes of operation in a world which could still be clearly understood, and clearly and successfully operated in early modern terms.

In social terms, too, it is difficult to see the early modern period ending in most of Europe in the early decades of the nineteenth century. At that point there certainly was no greater migration of population to towns and cities than had been the case before 1789. Nor can it be said that the ending of legal feudalism marked any real change for most of the population in any part of Europe, even including France. Indeed, in some areas, for instance in parts of Italy or in the Austrian and Prussian crown lands, the reforms of the Napoleonic period effectively meant social as well as economic retrogression. Far from being freed from servitude, except in the legal sense, the population was effectively subjected to a much more intense form of economic and social domination by the landlords. Perhaps that growing domination, and the gradual destruction of customary rights in the name of modernisation and freedom were an essential part of the process which led to the development of industrial economies and societies. Nonetheless it is clear that, even by 1850, over much of continental Europe the preconditions of modernity were being created rather than modernity itself.

Though there may be good reasons for starting the political modern age in 1789, it seems debatable whether the modern period in economic and social terms can be said to have started at the beginning of the nineteenth century. A more convincing date might well be 1850 or 1870, but even then modernisation can only be said to have begun in some parts of some European economies. Some European economies were only to achieve even a modicum of modernity in the twentieth century. For instance, much of Spain and much of southern and central Italy (and indeed many parts of the 'advanced' north of Italy such as the Veneto) can be said to have modernised only after the Second World War, and in some cases as late as the 1970s.

This continuance in Europe of early modern economies and early modern economics, albeit modified by the presence of some modernised sectors and areas, well into the nineteenth century, into the very core of the modern period, has profound implications for the way in which economic, social and political modernisation are interrelated. It is clear that, over most of Europe, political modernisation (the creation of the new nation-states, the creation of new, less autocratic administrative structures) proceeded well in advance of economic change, indeed in some cases can be seen as a precondition, if not a cause of that economic change. In this sense, political and perhaps social change were primary and economic change was secondary. Most of the great popular political events of the nineteenth century – the July Revolution in France in 1830, the Venetian and Milanese revolts in 1848, the March revolution of the same year in Austria and Germany, the June Days in Paris, even the Paris Commune of 1871 – occurred in economies which were resolutely and clearly pre-modern rather than modern. Again, the link between economic, social and political change is by no means a clear one, and, by extension, the appearance of modern political movements cannot be seen as evidence for the existence of modern economic structures.

What is clear, however, is the persistence of early modern economic and social structures well into the nineteenth and twentieth centuries. The early modern period and the early modern way of doing things did not simply curl up and die when faced with the supposedly superior modern mode of operation. This was no sudden, sweeping victory but rather a process of slow attrition which went on almost as long as the high period of industrialisation, and in many places for much longer.

The early modern period lasted, even on the traditional dating, for three and a half centuries, from the mid-fifteenth century to the end of the eighteenth. It is little over two hundred years since 1789 and already Europe seems to have entered a post-industrial age, in which confidence in the ability of the new methods to conquer all problems and to create universal wealth and happiness has been replaced by a much greater doubt about whether reliance on such intensive industrialisation was even a right direction to take. The relative lengths of the two periods point to one of the most important things about the early modern economic system. Taken as a whole the system was stable, efficient and effective. It provided a framework within which most of the population could and did live in reasonable prosperity and comfort, defined in their own terms. It is true that some did live in poverty, absolute as well as relative, as they do in modern Europe, and many did live precariously, always aware of the threat of poverty, but at least they had the means to plan and organise strategies to counteract and reduce that threat. At any one time the great mass of the population lived at a level above absolute want. Poverty and the relief of poverty are important topics in both economic and social history during this period, but it is clear that, except at times of great crisis, most people were not at or below bare subsistence level. Furthermore, the early modern system did not merely make possible a continuation of relative prosperity but in addition was able to generate and to manage a major increase and restructuring in consumption and in leisure – things which only the modern system is supposedly able to do.

The early modern system was also resilient. It permitted economies, societies, communities and families to survive not merely in good years and good periods but also through crises of a regional, national or even European scale of a type and an intensity which would in all probability cause serious difficulties for many modern economies. A crisis like the subsistence crisis of the 1590s, the crisis of the early 1630s or the 1690s, or the great crisis related to the French famine of the 1770s, were crises on a very different scale to most faced by any modern economy. At times of great crisis large areas of early modern Europe resembled a modern Third-World country struck by natural disaster: distribution broke down, large parts of the population became refugees, leaving their homes in search of food or other relief; towns were abandoned, land laid waste; all was apparent desolation. Yet within a few years, often within a single year, the economy and with it, society, began to recover, usually without any outside aid or help. The nearest modern parallel is perhaps the destruction of the European economy during the Second World War and the problems which Europe, especially Germany, faced in the immediate post-war years. To solve these problems in the late 1940s Europe had to rely on considerable help from outside. In the aftermath of the Thirty Years War European society had to help itself – and did so.

The resilience and flexibility of the early modern economic system help to explain its longevity and also its survival into the industrial period. It was a system which was especially geared to survival in times of adversity. By offering a range of strategies and a range of ways of approaching problems it was flexible, not relying on a single solution to achieve prosperity and not risking total loss if one element did not work out as predicted. The system also allowed a number of ways of achieving an economic goal; indeed it allowed for a number of possible aims, rather than insisting on all economic eggs going into one basket.

It is even possible to wonder whether the early modern mode and the early modern economy ever really went away. A great deal of modern economic history has tended to operate in terms of aggregates – nations or classes, for instance – or of corporate entities – companies, financial institutions, labour organisations – rather than in terms of individual and family strategy. The structure of the early modern economy made these family strategies the dominating feature in the whole economy. The great concentration of capital and of production which went with industrialisation meant that corporate aims and strategies became much more significant. It did not, however, mean that corporate and personal strategies became the same. There have frequently been periods in the modern European economy when individual and family strategies, for instance aiming for security or greater leisure rather than maximum income, have come into conflict with corporate aims. In this sense the triumph of modernity has never been complete. In particular, as consumption has reached higher and higher levels and new varieties of choice – of expenditure, employment, mode of living, for instance – have appeared, so the variety and flexibility which were so typical of the early modern period have reasserted themselves.

The great appeal of modernity was its promise, its apparent ability to create continuous growth, to combine stability and security with rapid growth and change. One of modernity's greatest triumphs was to change the population's general perceptions so that growth and progress, a constant and safe economic improvement, were seen as normal, as the reliable basis upon which individual strategies could and should be built. The years after the 1970s have done much to expose the promise as always having been something of a confidence trick. The history of the modern economy, especially in the period since 1914, is littered with periods of sharp, if not general, reversal. The history of the European economy since 1975 points increasingly to the insecurity of modern economic growth and above all to the personal and family insecurity which the modern reliance on a single income and a single employment involves. In many senses the family unit of the 1980s and the 1990s, with its multiple breadwinners, multiple jobs and readiness to change employments over the working lifespan, and its growing propensity to invest in security (such as pensions or real property), is no more than a revival or re-expansion of the early modern family and its strategies.

A multiplicity of choices and of strategies led to a variety of outcomes and to a variety of systems. The history of what I called, in the Introduction, the Fourth Age can no longer be seen simply in terms of the inevitable development of economies (or societies or political systems) towards one predetermined end point. The period was much too exciting, much too dynamic for that. Europe's history in these years was moving along many tracks rather than a single one; it was truly polymorphic and multifarious. This diversity was not a weakness, a lack of focus, but rather a source of strength, a flexibility of response and approach to real and immediate problems. This flexibility was not only or even chiefly limited to economic systems as a whole – nations, regions or even the whole continent – but also involved small communities and individual families. It raises the basic units of the economy – people – to a role of much greater dignity in their own history, since they were not merely the slaves of incomprehensible and inevitable historical or economic processes but did have real and vital choices to make, choices which made up the longer-term, grander history of the whole economic system.

What is also striking is that, despite the approach which is implicit in many of the theories of development, many systems were able to exist side-by-side without destroying each other. Indeed, it would not be unfair to say that the interpretation of this history offered in this book has strayed too far in the direction of creating a conflict between two systems, when in reality it is clear that they existed together happily and that, in particular, what has here been described as the system of southern prosperity, with its emphasis on widened ranges of choice and insurance through risk spreading, was also typical of much of Northern Europe throughout the early modern period and beyond, even in those areas and those communities which were most heavily 'modernised' by industrialisation in the nineteenth and twentieth centuries. It is also the case that the relationship between the systems was one of co-evolution and mutual influence rather than one of the overwhelming of one 'less efficient' system by a more 'efficient' one.

Both systems delivered prosperity to many areas of Europe during the period. It is no longer possible to polarise Europe before the mid-nineteenth century into a prosperous North or North-West and a poverty-stricken South. The problem of the South, of the Midi and the Mezzogiorno, is a nineteenth- and twentieth-century problem, not one of earlier ages. Europe between the fifteenth and the late eighteenth centuries clearly demonstrated that there were many roads to prosperity, rather than a single one, that 'modernity', in the sense of industrial society and all that involved, was not the only route to improvement in living standards and living conditions and that other values, like stability and security, can be just as important, and just as valuable, as growth.

The multivariate structure of the economy has many implications for other sectors of life and hence for other sectors of history. In particular, the realisation that economic change and economic structures are themselves related to and affected by change in other areas, such as social structures, ideas and attitudes and political systems, and that change in those areas may not be simply a consequence of economic change, must lead to a reassessment of the way in which both economic historians and other historians look at the way in which society and political systems are organised. It is no longer enough to discuss the economic dimensions of social change and social structure, nor to formulate patterns of social structure and social organisation which are based simply on Hegelian–Marxian views of social relationships dominated by relationship to the means of production or on the necessary conflicts and tensions between economic categories. Underlying the idea of economic multifariousness is also the idea of social multifariousness; it is no longer possible to categorise early modern people as 'owners', 'capitalists' or 'landless and oppressed peasants' because many families, even many individuals, would perfectly comfortably occupy all or most of these traditional categories during their lifetimes, and in many cases at one and the same time. It is also no longer possible to look at social relationships as being no more than the working-out of those inbuilt tensions. It is no longer possible to look at social history purely as the study of the parts which went to make up the whole, and to regard their interrelationships as being predetermined by a set of economic relationships which were inevitable and based on a relationship to ownership and control of the means of production.

The years between about 1450 and about 1800 constitute a clear and distinct period in the history of Europe and in the history of the European economy. Although in one very real sense they are a period of transition between the Middle Ages and the modernity of the nineteenth and twentieth centuries, in another it is dangerous and misleading to regard them as 'the Age of Transition'. It is not a period in which one system – the feudalism of the Middle Ages – is transformed into another – the Industrial World. The early modern period did create the modern world; the Industrial Revolution, whatever else it may be, was an early modern and not a modern event. However, as we have seen throughout this book, the early modern period was not simply or chiefly a period in which the ground was prepared for the inevitable triumph of industrialisation and industrial capitalism. The triumph, if that is what it was, of industrialisation came very late and, in some ways, almost accidentally as the result of particular circumstances, above all of specific crises, in relatively unstable sectors of the economy of Northern Europe.

The question of vocabulary haunts this book, and indeed any discussion of the historical role of this period. The now traditional designation of these centuries as early modern clearly implies that they were a period in which a form of the modernity of the nineteenth and twentieth centuries had developed, a stage on the way to that greater modernity. Again this is obviously and axiomatically true, but at the same time it does imply that it was this contribution to modernity rather than any individual contribution which was most significant. As has been argued, that modernity was there but it was only one element, and perhaps one of the less significant elements, of the overall picture of the period, which was much more complex, much more polymorphous and multifarious than the traditional designation allows. It is time that early modern historians began to develop a vocabulary of their own to distinguish the period in a way which does not make it simply the antechamber to modernity, which makes clear its very special claims to distinctiveness and to be considered *sui generis*. The possible terms suggested in the Introduction were suggested with the intention of seeking vocabulary which was neutral, which did not imply a place in a predetermined structure of historical development nor yet, and even worse, a subliminal judgement on the period. In particular, it is crucially important to find ways to express our growing understanding that the period of European history which stretches from the middle of the fourteenth century to the end of the eighteenth – or even later – was not just a period of a diluted form of the modernity which was to develop in the nineteenth and twentieth centuries, but rather one with its own distinctive and individual patterns of economic organisation, social structure, culture and political operation. It is only when we can get away from this linguistic subservience to a subsequent, and very different period, that it will be fully possible to appreciate and to study the 'Fourth Age' for what it was in itself rather than as a collection of origins for something else. Modernity as conceived in the later twentieth century was indeed inherent in the period which preceded it, indeed was created by it, but it is only a small part, and in terms of historical understanding an unimportant part of what the period was about and what its distinctive contribution was. It was, above all, an age of flexibility, of variety and of many different approaches to problems. It was, above all, an age which succeeded and would have continued to succeed.

NOTES

INTRODUCTION

1. F. Braudel, *Civilisation and Capitalism, 15th–18th Centuries*, Vol. 2, *The Wheels of Commerce* (trans. S. Reynolds, London, 1982), p. 231.
2. The classic statement of the relationship between Europe and the Americas in the early modern period is R. Davis, *Rise of the Atlantic Economies* (London, 1973).
3. There is no space in this book to discuss the whole issue of population and historical demography in the early modern period. The reader is referred to E. A. Wrigley and R. Schofield, *Population History of England, 1541–1871* (London, 1981) and J. Dupâquier et al., *Histoire de la population française*, Tome 2, *De la Renaissance à 1789* (Paris, 1988).

1 DEVELOPMENT AND CHANGE

1. In his *Principles of Economics*, published in 1890, Alfred Marshall established what was to be the basic framework of economic interpretation for much of the twentieth century.
2. H. Butterfield, *The Whig Interpretation of History* (London, 1931).
3. Perhaps the most famous and the most influential of these was W. W. Rostow's *The Stages of Economic Growth* (1st edn, Cambridge, 1960) which was originally conceived as a policy document for John F. Kennedy.
4. Malthus's *Essay on Population* was published, ironically, in 1797 at just the point when, over much of Europe, the system which it describes was coming to an end.
5. On France see M. Morineau, *Les Faux-semblants d'un démarrage économique. Agriculture et démographie en France au XVIIIe siècle* (Cahiers des Annales ESC, Paris, 1971).

2 STRATAGEMS AND SPOILS

1. To avoid making the following discussion too opaque, in future the term 'individual' will be used without qualification, but it must be remembered

that in this context, the individual was not necessarily an individual man or woman, but could be, and most frequently was, a family, kinship, community or business group.

2. The residual, which included such factors as chance as well as cultural factors, was often admitted to involve more than half of all the variability in many 'economic' situations.

3. This idea of a population which was largely at or below subsistence levels for much of the time was a very common one and can be found in many 'standard' works of both economic and social history. See, for instance, H. Kamen, *European Society 1500–1700* (London, 1984) and Jan de Vries, *The Economy of Europe in an Age of Crisis, 1600–1750* (Cambridge, 1976).

4. See C. Lis and H. Soly, *Poverty and Capitalism in Pre-Industrial Europe* (Brighton, 1982).

5. See, for instance, J. Lynch, *The Hispanic World in Crisis and Change, 1598–1700* (Oxford, 1992), p. 176.

6. The very term 'peasant' is a complex and difficult one. Most recent interpretations seek to avoid it as being too heavily loaded with assumptions. It is used here merely as a convenient shorthand, so should perhaps be understood to appear in inverted commas throughout.

7. See P. Goubert, *Beauvais et le Beauvaisis de 1600 à 1730* (Paris, 1960), p. 128.

8. See A. Pointrineau, *Remues d'hommes: essai sur les migrations montagnardes en France aux XVII et XVIII siècles* (Paris, 1983).

9. See, for instance, Daniel Roche's brilliant study, *Le Peuple de Paris: essai sur la culture populaire* (Paris, 1981).

10. J. P. Gutton, *Domestiques et serviteurs dans la France de l'ancien régime* (Paris, 1981), p. 8.

11. Pointrineau, *Remues d' hommes* and J. K. J. Thomson, *Clermont-de-Lodève, 1633–1789: Fluctuations in the Prosperity of a Languedocian Cloth-Making Town* (Cambridge,1982), p. 23.

12. It is very important to be careful here. To suggest that Europe saw the 'development' of the rich peasant during the early modern period should not be taken to mean that the rich peasant did not exist in the Middle Ages. What is quite clear is that throughout the archaeologically recent history of Europe, differentiation was a constant feature of virtually all agricultural systems.

13. The British in India were led into great difficulties by their insistence, in part ideological, on taking European concepts of landownership as the basis of their own economic and fiscal policies: E. T. Stokes, *The English Utilitarians and India* (Oxford, 1948).

14. E. M. Link, *The Emancipation of the Austrian Peasant, 1740–1798* (New York, 1974).

15. I have developed this idea further in P. J. Musgrave, 'City, small town and countryside in the early modern Veronese: the Parons of Pescantina and Verona, 1630–1797', in R. ni Neill (ed.), *Town and Countryside in Western Europe from 1500 to 1939* (Leicester, 1996), pp. 28–55.

16. See, for instance, A. Collomp, *La Maison du père: famille et village en Haute Provence aux XVII et XVIII siècles* (Paris, 1983), ch. 1.

17. The normal expectation is that economically things will improve, that prosperity is secure and growth in at least the medium and long term is certain,

is the most important change which has come over the European economy and, indeed, the European political situation as a result of 'industrialisation'; without such a change much of the development of the late twentieth-century European economy would have been impossible. The history of this change in perceptions is a fascinating one and one which merits much greater interest than it has yet received. There is a case, which will be in part reviewed in Chapter 3, that this change began in the early modern period and that it was a vital component in the development of industrialisation.

18. The crisis of the 1770s in France has been brilliantly discussed by Olwen Hufton in *The Poor of Eighteenth Century France* (Oxford, 1974). The crisis of the 1790s is usually only considered as a side-issue to the political and military events of the decade.

19. See P. J. Cain and A. G. Hopkins, *British Imperialism: Innovation and Expansion, 1688–1914* (London, 1993).

20. I have discussed these problems in the context of the spice trade in P. J. Musgrave, 'The economics of uncertainty', in D. H. Aldcroft and P. L. Cottrell (eds.), *Shipping, Trade and Commerce: Essays in Memory of Ralph Davis* (Leicester, 1981), pp. 9–21.

21. See Gutton, *Domestiques et serviteurs*, pp. 24, 170. In the second half of the eighteenth century, for instance, 70 per cent of all male servants in Paris owned at least one watch, and 20 per cent owned two or more. *Ibid.*, p. 185.

3 THE RISE OF A CONSUMER SOCIETY

1. E. Labrousse (ed.), *Histoire économique et social de la France*, Tome 2, *Des derniers temps de l'âge seigneurial aux préludes de l'âge industriel, 1660–1789* (Paris, 1970).

2. J. Thirsk, *Economic Policy and Projects: The Development of a Consumer Society in Early Modern England* (Oxford, 1978).

3. F. Braudel, *The Mediterranean and the Mediterranean World in the Age of Philip II* (trans. S. Reynolds, London, 1972), Vol. 1, p. 547.

4. This is apparent from the work of Daniel Roche on Paris (*Le Peuple de Paris: essai sur la culture populaire*, Paris, 1981), of Maurice Garden on Lyon (*Lyon et les Lyonnais aux XVIIe et XVIIIe siècles*, Paris, 1970) and of Paolo Malanima on rural Tuscany (*Il Lusso dei contadini: consumi e industrie nelle campagne toscane del 'sei e 'settecento*, Bologna, 1990).

5. On the *revendeurs* and *revendeuses* of Paris see Roche, *Le Peuple de Paris*, p. 187.

6. The study of rural, 'vernacular' housing on the Continent is only in its infancy, but there does seem to be considerable evidence from both northern and southern Europe that this general improvement in living conditions took place.

7. Although the potato was introduced into Europe in the early sixteenth century, and was cultivated on a small scale in the following 150 years, it was not until the late eighteenth century that it became a widely grown or economically important crop in Europe: R. N. Salaman, *The History and Influence of the Potato* (London, 1949).

8. On the importance of the curved chimney see Roche, *Le Peuple de Paris*, pp. 140–1.
9. J. Whalley, *Society and Religious Toleration in Hamburg, 1529–1819* (Cambridge, 1985), p. 174.
10. Bars, cabarets and *guinguettes* were important centres of sociability for all levels of society and for both sexes in many towns and cities in the eighteenth century. See Roche, *Le Peuple de Paris*, pp. 256–8; Garden, *Lyon et les Lyonnais au XVIII siècle*, pp. 266, 432 and K. Norberg, *Rich and Poor in Grenoble, 1600–1814* (Berkeley, 1985), p. 228.
11. In many towns and cities, the eighteenth century was to see the construction of special streets or areas for these promenades. The construction of the via Nuova in Verona was a conscious attempt to create a 'promenade'. In Hamburg the building of the *Jungfernsteig* in 1710 was a response to the growing habit of Hamburgers, rich and poor, of taking a promenade to the neighbouring town of Altona. This had begun as a result of the greater religious toleration of Calvinism in Altona compared with Lutheran Hamburg, but increasingly people went to Altona either for the walk or ride or for the cheaper goods, including food and drink, which were available there as a result of the conscious commercial policy of Altona's Danish rulers. Whalley, *Society*, p. 177.
12. On Tuscany see F. McArdle, *Altopascio: A Study in Tuscan Rural Society* (Cambridge, 1974) .
13. See, for instance, T. Robisheaux, *Rural Society and the Search for Order in Early Modern Germany* (Cambridge, 1989), p. 222 and C. R. Phillips, *Ciudad Real 1500–1750: Growth, Crisis and Readjustment in the Spanish Economy* (Cambridge, Mass., 1979), pp. 30, 32.
14. See, for instance, B. Porchnev, *Les Soulèvements populaires en France sous l'ancien régime* (Paris, 1963) and A. M. Lublinskaya, *French Absolutism 1620–1629* (Cambridge, 1969).
15. See W. Heide, 'Agriculture and agrarian society', in S. Ogilvie (ed.), *Germany: A New Social and Economic History*, Vol. II, *1630–1800* (London, 1996), pp. 63–99.
16. The best short summary of the whole discussion of 'proto-industrialisation' is P. Kriedte, H. Medick and J. Schlumbohm, *Industrialisation before Industrialisation* (trans. S. Burke, Cambridge, 1982).
17. See, for instance, Philips, *Ciudad Real*, p. 53 and D. Sella, *Crisis and Continuity: The Economy of Spanish Lombardy in the Seventeenth Century* (London and Cambridge, 1979), pp. 83–9.
18. Sella, *Crisis and Continuity*, pp. 113–16.
19. P. Mathias, *The First Industrial Nation: An Economic History of Britain 1700–1914* (2nd edn, London, 1983).
20. R. Gascon, *Grand Commerce et vie urbaine au XVI siècle: Lyon et ses marchands* (Paris and The Hague, 1971), Vol. 1, p. 83.
21. *Ibid.*, Vol. 1, p. 189.
22. T. J. A. Le Goff, *Vannes and its Region: A Study of Town and Country in Eighteenth Century France* (Oxford, 1981).
23. D. R. Ringrose, *Madrid and the Spanish Economy, 1560–1850* (Berkeley, 1983), p. 250.

24. See Gascon, *Grand Commerce*.
25. Rafts were important on rivers as different as the Adige in northern Italy (See G. Borelli (ed.), *Una Città e il suo fiume: Verona e l'Adige*, 2 vols., Verona, 1977) and the Vistula (see F. Braudel, *Civilisation matérielle, économie et capitalisme*, Vol. 1, *Les Structures du quotidien: le possible et l'impossible* (Paris, 1972, pp. 102–3).
26. The history of internal navigation, both on rivers and canals, is largely ignored in the literature; the best source of information in English on the development of internal navigation in France is H. McKnight, *Cruising French Waterways* (2nd edn London, 1991). Jan de Vries has studied the role of canal navigation in the northern Netherlands in *Barges and Capitalism: Passenger Transport in the Dutch Economy 1632–1839* (Utrecht, 1981).
27. Gascon, *Grand Commerce*, Vol. 1, p. 147.
28. de Vries, *Barges and Capitalism*.
29. Gascon, *Grand Commerce*, Vol. 1, pp. 157, 173.
30. *Ibid.*, Vol. 1, p. 132.
31. Robisheaux, *Rural Society*, p. 249.
32. In the eighteenth century 5000 cattle per annum were driven from Isigny in Normandy to Paris (M. El Kordi, *Bayeux aux XVII et XVIII siècles*, Paris, 1970, p. 191) while sheep and cattle from Normandy were fattened around Beauvais before being driven to Paris (P. Goubert, *Beauvais et le Beauvaisis de 1600 à 1730* (Paris, 1960) p. 118).
33. Braudel, *Civilisation matérielle*, Vol. 2, p. 192.
34. Governments were developing methods of passing information more rapidly, by semaphores or by heliographs, but these systems were confined to important political, diplomatic or military information. The fastest information travelled by normal means was around 200 km in a day: by the fastest sixteenth-century courier, news from Fontainebleau reached Lyon in two days (210 km per day): Gascon, *Grand Commerce*, Vol. 1, p. 191. See also Braudel, *Mediterranean*, Vol. 1, pp. 366–7.
35. Goubert, *Beauvais et le Beauvaisis*, p. 309.

4 THE ROLE OF THE STATE

1. E. Hecksher, *Mercantilism* (Stockholm, 1935).
2. See D. M. Palliser, *The Age of Elizabeth: England under the Later Tudors, 1547–1603* (2nd edn, London and New York, 1992), pp. 157–62 and N. G. Parker, *The Thirty Years War* (London, 1984), pp. 88–90.
3. See Olaf Mörke, 'Social structure' in S. Ogilvie (ed.), *Germany: A New Social and Economic History*, Vol. II, *1630–1800* (London, 1996), p. 147.
4. S. M. Schama, *Citizens: A Chronicle of the French Revolution* (London, 1989), pp. 90–2.
5. From time to time, of course, ministers like Colbert or Lerma sought to build up 'war chests', but they never succeeded except in the most limited short range.
6. D. R. Ringrose, *Madrid and the Spanish Economy, 1560–1850* (Berkeley, 1983), pp. 194, 232.

7. E. Le Roy Ladurie, 'Baroque et Lumières: la croissance économique', in G. Duby (ed.), *Histoire de la France urbaine*, Vol. 3, *La Ville classique de la Renaissance aux révolutions* (Paris, 1981), p. 362 and S. L. Kaplan, *Provisioning Paris: Merchants and Millers in the Grain and Flour Trade during the Eighteenth Century* (Ithaca and London, 1984).

8. J. P. Poussou, *Bordeaux et le Sud-Ouest au XVIII siècle: croissance économique et attraction urbaine* (Paris, 1983), p. 226.

9. A. Calabria and J. A. Marino (eds.), *Good Government in Spanish Naples* (New York, 1990).

10. A. Pointrineau, *Remues d'hommes: essai sur les migrations montagnardes en France aux XVII et xviii siècles* (Paris, 1983).

11. On Madrid see Ringrose, *Madrid and the Spanish Economy*; on St Petersburg see J. H. Bater, *St Petersburg: Industrialisation and Change* (London, 1976), chs. 1 and 2.

12. See E. Cochrane, *Florence in the Forgotten Centuries, 1527–1800: A History of Florence and the Florentines in the Age of the Grand Dukes* (Chicago and London, 1973), pp. 111–13.

13. See P. and S. Pillorget, *France baroque, France classique*, III, *Dictionnaire* (Paris, 1995), pp. 510–11.

14. Poussou, *Bordeaux et le Sud-Ouest*, pp. 233–4.

15. On Sète see J. K. J. Thomson, *Clermont-de-Lodève, 1633–1789: Fluctuations in the Prosperity of a Languedocian Cloth-Making Town* (Cambridge, 1982), p. 385.

16. P. Deyon, *Amiens, capitale provinciale: étude sur la société urbaine au XVII siècle* (Paris, 1967), p. 91.

17. Poussou, *Bordeaux et le Sud-Ouest*, p. 240.

18. See C. Hadfield, *British Canals: An Illustrated History* (7th edn, Newton Abbot, 1984).

19. See, for instance, J. K. J. Thomson, *A Distinctive Industrialisation: Cotton in Barcelona 1728–1832* (Cambridge, 1992).

20. E. Labrousse (ed.), *Histoire économique et social de la France*, Tome 2, *Des derniers temps de l'âge seigneurial aux préludes de l'âge industriel, 1660–1789* (Paris, 1970), pp. 367–83.

21. F. Vecchiato, *Pane e politica annonaria in Terraferma Veneta tra secolo XV e secolo XVIII: il caso di Verona* (Verona, 1979).

22. S. Kaplan, *Bread, Politics and Political Economy in the Reign of Louis XIV* (The Hague, 1976) and Schama, *Citizens*, pp. 305–9.

23. See C. W. Cole, *Colbert and a Century of French Mercantilism* (London, 1964).

24. See H. Kamen, *Spain in the Later Seventeenth Century, 1665–1700* (London, 1980), p. 75 and C. A. Hanson, *Economy and Society in Baroque Portugal 1668–1703* (London, 1981), p. 130.

25. Schama, *Citizens*, pp. 74–5.

26. The *guinguettes* of Paris, bars set up just outside the local customs barriers, were replicated by similar establishments outside the customs barriers of many other French towns and frequently were the goal of much of the population during their Sunday promenades. See D. Roche, *Le Peuple de Paris: essai sur la culture populaire* (Paris, 1981), p. 258 and M. Garden, *Lyon et les Lyonnais aux XVIIe et XVIIIe siècles* (Paris, 1970), p. 256.

27. See E. Le Roy Ladurie and J. Goy (eds.), *Tithe and Agrarian History from the Fourteenth to the Eighteenth Centuries: An Essay in Comparative History* (trans. S. Burke, Cambridge, 1982).

28. Pierre Goubert has calculated that, in the late seventeenth century, state taxation took perhaps 20 per cent of the total gross production of peasant holdings in the Beauvaisis, while tithe accounted for perhaps a similar proportion of total production. Goubert calculated that after taxation, tithe and rent, the farmer retained a minimum of 48 per cent of the gross production of the land. P. Goubert, *Beauvais et le Beauvaisis de 1600 à 1730* (Paris, 1960), pp. 180–2. Le Goff reckons that in the eighteenth century peasant landholders in the Vannetais retained 50–55 per cent of their harvest after tax, rent and tithe payments; T. G. A. Le Goff, *Vannes and its Region: A Study of Town and Country in Eighteenth Century France* (Oxford, 1981).

29. See T. Robisheaux, *Rural Society and the Search for Order in Early Modern Germany* (Cambridge, 1989), p. 162.

30. Taxation in the rural Veneto was largely collected by communal officials, appointed by the communes themselves. P. J. Musgrave, *Land And Economy in Baroque Italy: The Valpolicella, 1630–1797* (Leicester, 1992), pp. 17–18.

31. It is clear that, at the most local levels, the distinction between elite and mass was very weak, and that village leaders, who could become leaders on a much larger scale, were closely linked by family and other ties with the less prosperous members of local communities.

5 THE PROSPERITY OF THE SOUTH

1. J. R. Seeley, *The Expansion of England*, (1st edn, London, 1883).

2. F .C. Lane, *Venice, A Maritime Republic* (Baltimore, 1973), p. 291.

3. F. Braudel, *The Mediterranean and the Mediterranean World in the Age of Philip II* (trans. S. Reynolds, 2 vols., London, 1972), Vol. 1, p. 547.

4. See B. Stier and W. von Hippel, 'War, economy and society', in S. Ogilvie (ed.), *Germany: A New Social and Economic History*, Vol. II, *1630–1800* (London, 1996), pp. 233–62.

5. The term is Gramsci's.

6. Lane, *Venice*, pp. 431–4.

7. G. Galasso, 'Trends and problems in Neapolitan history in the age of Charles V', in A. Calabria and J. A. Marino (eds.), *Good Government in Spanish Naples* (New York, 1990).

8. It should be emphasised that this holds true whether the economy which is being discussed is that of a state or of an individual.

9. The terms 'capitalist' and (even more) 'pre-capitalist' are, of course, not Seeley's own.

10. Some historians have used 'Mediterranean' as a synonym for southern and 'Atlantic' for northern. As will become clear, these terms have as many difficulties as each other.

11. C. A. Hanson, *Economy and Society in Baroque Portugal, 1668–1703* (London, 1981), p. 185.

12. H. Kamen, *Spain, 1469–1714* (London, 1991), p. 99.

13. J. H. Elliot, *Imperial Spain 1469–1716* (London, 1963), pp. 51–6.

14. R. Gascon, *Grand Commerce et vie urbaine au XVI siècle: Lyon et ses marchands*, 2 vols. (Paris and The Hague, 1971), Vol. 1, pp. 122–69 and M. Garden, *Lyon et les Lyonnais aux XVIIᵉ et XVIIIᵉ siècles* (Paris, 1970), p. 377.

15. J. P. Poussou, *Bordeaux et le Sud-Ouest au XVIII siècle: croissance économique et attraction urbaine* (Paris, 1983), p. 240.

16. E. Le Roy Ladurie, *The Peasants of Languedoc* (Urbana, 1974), p. 229.

17. See G. L. Soliday, *A Community in Conflict: Frankfurt Society in the Seventeenth and Eighteenth Centuries* (Hanover, NH, 1974).

18. See J. Whalley, *Society and Religious Toleration in Hamburg, 1529–1819* (Cambridge, 1985), which is the only easily available treatment of early modern Hamburg in English.

19. J. de Vries, *European Urbanisation, 1500–1800* (London, 1984).

20. Most finance in the North also remained organised on a small-scale basis.

21. Calabria and Marino (eds.), *Good Government*, p. 11.

22. See J. Israel, *Dutch Primacy in World Trade 1585–1740* (Oxford, 1989).

23. For instance in Castile: D. E. Vassberg, *Land and Society in Golden Age Castille* (Cambridge, 1984), pp. 155, 203.

24. Marginal (high) land was being taken into cultivation in many parts of the sub-Alpine foothills in northern Italy until the early years of the seventeenth century (P. J. Musgrave, *Land and Economy in Baroque Italy: The Valpolicella, 1630–1797* (Leicester, 1992), p. 39).

25. In 1453 the population of Istanbul (Constantinople) was probably less than 50 000; by 1600 it had probably reached more than half a million. The first surviving record of the *celeps* system of forced sales of grain (and also livestock) being used in the Balkans dates from 1586. P. F. Sugar, *South-Eastern Europe under Ottoman Rule, 1354–1804* (Seattle, 1977), p. 125.

26. P. A. Clark (ed.), *The European Crisis of the 1590s: Essays in Comparative History* (London, 1985).

27. See C. M. Cipolla, *Cristofano and the Plague: A Study in the History of Public Health in the Age of Galileo* (London, 1973): *Faith, Reason and the Plague in Seventeenth Century Tuscany* (Hassocks, 1979) and *Fighting the Plague in Seventeenth Century Italy* (Madison, 1981). It was, however, not only southern cities which imposed regulations to prevent the spread of plague, which also interrupted trade; in Amiens, for instance, the measures imposed by the city government to stop the spread of plague contributed to the financial and subsistence crises in the city between 1629 and 1631: P. Deyon, *Amiens, capitale provinciale: étude sur la société urbaine au XVII siècle* (Paris, 1967), p. 19.

28. See Musgrave, *Land and Economy*, ch. 4.

29. N. Steensgaard, *Carracks, Caravans and Companies: The Structural Crisis in the European–Asian Trade in the Early Seventeenth Century* (Lund, 1973), pp. 182–5.

30. P. and H. Chaunu, *Séville et l'Atlantique, 1504–1650* (8 vols., Paris, 1955–59) and P. J. Bakewell, *Silver Mining and Society in Colonial Mexico: Zacatecas, 1546–1700* (London, 1971).

31. J. Gagliaro, *Germany under the Old Regime, 1600–1790* (London, 1991) and T. Robisheaux, *Rural Society and the Search for Order in Early Modern Germany* (Cambridge, 1989), p. 208.

32. It is important to remember that profit was by no means the only benefit financiers and merchants sought to obtain from their economic activities.

33. See. J. Casey, *The Kingdom of Valencia in the Seventeenth Century* (Cambridge, 1979).

34. F. McArdle, *Altopascio: A Study in Tuscan Rural Society* (Cambridge, 1974).

35. Both Barcelona and Marseilles were to develop important trades with America in the eighteenth century. C. Carrière, *Négociants Marseillais au XVIIIe siècle: contribution à l'étude des économies maritimes* (2 vols., Marseilles, 1976) and J. K. J. Thomson, *A Distinctive Industrialisation: Cotton in Barcelona 1728–1832* (Cambridge, 1992).

36. Garden, *Lyon et les Lyonnais*, pp. 275–84, Thomson, *A Distinctive Industrialisation* and J. K. J. Thomson, *Clermont-de-Lodève, 1633–1789: Fluctuations in the Prosperity of a Languedocian Cloth-Making Town* (Cambridge, 1982) pp. 21, 229, 307.

37. Poussou, *Bordeaux*, p. 232.

38. Galasso in Calabria and Marino, *Good Government*, p. 58.

39. T. Davies, *Famiglie Feudali siciliane: patrimoni, redditti, investimenti tra '500 e '600* (Caltanissetta, Rome, 1985), p. 93.

40. M. Lecce, *La Coltura del riso in territorio veronese* (Verona, 1958).

41. D. Cosgrove, *The Palladian Landscape: Geographical Change and its Cultural Representations in Sixteenth-Century Italy* (Leicester, 1993).

42. Garden, *Lyon et les Lyonnais*, pp. 405–13 and P. Malanima, *Il Lusso dei contadini: Consumi e industrie nelle campagne toscane del sie e settecento* (Bologna, 1990), pp. 11–56.

43. Thomson, *A Distinctive Industrialisation* and *Clermont-de-Lodève*, p. 385.

44. This was so in the case of Marseilles until at least the 1750s and 1760s. Carrière, *Négociants Marseillais*, p. 44.

45. Whalley, *Society*, p. 184.

6 THE PROSPERITY OF THE NORTH

1. J. Israel, *Dutch Primacy in World Trade 1585–1740* (Oxford, 1989).

2. *Ibid.*

3. The growth of urban populations was irregular, subject to periods of reversal and very patchy; although many towns grew, many also declined. See, for instance, P. Benedict (ed.), *Cities and Social Change in Early Modern France* (London, 1989), pp. 7, 28, 39.

4. J. Dupâquier et al., *Histoire de la population française*, Tome 2, *De la Renaissance à 1789*, p. 65.

5. E. T. Williams, *Capitalism and Slavery* (London, 1954).

6. On the Netherlands see Israel, *Dutch Primacy*, on Bordeaux, J. P. Poussou, *Bordeaux et le Sud-Ouest an XVIII siècle: croissance économique et attraction*

urbaine (Paris, 1983), p. 248; on Hamburg, J. Whalley, *Society and Religious Toleration in Hamburg, 1529–1819* (Cambridge, 1985), p. 91.

7. J. Israel, *The Dutch Republic: Its Rise, Greatness and Fall 1477–1806* (Oxford, 1995), p. 317.

8. See T. Robisheaux, *Rural Society and the Search for Order in Early Modern Germany* (Cambridge, 1989), p. 228.

9. It must be pointed out here that the traditional historiography is not really clear as to whether northern superiority was based in this period on the potential for the development of 'commercial capitalism', the existence of the preconditions for, or an early form of, that system, or on the existence of the system.

10. Poussou argues (*Bordeaux*, p. 263) that by the eighteenth century most of the agriculture of south-western France was geared to production for distant markets: by the mid-eighteenth century grain was being exported from Montauban to the West Indies (*ibid.*, p. 248).

11. Israel, *Dutch Primacy*.

12. It is also important to remember that by no means all joint-stock companies were successful, even before the South Sea Bubble and Law Scheme crises in England and France in the early eighteenth century.

13. C. R. Boxer, *The Dutch in Brazil 1624–1654* (Oxford, 1973).

14. It has to be said that, especially in the seventeenth century, accounting procedures were such that the calculation of profit and hence dividend was an extremely inexact process, and it is difficult to escape the conclusion that levels of dividend must have been set on political as much as on commercial grounds.

15. The most important of the early banks, the Amsterdam Exchange Bank, was established by the city government in 1609. The city government of Hamburg established its own bank in 1619: Whalley, *Society*, p. 9.

16. For a graphic discussion of the problems of subsistence crisis in eighteenth-century France see O. Hufton, *The Poor of Eighteenth Century France* (Oxford, 1974).

17. C. Lis and H. Soly, *Poverty and Capitalism in Pre-Industrial Europe* (Brighton, 1982).

18. D. Roche, *Le Peuple de Paris: essai sur la culture populaire* (Paris, 1981).

19. Hufton, *The Poor*.

7 EUROPE'S PLACE IN THE WORLD

1. A. G. Hopkins, *An Economic History of West Africa* (London, 1973), pp. 78–123.

2. V. Magalhães-Godinho, *L'Economie de l'empire portugais aux XV et XVI siècles* (Paris, 1969).

3. J. Eccles, *France in America* (New York, 1972).

4. T. M. Whitmore, *Disease and Death in Early Colonial Mexico: Simulating Amerindian Depopulation* (Boulder, 1992), pp. 201–7.

5. P. J. Bakewell, *Silver Mining and Society in Colonial Mexico: Zacatecas, 1546–1700* (London, 1971), pp. 121–9.

6. K. N. Chaudhuri, *The Trading World of Asia and the English East India Company circa 1660–1760* (Cambridge, 1978).

7. F. Braudel, *The Mediterranean and the Mediterranean World in the Age of Philip II* (trans. S. Reynolds, London, 1972), Vol. 1, p. 463.

8. See I. Schoffer and F. G. Gaastra, 'The import of bullion', in M. Aymard (ed.), *Dutch Capitalism and World Capitalism* (Cambridge and Paris, 1982), p. 224.

9. See P. J. Musgrave, 'The economics of uncertainty', in D. H. Aldcroft and P. L. Cottrell (eds.), *Shipping, Trade and Commerce: Essays in Memory of Ralph Davis* (Leicester, 1981), pp. 9–21.

10. These rights were the beginnings of claims to sovereignty, although it is fair to question just how significant those grants were in the eyes of the rulers who were granting them.

11. The clearest and most accessible description of the development of these African–European partnerships is in Hopkins, *An Economic History*, ch. 3.

12. On this see I. A. Akinjogbin, *Dahomey and its Neighbours 1708–1818* (Cambridge, 1967).

13. That the interruption of supply could have disastrous consequences was clear; it had been demonstrated by the effects of the failure of the Dutch West India Company to gain control of the ports which supplied slaves to Brazil in the mid-seventeenth century on the economy of northern Brazil, and hence on the stability of the company's conquest of the region. See C. R. Boxer, *The Portuguese Seaborne Empire, 1415–1825* (London, 1969).

14. J. Whalley, *Society and Religious Toleration in Hamburg, 1529–1819* (Cambridge, 1985), p. 9.

15. R. B. Sheridan, *Sugar and Slavery: An Economic History of the British West Indies, 1623–1775* (Barbados, 1974), and R. S. Dunn, *Sugar and Slaves: the Rise of the Planter Class in the English West Indies, 1624–1713* (London, 1973).

16. See C. A. Hanson, *Economy and Society in Baroque Portugal 1668–1703* (London, 1981) and A. H. de Oliveira Marques, *History of Portugal*, Vol. I, *From Lusitania to Empire* (New York and London, 1972), pp. 431–79.

17. J. Israel, *Dutch Primacy in World Trade 1585–1740* (Oxford, 1989).

18. Dunn, *Sugar and Slaves*, p. 67.

19. D. E. Vassberg, *Land and Society in Golden Age Castille* (Cambridge, 1984), p. 165.

20. J. Lynch, *The Hispanic World in Crisis and Change, 1598–1700* (Oxford, 1992), p. 325.

21. *Ibid.*, p. 217.

22. See J. P. Poussou, *Bordeaux et le Sud-Ouest au XVII siècle: croissance économique et attraction urbaine* (Paris, 1983), pp. 231, 239, 242; P. Goubert, *Beauvais et le Beauvaisis de 1600 à 1730* (Paris, 1960), p. 134; P. Deyon, *Amiens, capitale provinciale: étude sur la société urbaine au XVII siècle* (Paris, 1967), pp. 162, 168 and D. R. Ringrose, *Madrid and the Spanish Economy, 1560–1850* (Berkeley, 1983), p. 219.

23. J. K. J. Thomson, *Clermont-de-Lodève, 1633–1789: Fluctuations in the Prosperity of a Languedocian Cloth-Making Town* (Cambridge, 1982), p. 385.

24. J. K. J. Thomson, *A Distinctive Industrialisation: Cotton in Barcelona 1728–1832* (Cambridge, 1992), p. 38.

25. Lynch, *The Hispanic World*, pp. 336–7, Hanson, *Economy and Society*, pp. 244–7.

26. The classic discussion of the scale and pattern of bullion imports from the New World through Seville is P. and H. Chaunu, *Séville et l'Atlantique, 1504–1650* (8 vols., Paris, 1956–59). There is a discussion of the volume of imports after 1650 in Lynch, *The Hispanic World*, p. 228.

27. Israel, *Dutch Primacy*.

SELECT BIBLIOGRAPHY

No bibliography of the economic history of early modern Europe can realistically aim to be complete, and this one is no different. The number of books, articles, pamphlets and other material being produced each year is immense and is growing as the fascination of the period draws more scholars, amateur as well as professional, to it. This massive profusion of material has also other problems associated with it. In many European countries – Italy and Germany spring to mind, but others such as Spain or France have similar, if less severe, problems – most research is carried on at a local level. As a result most work is published locally, often privately, and information on newly published material is often extremely difficult to obtain, even within the country, or region, involved. Even more, such material is almost unobtainable outside a very limited geographical range and often totally unobtainable outside its country of production. Language, too, presents an obvious problem. This bibliography is inevitably slanted towards those languages – English, French, Italian and (Castilian) Spanish – of which the author has a working knowledge; it is lacking in those languages – German, Dutch, the Scandinavian and Eastern European languages – where I have little or no knowledge.

This bibliography is not intended therefore to provide a complete listing of all items which have some relevance to the topic, but rather to provide at least a starting point for further reading. No attempt has been made to include items on the British Isles except where they have some relevance to the wider European context. This is not a list of all works cited in the main body of the book.

General Works

Surprisingly few works have considered the economic history of Europe as a whole during this period. Two, however, stand out as being of major significance. The first is J. de Vries, *The Economy of Europe in an Age of Crisis 1600–1750* (Cambridge, 1976). In many ways this is the book which has influenced most historians working on the period most profoundly, and the one which comes closest to encapsulating the 'traditional' approach which has been discussed in this book. It is, of course, unfair to de Vries's vision and knowledge to suggest that his interpretation is purely and simply a 'traditional' one, but he himself would accept that his work is clearly within the central tradition of a single pattern of modernisation through capitalism and industrialisation.

The second, in very many ways much different to de Vries, is Fernand Braudel's *Capitalism and Civilisation: 15th–18th Centuries*, 2 vols. (trans. S. Reynolds, London, 1982). Like all of Braudel's work, it is striking by its inclusiveness and breadth of information and interpretation; it is also striking for its imaginative use of graphic material. Its very scale makes it difficult to use as a general introduction to the whole field, even though each and every section has much of interest. In many ways, Braudel's interpretation is again a very traditional one, seeing the history of the period in essentially developmental and 'modernising' terms. Many reviewers were disappointed with *Capitalism and Civilisation* when it first appeared, if only because it failed to provide the sort of revolutionary insights which his earlier *The Mediterranean and the Mediterranean World in the Age of Philip II* (1972) had done. It is still one of the best and most fascinating ways into this fascinating period, not least because Braudel links the patterns of economic change he is describing with economic and cultural change.

A third work, Ralph Davis's *Rise of the Atlantic Economies* (London, 1973), does not claim to be an economic history of the whole of Europe, but rather concerns itself with the development of the Atlantic west of Europe and its relationship, above all to the developing economies of the Americas. It is firmly rooted in the traditional historiography of modernisation and industrialisation but has many valuable insights which guarantee its continuing importance.

Berg, M. (ed.), *Markets and Manufacture in Early Industrial Europe* (London, 1991).

Braudel, F., *The Mediterranean and the Mediterranean World in the Age of Philip II* (trans. S. Reynolds, 2 vols., London, 1972).

Clark, P. A. (ed.), *The European Crisis of the 1590s: Essays in Comparative History* (London, 1985).

——, *Small Towns in Early Modern Europe* (Cambridge, 1995).

de Vries, J., *European Urbanisation, 1500–1800* (London, 1984).

Guttman, M. P., *Toward the Modern Economy* (Philadelphia, 1988).

Kamen, H., *European Society, 1500–1700* (London, 1984).

Kriedte, P., Medick, H. and Schlumbohm, J., *Industrialisation before Industrialisation* (trans. S. Burke, Cambridge, 1982).

Le Roy Ladurie, E. and Goy, J. (eds.), *Tithe and Agrarian History from the Fourteenth to the Eighteenth Centuries: An Essay in Comparative History* (trans. S. Burke, Cambridge, 1982).

Lis, C. and Soly, H., *Poverty and Capitalism in Pre-Industrial Europe* (Brighton, 1982).

Rapp, R. T., 'The unmaking of the Mediterranean trade hegemony: international trade rivalry and the commercial revolution', *Journal of Economic History*, 35:3, pp. 499–525, 1975.

Taylor, B., *Society and Economy in Early Modern Europe 1450–1789* (London, 1989).

van der Wee, H., *The Rise and Decline of Urban Industries in Italy and the Low Countries* (Leuven, 1988).

Walter, J., *Famine, Disease and the Social Order in Early Modern Europe* (London, 1989).

France

Agulhon, M., *La Sociabilité méridionale* (Aix-en-Provence, 1966).

——, *Vie sociale en Provence intérieure au lendemain de la révolution* (Paris, 1971).

Bardet, J. P., *Rouen aux XVII et XVIII siècles* (Paris, 1983).

Baudry, A., *Subsistances et population en Périgord 1740–1789* (Bordeaux, 1970).

Beauroy, J., *Vin et société à Bergerac du XIV au XVIII siècle* (Stanford, 1977).

Beik, W., *Absolutism and Society in Seventeenth Century France: State Power and Provincial Aristocracy in Languedoc* (Cambridge, 1985).

Benedict, P., *Rouen during the Wars of Religion* (Cambridge, 1981).

Benedict, P. (ed.), *Cities and Social Change in Early Modern France* (London, 1989).

Bercé, Y.-M., *History of Peasant Revolts: The Social Origins of Revolution in Early Modern France* (London, 1990).

Butel, P., *Les Négociants bordelais, l'Europe et les Iles au XVIII siècle* (Paris, 1974).

Carrière, C., *Négociants marseillais au XVIIIe siècle: contribution à l'étude des économies maritimes* (2 vols., Marseilles, 1976).

Castets, R., *Marchands et négociants à Nérac dans la deuxième moitié du XVIII siècle* (Bordeaux, 1970).

Chaunu, P., *La Mort à Paris: XVI, XVII, XVIII siècles* (Paris, 1978).

Chaussinnand-Nogaret, G., *Les Financiers de Languedoc au XVIII siècle* (Paris, 1970).

Cole, C. W., *Colbert and a Century of French Mercantilism* (London, 1964).

Collins, J. B., 'The role of Atlantic France in the Baltic trade: Dutch traders and Polish grain at Nantes 1625–1675', *Journal of European Economic History*, 13 (1984), pp. 239–89.

Collomp, A., *La Maison du père: famille et village en Haute-Provence aux XVII et XVIII siècles* (Paris, 1983).

Croix, A., *La Bretagne aux XVI et XVII siècles: les hommes, la mort, la foi* (Paris, 1981).

Davis, N. Z., *Society and Culture in Early Modern France* (Stanford, 1975).

Deyon, P., *Amiens, capitale provinciale: étude sur la société urbaine au XVII siècle* (Paris, 1967).

Dupâquier, J. et al., *Histoire de la population française*, Tome 2, *De la Renaissance à 1789* (Paris, 1988).

Durand, Y., *Les Fermiers généraux au XVIII siècle* (Paris, 1971).

Duwald, J., *The Formation of a Provincial Nobility: The Magistrates of the Parlement of Rouen, 1499–1610* (Princeton, 1980).

——, *Pont-St-Pierre 1398–1789: Lordship, Community and Capitalism in Early Modern France* (Berkeley, 1987).

Eccles, J., *France in America* (New York, 1972).

El Kordi, M., *Bayeux aux XVII et XVIII siècles* (Paris, 1970).

Fairchilds, C., *Domestic Enemies: Servants and their Masters in Old Regime France* (Baltimore, 1984).

Farr, J. R., *Hands of Honor: Artisans and their World in Dijon, 1550–1650* (Ithaca and London, 1988).

Frêche, G., *Toulouse et la région Midi-Pyrénées au siècle des Lumières* (Paris, 1974).

Gallet, J., *La Seigneurie bretonne 1450–1680: l'exemple du Vannetais* (Paris, 1983).

Garrioch, D., *Neighbourhood and Community in Paris 1740–1790* (Cambridge, 1986).

Gascon, R., *Grand Commerce et vie urbaine au XVI siècle: Lyon et ses marchands* (2 vols., Paris and The Hague, 1971).

Goubert, P., *Beauvais et le Beauvaisis de 1600 à 1730* (Paris, 1960).

Gutton, J. P., *Domestiques et serviteurs dans la France de l'ancien régime* (Paris, 1981).

Hoffman, P. T., *Church and Community in the Diocese of Lyon 1500–1789* (New Haven, 1984).

Hufton, O., *Bayeux in the Late Eighteenth Century: A Social Study* (Oxford, 1967).

——, *The Poor of Eighteenth Century France* (Oxford, 1974).

Jacob, H., *La Vie économique à Conflans dans la deuxième moitié du XVIII siècle* (Grenoble, 1971).

Jones, C., *Charity and Bienfaisance: The Treatment of the Poor in the Montpellier Region 1740–1805* (Cambridge, 1983).

Kaplan, S., *Bread, Politics and Political Economy in the Reign of Louis XIV* (The Hague, 1976).

Kaplan, S. L., *Provisioning Paris: Merchants and Millers in the Grain and Flour Trade during the Eighteenth Century* (Ithaca and London, 1984).

Kaplow, J., *The Names of Kings: The Parisian Labouring Poor in the Eighteenth Century* (New York, 1972).

Labrousse, E., *Histoire économique et social de la France*, Tome 2, *Des derniers temps de l'âge seigneurial aux préludes de l'âge industriel, 1660–1789* (Paris, 1970).

Le Goff, T. J. A., *Vannes and its Region: A Study of Town and Country in Eighteenth Century France* (Oxford, 1981).

Le Roy Ladurie, E., *The Peasants of Languedoc* (Urbana, 1974).

Léon , P. et al., *Aires et structures du commerce française au XVIII siècle* (Lyon, 1975).

Lublinskaya, A. M., *French Absolutism 1620–1629* (Cambridge, 1969).

Morineau, M. 'Budgets populaires en France au XVIII siècle', *Revue d'histoire économique et sociale* (1972), pp. 204–37, 449–81.

Norberg, K., *Rich and Poor in Grenoble, 1600–1814* (Berkeley, 1985).

Parker, D., *La Rochelle and the French Monarchy: Conflict and Order in Seventeenth Century France* (London, 1980).

Perrot, J.-C., *Genèse d'une ville moderne: Caen au XVIII siècle* (Paris, 1975).

Pointrineau, A., *La Vie rurale en Basse Auvergne au XVIII siècle* (Aurillac, 1966).

——, *Remues d'hommes: essai sur les migrations montagnardes en France aux XVII et XVIII siècles* (Paris, 1983).

Porchnev, B., *Les Soulèvements populaires en France sous l'ancien régime* (Paris, 1963).

Poussou, J. P., *Bordeaux et le Sud-Ouest au XVIII siècle: croissance économique et attraction urbaine* (Paris, 1983).

Price, J. M., *France And the Chesapeake: A History of the French Tobacco Monopoly 1684–1791 and its Relationship to the British and American Tobacco Trades* (2 vols., Ann Arbor, 1973).

Riley, J. C., *The Seven Years War and the Old Regime in France; The Economic and Financial Toll* (Princeton, 1986).

Roche, D., *Le Peuple de Paris: essai sur la culture populaire* (Paris, 1981).

Schwartz, R. M., *Policing the Poor in Eighteenth Century France* (Chapel Hill, 1988).

Thomson, J. K. J., *Clermont-de-Lodève, 1633–1789: Fluctuations in the Prosperity of a Languedocian Cloth-Making Town* (Cambridge, 1982).

Spain and Portugal

Alvarez, G. A., *Las Crisas agrarias en la España moderna* (Madrid, 1970).

Boxer, C. R., *The Portugese Seaborne Empire, 1415–1825* (London, 1969).

Casey, J., *The Kingdom of Valencia in the Seventeenth Century* (Cambridge, 1979).

Chaunu, P. and H., *Séville et l'Atlantique, 1504–1650* (8 vols., Paris, 1956–59).

de Oliveira Marques, A. H., *History of Portugal*, Vol. I, *From Lusitania to Empire* (New York and London, 1972).

Disney, A. R., *The Twilight of the Pepper Empire: Portuguese Trade in South Western India in the Early Seventeenth Century* (Cambridge, Mass., 1978).

Hanson, C. A., *Economy and Society in Baroque Portugal 1668–1703* (London, 1981).

Kamen, H., *Spain in the Later Seventeenth Century, 1665–1700* (London, 1980).

——, *Spain, 1469–1714* (London, 1991).

Livermore, H., *History of Portugal* (Cambridge, 1969).

Lynch, J., *The Hispanic World in Crisis and Change, 1598–1700* (Oxford, 1992).

Magalhães-Godinho, V., 'Le problème du pain dans l'empire portugaise XV–XVI siècles: blé d'Europe au blé des Iles', *Revista di economia*, 12 (fasc. 3) (1959), pp. 87–113.

——, *L'Economie de l'empire portugais aux XV et XVI siècles* (Paris, 1969).

Phillips, C. R., *Ciudad Real 1500–1750: Growth, Crisis and Readjustment in the Spanish Economy* (Cambridge, Mass., 1979).

Reher, D. S., *Town and Country in Pre-Industrial Spain: Cuenca 1550–1870* (Cambridge, 1990).

Ringrose, D. R., *Madrid and the Spanish Economy, 1560–1850* (Berkeley, 1983).

Thomson, J. K. J., *A Distinctive Industrialisation: Cotton in Barcelona 1728–1832* (Cambridge, 1992).

Vassberg, D. E., *Land and Society in Golden Age Castille* (Cambridge, 1984).

Germany and Austria

Beneke, G., *Society and Politics in Germany 1500–1750* (London, 1974).

Blanning, T. C. W., *Reform and Revolution in Mainz, 1743–1806* (Cambridge, 1974).

Dickson, P. G. M., *Finance and Government under Maria Theresa, 1740–1780* (2 vols., Oxford, 1987).

Evans, R. J. W., *The Making of the Habsburg Monarchy 1550–1700* (Oxford, 1979).

Freidrichs, C. R., *Urban Society in an Age of War: Nördlingen 1580–1720* (Princeton, 1979).

Gagliaro, J., *Germany under the Old Regime, 1600–1790* (London, 1991).

Hsia, P.-C., *Society and Religion in Münster 1535–1618* (New Haven, 1984).

Ingrao, C., *The Habsburg Monarchy* (London, 1994).

Liebel, H., *Enlightened Bureaucracy vs. Enlightened Despotism in Baden 1750–1792* (Philadelphia, 1965).

Link, E. M., *The Emancipation of the Austrian Peasant, 1740–1798* (New York, 1974).

Newman, K., 'Hamburg in the European economy, 1660–1750', *Journal of European Economic History*, 14:1 (1985), pp. 57–94.

Ogilvie, S. (ed.), *Germany: A New Social and Economic History*, Vol. II, *1630–1800* (London, 1996).

Rebel, H., *Peasant Classes: The Bureaucratisation of Property and Family Relations Under Early Habsburg Absolutism* (Princeton, 1983).

Robisheaux, T., *Rural Society and the Search for Order in Early Modern Germany* (Cambridge, 1989).

Sabean, D., *Power in the Blood: Popular Culture and Village Discourse in Early Modern Germany* (Cambridge, 1984).

Scott, T., *Freiburg and the Breisgau: Town–Country Relations in the Age of the Reformation and Peasants' War* (Oxford, 1986).

Soliday, G. L., *A Community in Conflict: Frankfurt Society in the Seventeenth and early Eighteenth Centuries* (Hanover, NH, 1974).

Strauss, G., 'Protestant dogma and city government: the case of Nuremberg', *Past and Present*, 36 (1967), pp. 38–58.

Taylor, R., *Berlin and its Culture: A Historical Portrait* (New Haven and London, 1997).

Vann, J. A., *The Making of a State: Württemberg 1593–1793* (Ithaca, 1984).

Walker, M., *German Home Towns: Community, State and General Estate 1648–1871* (Ithaca and London, 1971).

Whalley, J., *Society and Religious Toleration in Hamburg, 1529–1819* (Cambridge, 1985).

The Netherlands

Aymard, M. (ed.), *Dutch Capitalism and World Capitalism* (Cambridge and Paris, 1982).

Bogucka, M., 'Amsterdam and the Baltic in the first half of the seventeenth century', *Economic History Review*, 2nd ser., 26 (1973), pp. 433–47.

Boxer, C. R., *The Dutch in Brazil 1624–1654* (Oxford, 1973).

Collins, J. B., 'The role of Atlantic France in the Baltic trade: Dutch traders and Polish grain at Nantes 1625–75', *Journal of European Economic History*, 13 (1984), pp. 239–89.

Davids, K. and Noordgraaf, L. (eds.), *The Dutch Economy in the Golden Age* (Amsterdam, 1993).

Davies, D. W., *A Primer of Dutch Seventeenth Century Overseas Trade* (The Hague, 1961).

de Vries, J., *The Dutch Rural Economy in the Golden Age 1500–1700* (New Haven, 1974).

——, *Barges and Capitalism: Passenger Transport in the Dutch Economy 1632–1839* (Utrecht, 1981).

Faber, J. A., 'The decline of the Baltic grain trade in the second half of the seventeenth century', *Acta Historia Neerlandicae*, 1 (1966), pp. 108–31.

Glamann, K., *Dutch–Asiatic Trade 1620–1740* (Copenhagen and The Hague, 1958).

Goslinga, C. C., *The Dutch in the Caribbean and in the Guianas 1680–1791* (Assen, 1985).

Gutman, M. P., *War and Rural Life in the Early Modern Low Countries* (Princeton, 1980).

Israel, J., *Dutch Primacy in World Trade 1585–1740* (Oxford, 1989).
——, *The Dutch Republic: Its Rise, Greatness and Fall 1477–1806* (Oxford, 1995).
Prakash, O., *The Dutch East India Company and the Economy of Bengal 1630–1720* (Princeton, 1985).
Price, J. L., *Culture and Society in the Dutch Republic in the Seventeenth Century* (London, 1974).
Raychaudhuri, T., *Jan Compagnie in Coromandel* (The Hague, 1962).
Schama, S. M., *The Embarrassment of Riches: An Interpretation of Dutch Culture in the Golden Age* (London, 1987).
Smith, G. L., *Religion and Trade in New Netherland* (Ithaca, 1973).

Italy

Borelli, G. (ed.), *Una Città e il suo fiume: Verona e l'Adige* 2 vols. (Verona, 1977).
Burr Litchfield, R., *Emergence of a Bureaucracy: The Florentine Patricians, 1530–1790* (Princeton, 1986).
Calabria, A. and Marino, J. A. (eds.), *Good Government in Spanish Naples* (New York, 1990).
Cancila, O., *Impresea, redditti, mercato nella Sicilia moderna* (Bari, 1980).
Cavallo, S., *Charity and Power in Early Modern Italy: Benefactors and Their Motives in Turin, 1541–1789* (Cambridge, 1995).
Cipolla, C. M., *Cristofano and the Plague: A Study in the History of Public Health in the Age of Galileo* (London, 1973).
——, *Faith, Reason and the Plague in Seventeenth Century Tuscany* (Hassocks, 1979).
——, *Fighting the Plague in Seventeenth Century Italy* (Madison, 1981).
Cosgrove, D., *The Palladian Landscape: Geographical Change and its Cultural Representation in Sixteenth-Century Italy* (Leicester, 1993).
Davies, T., *Famiglie feudali Siciliane: patrimoni, redditti, investimenti tra '500 e '600* (Caltanissetta, Rome, 1985).
Delille, G., *Famille et propriété dans la Royaume de Naples XV–XIX siècles* (Rome and Paris, 1985).
Doria, G., *Uomini e terre di un borgo collinare* (Geneva, 1968).
Fasano-Guarini, E., *Potere e società negli Stati Regionali Italiani del '500 e '600* (Bologna, 1974).
Galasso, G., *Economia e società nella Calabria del '500* (Naples, 1967).
Georgelin, J., *Venise au siècle des Lumières* (Paris, 1978).
Klapisch-Zuber, C., *Les Maîtres du marbre: Carrara 1300–1600* (Paris, 1969).
Lane, F. C., *Venice: A Maritime Republic* (Baltimore, 1973).
Lecce, M., *La Coltura di riso in territorio veronese* (Verona, 1958).
Malanima, P., *Il Lusso dei contadini: consumi e industrie nelle campagne toscane del 'Sei e 'Settecento* (Bologna, 1990).
Marino, J. A., *Pastoral Economies in the Kingdom of Naples* (Baltimore, 1988).
Mazzaoui, M. F., *The Italian Cotton Industry in the Later Middle Ages, 110–1600* (Cambridge, 1981).
McArdle, F., *Altopascio: A Study in Tuscan Rural Society* (Cambridge, 1974).
Musgrave, P. J., *Land and Economy in Baroque Italy: The Valpolicella, 1630–1797* (Leicester, 1992).

——, 'City, small town and countryside in the early modern Veronese: the Parons of Pescantina and Verona 1630–1797', in R. ni Neill. (ed.), *Town and Countryside in Western Europe from 1500 to 1939* (Leicester, 1996).

Pullan, B. (ed.), *Crisis and Change in the Venetian Economy* (London, 1968).

Rapp, R. T., *Industry and Economic Decline in Seventeenth Century Venice* (Cambridge, Mass. and London, 1976).

Sella, D., *Crisis and Continuity: The Economy of Spanish Lombardy in the Seventeenth Century* (London and Cambridge, 1979).

Storia d'Italia: dalla caduta del Impero Romano al secolo XVIII (Turin, 1974).

Ulvioni, P., *Il gran castigio di Dio: carestia ed epidemie a Venezia e nella Terra Ferma 1628–32* (Milan, 1989).

Vecchiato, F., *Pane e politica annonaria in Terraferma Veneta tra secolo XV e secolo XVIII: il caso di Verona* (Verona, 1979).

Woolf, S. J., *A History of Italy 1700–1860: The Social Constraints of Political Change* (London, 1979).

Miscellaneous

Akinjogbin, I. A., *Dahomey and its Neighbours 1708–1818* (Cambridge, 1967).

Bakewell, P. J., *Silver Mining and Society in Colonial Mexico: Zacatecas, 1546–1700* (London, 1971).

Bater, J. H., *St Petersburg: Industrialisation and Change* (London, 1976).

Cain, P. J. and Hopkins, A. G., *British Imperialism: Innovation and Expansion, 1688–1914* (London, 1993).

Chaudhuri, K. N., *The Trading World of Asia and the English East India Company circa 1660–1760* (Cambridge, 1978).

——, *Trade and Civilisation in the Indian Ocean: An Economic History from the Rise of Islam to 1750* (Cambridge, 1985).

Dunn, R. S., *Sugar and Slaves: The Rise of the Planter Class in the English West Indies, 1624–1713* (London, 1973).

Frangakis-Syrett, E., *The Commerce of Smyrna in the Eighteenth Century* (Athens, 1992).

Hecksher, E., *Mercantilism* (Stockholm, 1935).

Hopkins, A. G., *An Economic History of West Africa* (London, 1973).

Musgrave, P. J., 'The economics of uncertainty', in D. H. Aldcroft and P. L. Cottrell (eds.), *Shipping, Trade and Commerce: Essays in Memory of Ralph Davis* (Leicester, 1981), pp. 9–21.

Rostow, W. W., *The Stages of Economic Growth* (1st edn, Cambridge, 1960).

Sheridan, R. B., *Sugar and Slavery: An Economic History of the British West Indies, 1623–1775* (Barbados, 1974).

Steensgaard, N., *Carracks, Caravans and Companies: The Structural Crisis in the European–Asian Trade in the Early Seventeenth Century* (Lund, 1973).

Sugar, P. F., *South-Eastern Europe under Ottoman Rule, 1354–1804* (Seattle, 1977).

Tracey, J. D. (ed), *The Rise of Merchant Empires: Long-Distance Trade in the Early Modern World 1350–1750* (Cambridge, 1990).

Williams, E. T., *Capitalism and Slavery* (London, 1954).

INDEX